Children Who Commit Acts of Serious Interpersonal Violence

Children Who Commit Acts of Serious Interpersonal Violence

Messages for Best Practice

*Edited by Ann Hagell
and Renuka Jeyarajah-Dent*

Foreword by Florence Bruce

Jessica Kingsley Publishers
London and Philadelphia

First published in 2006
by Jessica Kingsley Publishers
116 Pentonville Road
London N1 9JB, UK
and
400 Market Street, Suite 400
Philadelphia, PA 19106, USA

www.jkp.com

Library of Congress Cataloging in Publication Data
Children who commit acts of serious interpersonal violence : messages for best practice /
edited by Ann Hagell and Renuka Jeyarajah-Dent. -- 1st American paperback ed.
p. cm.
Includes bibliographical references and index.
ISBN-13: 978-1-84310-384-4 (pbk. : alk. paper)
ISBN-10: 1-84310-384-2 (pbk. : alk. paper) 1. Children and violence--Prevention. 2.
Violence in children--Prevention. I. Hagell, Ann. II. Jeyarajah-Dent, Renuka.
HQ784.V55C454 2006
364.36--dc22

2006014165

British Library Cataloguing in Publication Data
A CIP catalogue record for this book is available from the British Library

ISBN-13: 978 1 84310 384 4
ISBN-10: 1 84310 384 2

Printed and bound in Great Britain by
Athenaeum Press, Gateshead, Tyne and Wear

Contents

Appendices: Brief commentaries 201

List of tables

List of figures

List of boxes

Acknowledgements

A large number of people were very helpful to us while we prepared this volume, and we are grateful to all of them. The Oak Foundation has generously funded both fieldwork and conferences that have formed part of this programme of work undertaken by NCH – The Bridge Child Care Development Service, and its interest in our work is much appreciated. In particular we are grateful to Florence Bruce, Senior Programme Officer on the Child Abuse Programme, for her support.

Many busy practitioners have shared their time with us over the last couple of years, and we hope that we have captured something of the challenges of their work, and the thought and care that goes into it. In addition, one enormous privilege for us has been working with people from a range of countries in the preparation of these chapters. We are particularly grateful to people who were not writing (or talking) in their first language for the extra effort involved on their part in making the collaboration work. We personally benefited from the international exchange in all sorts of ways, and one of our main hopes for this volume is that some of the comparative work can be shared more widely.

Finally, we would like to acknowledge the support of the staff of NCH – The Bridge Child Care Development Service, and in particular Elaine Anderson, both for their help with the fieldwork but also for doing so many of the small, invisible but important tasks that go with this type of editing job.

Foreword

This book addresses the needs of a particular group of children who present not as victims but as perpetrators. Their vulnerability is difficult to recognise and accept because their victims, often vulnerable children themselves because of age or disability, are immediately more deserving of sympathy and help. However, the work of NCH – The Bridge Child Care Development Service, especially through its analysis of particular cases involving the lives of children who had been abused, served to illustrate once again that it is often sad children who do bad things. It is not uncommon to hear about neighbourhood children who are disruptive or terrorising and to hear, at least through gossip, that caring relationships for them have always been fraught. It is perhaps then not surprising that children with abusive and neglectful home lives are often over-represented in the statistics relating to imprisonment and crime. They are also over-represented in statistics relating to prostitution, homelessness, drug dependency and other factors associated with social exclusion and crime. Therefore, while taking steps to protect society at large, our commitment to all children dictates that we should try to understand how this happens and begin to work actively to stop it.

For this reason I am delighted that the Oak Foundation, which commits its resources to address issues of global and social concern, was able to fund the initiative that brought European organisations together to discuss this group of children and resulted in this impressive book. It would appear that we know how to describe these children and at least some of the factors that contribute towards their later dangerous behaviour. What we need to do now is to provide reliable services for them. I hope this book will be a step in that direction.

Florence Bruce
Senior Programme Officer, Child Abuse Programme
Oak Foundation

Part 1
Backgrounds
and characteristics

1

Introduction and context

Ann Hagell and Renuka Jeyarajah-Dent

Background

During the last few years a number of child death inquiries in England and Wales have shown that there are particular placement and treatment difficulties with respect to children who may be a danger to others or to themselves, but who somehow fall between diagnostic and service boundaries (Bridge Child Care Development Service 2001). In some tragic cases, the inquiries reveal, this has resulted in death or injury to other children or adults who are in the vicinity of these children. Even when such situations do not result in tragedy, anecdotal evidence suggests that most local authorities in England and Wales are responsible for a small group of children who may have committed or may be at risk of committing serious interpersonal violence. They may have overlapping mental health problems and be very difficult to place in company with other children. There is evidence that treatment facilities for these children are limited and unregulated (Stuart and Baines 2004) and that they pose particular challenges for agencies who do not know what to do with them. As a result there is a tension between meeting the children's needs and protecting society, which may result in compromises of care that contribute further to the risk that they will continue to pose a danger.

NCH – The Bridge Child Care Development Service (NCH – The Bridge), of which Renuka Jeyarajah-Dent is Director, became particularly interested in the needs of children who commit serious interpersonal violence through an inquiry into the murder of a young boy by another young person (The Bridge Child Care Development Service 2001). Public response to the event was typically, and perhaps understandably, one of anger and vilification of the offender but the inquiry uncovered the latter's own neglect and abuse throughout his childhood. In fact concern about his welfare and offending in relation to sexual assault of other children had led to a three-year treatment order at a specialist facility whilst in the care of the local authority. However, the validity of the treatment package and the lack of recorded educational intervention and inter-agency planning caused the inquiry panel particular concern. The perpetrator ended up in prison, and research into the lives of young men incarcerated repeatedly suggests that a significant proportion of other children in prison will share a history of chronic abuse and neglect (Boswell 1995; Goldson 2002).

The extent of the problem that these children posed for social care agencies, and the extent to which this was a particular problem of UK service patterning, became of interest to NCH – The Bridge. It seemed likely that this situation also arose within the rather different social care contexts of other European countries. The children may be quite similar, but the ways in which they are dealt with may be different and it may be possible to learn from these differences. Together with Ann Hagell, a researcher with particular interest in the emotional and behavioural difficulties faced by adolescents, NCH – The Bridge built up a programme of projects supported by the Oak Foundation in the early 2000s looking into the different challenges presented by very 'difficult to place' children. At the very crux of the work was this central paradox concerning the need to protect and respond to the needs of these very vulnerable children, yet also to ensure they do not harm others in the process.

This book is thus concerned with describing these children and their needs and the extent of the problem in relation to meeting these needs. In this sense it is an exercise in 'taking stock'. Where possible, it also describes innovative and good practice in the care and treatment necessary to enable these children to progress towards the five outcomes for children described in the England and Wales Children Act 2004 and encompassed in the UN Convention on the Rights of the Child. These outcomes are: to be kept safe, to achieve economic well-being, to be healthy, to make a positive contribution and to enjoy and achieve. Clearly, achieving these outcomes is a challenge in relation to these children and requires close inter-agency work but, if it can be done, everyone will benefit. Specifically this book aims to:

- highlight the plight of, and extent of the problem posed by, potentially dangerous children who fall between agencies and are difficult to place

- document current strategies for dealing with them

- encourage agencies and policymakers to think creatively about how best to intervene and to support good practice

- raise the quality of discussion over issues of managing risk and public protection while at the same time actively managing care and providing successful intervention.

Some definitional issues

Writers in the UK-based social care world often comment on our lack of a 'common language' when talking about children, child development and child social care in a multidisciplinary environment. There is no doubt that different professional groups have their own ways of discussing issues that reflect the way they view the world. We discovered that we had a particular problem, for example, with the phrase that we began with when we first set about some of our joint work around ten years ago. Back in those days, as British psychologists, we both felt reasonably comfortable with the word 'dangerous' used either with respect to parents or children in the context of child abuse. By this we meant a literal definition of children or adults whose behaviour could put others at risk of danger, but it was a salutary lesson to us how offensive this term could be not just to others in different disciplines, but also to others in different European countries. Our initial studies of parents who kill their children were, after considerable debate, entitled 'dangerous care' rather than 'dangerous parents' (e.g. Hagell 1998), to imply that the danger lay in the behaviour and that we were not implying charactological (unmodifiable) evil. On reflection our concern to highlight danger arose from our starting place – inquiries investigating the death of children at the hands of other people who seemed to have been in touch with services but where the warning signs were missed. Shouting 'danger', we felt, was crucial at the time to make us all face what it was we were talking about.

Still we have modified our use of the term and have avoided it as a title for this book. Readers will find, though, that it does inevitably crop up in places. Where it does, we mean something that arises out of a combination of the individual and the situational pressures on their behaviour. This might be called 'risk' in different settings, but we have continued to use the word danger on occasions to imply very serious risk, or risk of awful consequences, rather than lower levels of risk. The choice to use the term is our own though, and not necessarily a choice that would be shared by our various collaborators.

Moving on, we turn to the term 'child'. We will not be the first to point out that even what seems a reasonably straightforward construct such as childhood turns out to be a moveable feast. Article 1 of the Convention on the Rights of the Child defines a child as 'every human being below the age of eighteen years unless, under the law applicable to the child, majority is attained earlier'. As a result, international law increasingly uses the benchmark of 18 years as the age below which special protection should be afforded. For example, the vast majority of states recognise 18 years as the age when individuals reach the necessary intellectual maturity to participate in the political process including voting in elections. There are, of course, many examples where childhood officially ends at age 16 (particularly if young men are required to fight wars), but in this volume we are essentially thinking about young people aged up to 18 years old. It is worth noting, though, that in some countries and particularly in the UK, the period from 16 to 18 years is a bit of a no man's land in terms of rights and responsibilities.

We have also debated the terms violence, violent or grave crime, and serious offending. This was particularly difficult because the starting point had been children who were potentially at risk of perpetrating serious or grave crimes against other children, considered to be so because of a variety of warning signs, but not necessarily children who had already committed such acts. It was the handling of potential risk (or danger) that seemed to pose the real challenges to practice – and to definitions. We were concerned about managing the risk that they would seriously injure another person, either sexually or through physical violence. By seriously, we meant a behaviour or offence that would carry a significant penalty, such as intensive supervision or custody, if the perpetrator were successfully prosecuted in a court of law.

Identifying the issue

Which children are we talking about?

The previous sections begin to give an idea about the group of children with whom we were concerned, and who form the focus of this book. The key issue is the management of children where there is good evidence from their past histories that they may pose a risk to themselves or others. Agencies then have a duty to protect other children from them as well as to protect these children themselves. As we have seen, the local authority is likely to have a duty of care for these children because of child abuse or neglect or the serious risk of it, or in fact because carers have simply said they cannot cope with the demands posed. These children often have a multiplicity and/or complexity of needs and a number of different agencies and practitioners are involved in their care, making placement needs more complicated to define, expensive and thus unusual. In the UK the group is sometimes generically referred to as 'the most difficult to place' (although this phrase can have other meanings within the adoption field). These challenging children are also of interest to academics and social policy makers.

It is important to acknowledge at the outset that the children who form the focus of this project represent a heterogeneous group. The types of young people we were particularly interested in include:

- looked after children who have been seriously physically violent towards their families, carers or other children, but who are not being prosecuted or dealt with by the criminal justice agencies

- looked after children who are suspected of (or unprosecuted for) serious sexual abuse of others

- children who have committed homicide (murder or manslaughter) but are being placed outside prison service accommodation (local authority secure accommodation or secure psychiatric wards) or have been released from custody

- other cases where there is concern (due to high levels of risk factors and some signs of disturbed behaviour) that the child has potential to be dangerous, either sexually or through violence.

The likely needs of these children

Several of the chapters in this book bring together up-to-date information on the needs of the children in this 'difficult to place' group, and we do not want to pre-empt this information, but it is worth noting that we know already from practitioners and limited research that these children are likely to have both very problematic backgrounds and very problematic foregrounds at the time of intervention. They are likely to have severe and chronic problems in their daily lives – crises but also ongoing challenges, including family crises but also relating to behaviour problems; they have a high chance of becoming young parents despite problems in making and enduring relationships both with adults and peers; very low educational achievement (around 7% of children in care as a whole get five GCSEs or more at 16 years of age compared with over 50% of the general population; results for the very difficult to manage group will stand at around zero); that their emotional health is likely to be compromised, resulting in, amongst other things, high levels of self-harm and anger.

We are also often told that these children are difficult to assess, falling between diagnoses, and that in order to deal with their needs there is a range of professional, administrative and legal frameworks with which staff have to be familiar. We also know, before we start, that the problems of these children cannot be met effectively by a single agency, so there is likely to be interface between childcare agencies and other agencies over what to do.

Overview of chapters

The first part of this book focuses on the backgrounds and characteristics of children too dangerous to be placed in the company of others. Professor Susan Bailey (Chapter 2) outlines the key characteristics and patterns of need shown by these children and includes information relating to the coverage and size of the problem, operational definitions, causal relationships and an understanding of the child within an ecological perspective. Professor Bailey comes from a psychiatric health perspective but acknowledges the importance of a needs-led approach to intervening in the lives of these children which by definition involves many agencies and children and families themselves in prioritising and meeting these needs.

Professor Friedrich Lösel and Dr Doris Bender (Chapter 3) then look at risk factors for the broad group in general. They summarise what is known about what leads to some children being potentially dangerous. There are in fact a number of reviews into research on what causes antisocial behaviour but here the authors consider the more extreme end of the antisocial distribution, a group of children on whom less is known. Professor Lösel and Dr Bender begin to consider the psychometric tools that can be used to group these risk factors in the identification of children requiring further intervention, which is further commented on by Dr Paul Tiffin and Graeme Richardson in Appendix 1.

In Chapters 4 and 5, Dr Eileen Vizard, Paul Nieuwbeerta and Dr Peter van der Laan consider two specific subgroups of the children addressed in this book. Dr Vizard writes about the needs of children who sexually abuse – a group of children who pose particular challenges for carers both within the family and when placed in substitute care. Through a presentation of important literature in this field, Dr Vizard considers what makes this group different from others and how assessment models and treatment approaches will differ, thus leading to messages for service development and policy. Paul Nieuwbeerta and Dr van der Laan look at another group of children who invoke an emotive response from society, namely children who murder. These children form a small but critically important subgroup, especially because of the media attention and associated policy and practice discussions that they may invoke. Nieuwbeerta and van der Laan have collected unique data on all murder and manslaughter cases in the Netherlands in the period 1992 to 2001. Their chapter summarises information from this study on the characteristics of these children and their victims, the circumstances of the offence, risk factors and judicial outcomes. Learning more about these children will help us with the understanding and treatment of the broader group.

The second part of the book deals with outcomes and practical considerations. Chapter 6 by Dr Ann Hagell and Dr Patricia Moran describes what is known about these children in relation to interventions that work. In Chapter 7, Professor Gwyneth Boswell looks at an intervention in detail by describing a set of research projects exploring the different outcomes for children who are subject to treatment in a therapeutic community, an ordinary prison service young offenders institution and an enhanced prison service provision. Professor Boswell has longstanding experience in investigating the backgrounds and outcomes for children who are among the most difficult for systems to deal with. Through her description of the research project she addresses the implications for the treatment and management of the children considered by this book.

Dr Kevin Epps has worked for many years in treatment facilities for the most disturbed and 'difficult to place' children within our social care system. In Chapter 8 he draws upon his experience to comment on what we know from the past and how, even in the context of changing legislation and types of pro-vision, we should be careful not to forget what we already know about the best forms of provision.

In Chapters 9, 10, 11 and 12 the comparative field study funded by the Oak Foundation is described by the teams of Dr Ann Hagell in England, Dr Helen Agathonos in Greece and Dr Doris Bender in Germany. The study com-prised a survey of social care staff in the three countries to assess how many children of the type this book is dealing with raise challenges to care provision, how they are dealt with and what is essential in good practice terms. Both the similarities and differences between countries were revealing and interesting. Part 2 of the book is drawn together at the end in our Conclusions chapter, where we draw out some of the messages for good practice based on what we know already, and start to formulate the questions for continued work in this area.

At the end of the book is a collection of brief commentaries that illustrate the complexity of the work with this group of children and service response to it from a range of countries and professional backgrounds. These brief com-mentaries were invited from other delegates at the conference on which this book was based, and are intended to achieve a flavour of how wide the interest is in this group, and how many related issues impact on the key issues of the care for these children. In Appendix 1, Dr Paul Tiffin and Graeme Richardson draw on their own practice experience in the UK to offer more thoughts on the use of structured instruments in assessments. In Appendix 2, Professor Robert Vermeiren looks at some of the issues in making diagnoses of psychiatric disorder based on existing ways of classifying disorder. In Appendix 3, Dr Jean Harris-Hendriks considers disordered attachments and psychological trauma, while Paul Devonshire (Appendix 4) raises issues of autistic spectrum disorders. David Derbyshire (Appendix 5) describes the tensions in coordinating services for children with dangerous behaviour from a social care perspective, whilst Daniela Kolarova (Appendix 6) describes the situation in Bulgaria where services are at an early stage of development. Maria Ternovskaya, Maria Kapilina and Tatiana Gubina write about a project that they consider to be proving successful in the Russian Federation (Appendix 7).

Conclusions

Anecdotal information from practitioners led us to believe from the outset that we had a reasonably clear idea of what social and healthcare staff were dealing with in England and Wales at least. Most agencies seemed to have in their care a small group of children who posed a serious risk to other children. These children were often disturbed themselves, and usually came from very dis-turbed backgrounds. For some reason early intervention has not kicked in, or has not worked, so that by the time they rise to the top of the 'needs' pile they are very complex cases requiring significant multi-agency action.

However, it was not clear at the outset how much robust information existed on the particular needs of this small and demanding group, nor whether the literature offered much understanding about different subgroups. Is this group different to other worrying groups of children in any way or is it just that they have more needs and this makes it more complicated to provide a service? We were unaware what was known about how best to both deal with their day-to-day demands and also the particular value of any potential therapeutic intervention. It was also clear that children went down different routes and received varying services depending on whether they were picked up by education, youth justice, social or health services. We were interested in the importance of the interaction between the initial problems and the welfare agencies' responses in determining the types of experiences the children might be subject to. We wanted to know a bit more about the tensions between managing the day-to-day lives of these children in a way that paid attention to their rights as well as those of others around them, combined with the tensions of trying in fact to improve outcomes for them. The chapters in this volume begin the process of addressing some of these questions.

References

Boswell, G.R. (1995) *Violent Victims: The Prevalence of Abuse and Loss in the Lives of Section 53 Offenders.* London: The Prince's Trust.

Bridge Child Care Development Service (2001) *Childhood Lost: Part 8 Case Review Overview Report.* London: Bridge Publishing House.

Goldson, B. (2002) *Vulnerable Inside: Children in Secure and Penal Settings.* London: The Children's Society.

Hagell, A. (1998) *Dangerous Care.* London: Policy Studies Institute.

Stuart, M. and Baines, C. (2004) *Safeguards for Vulnerable Children: Three Studies on Abusers, Disabled Children and Children in Prison.* York: Joseph Rowntree Foundation.

2

Difficult to place children
Key characteristics, challenges and opportunities
Susan Bailey

Introduction

As a number of commentors have noted, children and adolescents hold a difficult place in our society, often serving as a convenient peg on which to hang the
free-floating anxiety about a range of societal ills, including crime and disorder.
There is a clear need to refocus, however, on children's and adolescents' particular needs. The child should be seen as an individual rather than as flotsam and
jetsam being buffeted through a system by the prevailing winds of policy
and/or service change. We need to cut through the administrative policy and
professional jargon and challenge the jurisdictions of health justice care and
education to come together to delineate effective needs-led services for
children with complex needs, some of whom present as high risk to others by
virtue of conduct disorder and/or more formal mental disorder (Little and
Bullock 2004).

None of this is more obvious than in the sphere of children who are very
behaviourally difficult. Without dismissing the value of diagnosis, there
is sometimes understandable frustration, particularly on the part of social
workers, that despite the young person displaying an array of bizarre behaviours, the child and adolescent mental health assessment ends with the words
'not formally mentally ill', with the result that the client is not viewed as
suitable for hospital treatment. In truth young people who become potential
candidates for long-term security present problems that cannot be met effectively by a single agency or intervention. The serendipitous nature of the career
routes of these children is well documented. Children enter one system and stay
within it when their needs would be better met by another.

The life paths of troubled children

As a starting point, it is useful to be reminded of the trajectories that these very difficult and challenging young people are likely to take. We cannot deal with them as if they live in a particular time or moment; we have to consider the pathway that they are on. Work at the Dartington Social Research Unit, for example, in the 1980s and 1990s resulted in a useful emphasis on compiling a picture of each child that begins at birth and covers all areas of a child's life. Decisions that a young person and his or her carers make then affect the young person's life chances, and it is only by understanding this that we can make an accurate prognosis about outcomes for that child. The idea of life route is an important conceptualisation for mental health workers because it incorporates the influence of the individual's personality on conduct. For very difficult young people, behavioural patterns reflect pathological conditions such as conduct, emotional or mixed disorders. Pressing problems of running away, violence and offending need to be taken into account in any assessment. The other dimension is 'process', defined as the decisions made by professionals or courts in response to the young person's life route and which affect his or her life chances. Whether an adolescent is picked up by education, child guidance, social or health services will certainly make some difference to his or her long-term experience and possibly to outcomes.

This approach incorporates the background, circumstances, needs and pathologies of young people and their families as well as the interventions fashioned to ease difficulties. As such, it brings together two streams of research that are rarely connected. With so many variables contributing to an outcome, it helps if the interaction between the decisions of the child and family on the one hand and those of support agencies on the other is subsumed under the single term 'career route'. Decisions made at successive moments in a career will influence what happens subsequently. 'Career routes', so defined, are a useful way of categorising the situations of children and young people in need, responding dynamically rather than statically as we know needs change over time and circumstances.

As a result of their experience, the very difficult young people referred to welfare and control agencies for help will follow several different career routes and the subsequent classification developed by Dartington (see below) provides more than a taxonomy: it has predictive value, encouraging us to state within a reasonable margin of error what a troubled adolescent's future life chances will be. Prediction is a notoriously complicated process in childcare, especially in view of those individuals who display risk factors but do not succumb to the behaviour being predicted – 'false positives'. Predicting the future for young people known to be very difficult, however, is somewhat easier since the starting point is the high-risk case already known to welfare or control agencies (Little 2002). The Dartington study of long-stay secure treatment units in England identified five groups of young people (Bullock, Little and Millham 1998):

1. those long in local authority care who exceed the capabilities of good open residential provision

2. those long dealt with by special education, school psychology and mental health services

3. those previously unknown to control and welfare agencies whose behaviour deteriorates in mid-adolescence

4. those who commit a one-off grave crime

5. persistent delinquents who also commit a serious offence.

Such a classification would be of limited interest if the five groups had no pre-dictive power but, with a reasonable degree of confidence, Bullock and colleagues are able to say what a long-term state care case (group 1) or an 'adolescent eruptor' (group 3) will be doing in two or five years' time. There is some indication about where they will be living, what kinds of family and social relationships they will enjoy, how much trouble they will get into and whether they will go to school, get a job, fall ill or move about. Further, they argue that, once known to health, education and social services, most cases behave predictably and that this information can be used to design an effective response to young people's problems.

Others have also offered descriptions of the developmental pathways to aggression in adolescence and adulthood, and these continue to be refined. Thus Loeber and Hay (1994) described four groups of young people:

1. those who desist from aggression

2. those whose aggression is stable and continues at the same level

3. those who escalate in the severity of their aggression and make the transition into violence

4. a group who show a stable pattern of aggression.

A systematic method to achieve effective services accurately targeted at the right children is essential. Little and Bullock (2004) stress that much has been written about linking the concepts of needs, threshold, services and outcome and note that some research teams have worked closely with local authorities to put these ideas into practice. The aim of these exercises is to encourage agencies to move from offering isolated initiatives to ones that prioritise risk, introduce eligibility criteria, encourage practitioners to respond creatively to the needs of children and families and adopt a perspective that sees all services as integral to a continuum, each part of which is useful to different individuals at different moments in their care careers.

Although this has been a principle of child protection for some time, it has been a late arrival to the scene of dangerous, high need adolescents. This may be because it is not easy to achieve. Children's marginality is frequently accompanied by their notoriety: any single individual can encompass both welfare and justice concerns. All too often, such young people have been marginal to available interventions and the specialism of the specialist centres becomes their ability to 'pick up the pieces' as opposed to delivering validated therapy. This finding resonates with the responsibilities that have been placed upon Community Adolescent Forensic Services across the UK. Moreover, the public consensus is often that the young person should be locked up, even though he or she is usually a victim of abuse and disadvantage (Bailey and Whittle 2004): hence the high proportion of young people with learning difficulties and mental health disorders in detention (Chitsabesan et al. 2005; YJB 2005).

Risks and characteristics

Accumulated risk is the real problem in the lives of very challenging children. Knowledge of risk factors is essential in planning prevention programmes. A risk factor is a characteristic of an individual or his environment that (a) is present before the onset of the disorder; and (b) increases the risk of disorder in individuals exposed to that factor, compared with those who are not. Although cross-sectional studies can provide important clues about risk factors, longitudinal studies are usually necessary to confirm them. Longitudinal research on the precursors of antisocial personality disorder (ASPD) does however have some limitations (Loeber, Burke and Lahey 2002a). The relatively low rate of ASPD in the general population means that few studies have had enough cases, and those that do have rarely had the resources to assess all relevant risk factors using state-of-the-art measures. Much of what we know comes from either high-risk studies or from general population studies in which the outcome has been antisocial behaviour of one kind or another but not ASPD as such. However, in attempting to work with any individual who has committed a violent act, the question to be answered is why this individual has behaved in this unique fashion on this occasion.

In cases of serious violence, experience of past violence is clearly a major risk. Some of the work in this field has, for example, concentrated on the impact of violence on children who have experienced war and subsequently become refugees. *Minefields in their Hearts* (Apfel and Bennet 1996) deals with the mental health issues of children in war. UNICEF estimates that whereas in 1900 the ratio of civilian to military casualties was about 1:9, it now stands at 8:1. Children constitute a significant proportion of these civilian casualties. Some countries – most often described in the USA but of increasing relevance to the UK – have chronic community violence in 'urban war zones', which affect the development of children (Kotlowitz 1991).

Garbarino (2001) sets out an ecological framework to explain the processes and condition that transform the 'developmental challenge' of violence into developmental harm in some children:

- an accumulation-of-risk model for understanding how and when children suffer the most adverse consequences of exposure to community violence and go beyond their limits of resilience

- the concept of 'social maps' as the product of childhood experiences

- the concept of trauma as a psychological wound

- children are embedded in families

- families are embedded in neighbourhoods

- embedded within neighbourhoods are schools.

The idea is that risk accumulates whilst opportunity ameliorates. As negative (pathogenic) influences increase, the child may exceed his or her breaking point: consequently as a positive (salutogenic) influence increases, the probability of recovery and enhanced development increases.

The developmental model predicts that children and adolescents most at risk for negative consequences associated with community violence are those who already live in the context of accumulated risk – the socially marginalised, those with fractured families and those with caregivers who have mental health problems or who are addicted to substances. By contrast, children who approach their community violence experience from a position of strength – with the salutogenic resources of social support, intact and functional families, and parents who model social competence – can accept better the developmental challenges posed by community violence and deal with them more positively in the long run (even if they show short-term disturbance). This model applies whether the experience is of actual war or 'urban war zones' (Garbarino and Kostelny 1996).

Chapter 3 in this volume provides a detailed review of the research on the main risk factors for serious antisocial behaviour, and so we do not go into detail in this chapter. Suffice it to say at this stage that there have now been a number of thorough reviews of the literature undertaken, and these tend to agree on the main candidates (Farrington 2003; Loeber, Green and Lahey 2003; Rutter, Giller and Hagell 1998) and from some of the best-known longitudinal studies, including the Cambridge Study (Farrington 1995), the Pittsburgh studies (Loeber *et al.* 2002b), and the Dunedin Study (Moffitt *et al.* 2002) and risk assessment instruments (e.g. Borum, Bartel and Forth 2002). These are summarised in Table 2.1 (Harrington and Bailey 2003).

Table 2.1 Child and adolescent risk factors
for antisocial behaviour in adulthood

Risk factor	Age	Adult outcome	Reference
Temperament/personality			
Undercontrolled	3	Aggression	(Caspi 2000)
Impulsive	8–10	Offending	(Farrington 1995)
Hyperactive	13	Violence	(Klinteberg *et al.* 1993)
Callous	7–12	ASPD	(Loeber *et al.* 2002a)
Low IQ and low educational achievement	4–11	Arrests	(Moffitt 1993)
Psychopathology			
Depression	14	ASPD	(Kasen *et al.* 2001)
Oppositional disorder	7–12	ASPD	(Loeber *et al.* 2002a)
Conduct disorder	9–16	ASPD	(Harrington *et al.* 1991)
Substance abuse	7–12	ASPD	(Loeber *et al.* 2002a)
Parents and parenting			
Antisocial parent	8–10	Offending	(Smith and Farrington 2004)
Poor supervision	8	Offending	(Farrington 1995)
Abuse	<12	Violence	(Widom 1989)
Violence between parents	3–16	Violence Violence to children	(Moffitt and Caspi 2003)
Deviant peer group	11–16	Offending	(Lipsey and Derzon 1998)
High delinquency school	11	Offending	(Farrington 1995)

Conduct disorder, antisocial personality disorder and psychopathy are often seen as developmental disorders that span the life course and the terms are sometimes used interchangeably. There are, however, significant differences between them and their associated correlates. Whereas conduct disorder and antisocial personality disorder primarily focus on behavioural problems, psychopathy, as described by Hare (1991), emphasises deficits in affective and interpersonal functioning. Psychopathy is seen as a higher order construct, which can now be reliably assessed in adults.

Overall, the research would suggest that young people who commit the most serious types of violence (juvenile homicide) are a heterogeneous group, with often abusive family backgrounds and a range of personal problems. We have selected three key areas of the characteristics of these children to explore in more detail in the next sections: trauma in their lives; the role of communities and gangs; and the overlap with mental health problems.

The role of trauma in creating psychological wounds

For some children the level of their fright exceeds the actual dangers they face; for others, the fact of the matter is they are surrounded by violence – the world for them is a dangerous place, and they experience trauma. Trauma arises when a child cannot give a meaning to dangerous experiences. The result is over-whelming negative emotion and cognition. Young children, in particular, have not developed fully functioning systems to modulate arousal and trauma. This can result in an inability to handle effectively the physiological responses of stress in situations of threat. The process required to 'understand' traumatic experiences can have pathogenic side effects and the child may be forced into patterns of behaviour, thought and feelings that are themselves 'abnormal' compared with the untraumatised healthy child.

Children and adolescents exposed to acute danger may develop symptoms of post-traumatic stress disorder (PTSD). These manifest themselves as sleep disturbance, daydreaming, revelations of trauma in play, extreme startle re-sponses, emotional numbing and diminished expectations for the future. Trauma can also result in alterations in brain chemistry that can impair social and academic performance (Osofsky 1995; Pynoos and Nader 1988). In some cases trauma may be seen as a significant aetiological factor for violent behaviour due to its adverse effects on psychological functioning, academic performance and normal parent–child relationships.

As difficult and damaging as acute trauma can be in the lives of children who in turn become violent, their neighbourhood and family experiences can also have a profound influence, particularly if these environments are chroni-cally traumatic. Garbarino (1995) describes chronic traumatic danger as rewriting the child's story, redrawing the child's social map, and redirecting behaviour. Trauma represents an enormous challenge to any individual's understanding of the meaning and purpose of life. Children start life with a need and expectation of care, protection and love. When this need is absolutely violated, some children will seek out a negative universe on the grounds that anything is better than nothing. This can result in extreme acts of violence later in life (Douglas and O'Shaker 1995). Importantly, it also has implications for identity: when faced with the prospect of psychic annihilation, human beings will even opt for negative identities (Gilligan 1996).

The community context for the development of serious violence (Bailey and Dolan 2004)

Community violence and its consequences can make children prime candidates for involvement in social groups that augment or replace families and offer a sense of affiliation and security and perhaps a sense of revenge. In urban settings this can mean gangs. It is difficult accurately to ascertain the extent of the gang problem owing to varying definitions of what constitutes a gang. However, it is recognised that youth gangs are widespread and beginning to include non-urban areas.

The USA and inner city areas of Britain have seen a proliferation in youth gangs. In the USA, an 11-city survey of eighth-graders found that nine per cent were gang members and seven per cent had been at some time in their lives (Esbensen and Osgood 1997). Research indicates that the USA has seen several distinct periods of gang proliferation (Curry and Decker 1998). The gravest cause for concern in recent years has been the association with weapons of greater lethality (Block and Block 1993; Miller 1992) and drug trafficking (Miller 1992; Thornberry 1998). There are several factors that influence youth gang membership, including community, family, school, peer group and individual factors. Howell (1998) reported that low community integrity, poverty, parental absence/lack of supervision, academic underachievement, peer influences and drug use were significant predictors of gang membership, and similar findings were reported in a Seattle study (Hill et al. 1996; Kosterman et al. 1996). Gang membership tends to be associated with lower social class and decaying urban areas, and ethnic-minority groups predominate (Miller 1974; Spergel 1995).

The mean age of gang members tends to be 17 years (Curry and Decker 1998), but older individuals are found in cities with longer histories of gang-related activity (Spergel 1995). Gang membership is often viewed in terms of its degree of organisation (Gordon 1994). Three other types of gang have been identified:

- organised/cooperative – strong leadership and a focus on illegal monetary gain

- territorial – belonging to a specific neighbourhood or turf

- scavenger – no strong leadership, but engaged in petty criminal activity.

Compared with non-gang adolescents, gang members commit serious and violent offences at significantly higher rates (Bjerregaard and Smith 1993; Esbensen and Huizinga 1993; Thornberry, Huizinga and Loeber 1995). The use of violence is a key characteristic distinguishing gangs from other adolescent peer groups (Horowitz 1983; Sanders 1994). It serves to maintain organisation within the gang and control gang members (Decker and Van Winkle 1996). While there is a perception that gang violence is a significant threat to society, work by Block et al. (1996) indicates that of 1000 gang-related homicides in Chicago between 1987 and 1994, 75 per cent were between gangs, 11 per cent were within gangs and 14 per cent involved non-gang victims. Disputes were usually over turf and the violent episodes occurred within a mile of the attackers' residence.

Schools also form an important part of the community context of these children's lives. There are a number of factors in school environments that may contribute to violence among schoolchildren. These include academic failure due to bullying, exclusion or underlying mental health and behavioural disorders such as attention deficit hyperactivity disorder (ADHD). Looking first at bullying, this is characterised by:

- repeated predatory activity designed to intimidate, physically harm, and in some cases elicit personal items from individuals under the threat of force

- an imbalance of power between bully and victim

- repeated harm over time

- for schoolchildren bullying affects their perceptions of safety and the overall quality of their school experience

- fear, with the potential to make students practise avoidance techniques to stay out of harm's way.

In addition to bullying, the onset of attention problems such as ADHD occurs during the preschool period, a key period when aggression manifests itself in some children (Barkley 1990, 1997). Longitudinal studies show that children with attention problems exhibit increased levels of aggression in childhood, adolescence and adulthood. A major cluster of individual risk factors is starting to emerge which include hyperactivity, impulsive attention problems, clumsiness, daring or risk taking and other elements of ADHD (Hagell and Shaw 1996). These factors are closely linked to childhood conduct disorder. Lynam (1996) has argued that children who had both hyperactivity impulsivity/attention deficit and conduct problems were at risk of serious adult antisocial behaviour and personality disorder.

Obviously these children are very difficult to manage in the school setting, and children who have frequent disagreements with peers do not make friends. Very aggressive children are rejected by their peers, a process which can start in the early school years. Aggressive children who are rejected show more diverse and severe conduct problems. Moreover, peer rejection promotes an association with antisocial peers; dyadic relationships are then formed that provide the focus for peer-diverted aggression. Victims often lack social skills and can be aggressive themselves. Repeatedly victimised young people are more likely to become aggressors as well. Aggressive young people may make alliances, bullying others, which results in the emergence of aggressive peer groups and gangs where the individual's rate of violence usually increases. These groups may appear attractive to other previously non-aggressive young people, adding to the group late-onset aggressive adolescence.

Most school-related violence is linked to competition for status among peers. The presence of gangs in schools increases the likelihood of victimisation for non-gang members. An additional emerging peer-related concern is that of sexual assault, particularly within the context of dating.

Overlaps between serious antisocial behaviour and mental health problems

An important characteristic of serious interpersonal violence in children is the overlap of this behaviour with the experience of mental health problems. This is crucial for understanding the problem, but even more so for intervening. Estimates suggest that as many as a third to two thirds of young offenders in the youth justice system have mental health needs (Hagell 2004). Looking at the progress since the early 1990s in meeting the mental health needs of young offenders, we have come some way down the road of reform. In Bailey (1992) I noted that mental health services for juvenile offenders would need to function effectively within a complex, ever-changing system. This requires being alert to the total clinical profile of the individual and not just referred offence behaviour, being proactive in multi-agency liaison and treatment programmes and making the best use of scarce research resources. At the time, the increase in violent acts committed by adolescents together with concern about the quality of care and treatment offered to juvenile offenders had caught the attention of the public and politicians, leading to persistent demands for action. The challenge was to bring together the various agencies involved to deliver integrated care.

Heightened concern at this time was epitomised by Liebling's (1993) comprehensive study of suicide and self-injury amongst young offenders. As well as describing the components that made up the vulnerability and situational triggers, their varying contribution to individual crises and their possible protecting agents, she made suggestions for the safer care of juveniles in custody. In 2004, levels of suicide in youth custody in the UK remain high, although there has been much work on how to meet young people's needs safely, for instance, by improving health provision in the establishments and transferring health responsibility in prisons to the National Health Service (NHS). By 2006 all local primary care trusts in England will be commissioning health services for prisons in their area. We have also seen the development of forensic secure mental health beds, now nationally commissioned. Indications of this change include the current provision of NHS beds in Newcastle, Manchester, Birmingham and London.

Other developments aimed at improving the mental health of young offenders concern practice and training. The Youth Justice Board has complemented its assessment tool (ASSET) with a mental health screening tool for use by youth justice workers (YJB 2003). This has been developed by myself and colleagues, multi-agency teams brought together as part of a major overhaul of working in Manchester, and used in training health workers in youth offending teams, staff in youth offender institutions and local authority secure children's homes.

Mental health awareness training has also been rolled out into the youth justice system under the umbrella of a children's National Service Framework. Strategies are in place to implement a 'fit for purpose' workforce that can take a developmental approach to working with young people wherever they are in the system. Child and adolescent primary mental health care workers act as facilitators to improve joint working and local access to services between youth offending teams and Child and Adolescent Mental Health Services (CAMHS).

Research is contributing to the improvement of services. The availability of official statistics and the increasing quality and sophistication of research data, particularly the longitudinal studies, mean that research can now inform both policymakers and practitioners about those interventions most likely to reduce reoffending rates in young people and have a positive impact on their mental health. This is apparent in several areas. In a review of the literature I have brought together findings on the background, nature, assessment, treatment and outcomes of those young people who have committed grave crimes (Bailey 1997a). Boswell (1995) vividly describes the prevalence and nature of abuse and loss in the lives of such offenders, as well as research on the nature of the medical, legal, clinical, assessment and treatment interventions with adolescents who murder (Bailey 1996, 1997b). The literature also examines the challenges of working directly with sadistic and violent young people using verbal and non-verbal therapies and the psychosocial characteristics of juvenile sex offenders (Dolan et al. 1996).

Chicchetti and Newcombe (1997) have highlighted the importance of developmental psychopathology as the bridge across fields of study that span the lifecycle and have clarified the process underlying adaptation and maladaptation, as well as the best means of preventing or ameliorating psychopathology. The application of this approach to the field of adolescent offenders offered a positive way forward for future research. Thus, by the turn of the millennium, psychosocial and biological factors placing young people at risk of offending and of developing mental health problems were well established in the national and international literature (Bailey 1999).

Following on from epidemiological and needs surveys of young people referred to CAMHS, specific studies were undertaken in the field of child and adolescent forensic mental health. These revealed a lack of appropriate services to meet the needs of young people at the interface of mental health and criminal justice. This major national survey highlighted the perceived extent and severity of psychiatric disorders among young people placed in different secure provision, whether in social care or penal establishments.

With like-minded practitioners and researchers in Manchester, we have paralleled some of the thinking of the Dartington team with the development and validation of the Salford Needs Assessment Schedule for Adolescents (Kroll *et al.* 1999). This provided the starting point for a series of research projects looking at the mental health needs of young people in the criminal justice system, both within youth offending teams and secure units. We utilised this schedule not only in dissemination to increase understanding of the mental health needs of young people in the criminal justice system but also to develop mental health screening tools and frameworks for intervention. The studies included the 'Psychosocial Needs of Boys in Secure Care for Serious or Persistent Offending', the first prospective longitudinal study of its kind (Harrington *et al.* 2005; Kroll *et al.* 2002).

The prevention of antisocial personality disorder

A proportion of children who commit the most serious violent and sexual offences will be exhibiting the early signs of personality disorder. The prevalence of antisocial personality disorder in the general population is approximately 2 per cent (Coid 2003; Torgersen, Kringlen and Cramer 2001). Antisocial personality disorder is associated with much social handicap and once established it is hard to treat, so there are strong arguments for trying to find ways to intervene in childhood or adolescence. There is also an association with increased morbidity and mortality. Individuals with antisocial personality are at increased risk of death through accidents, suicide, substance abuse and murder (Robins and Rutter 1990).

It is sometimes argued that preventing mental disorder will not only improve health but also save money. Indeed, there is evidence that antisocial personality is associated with a variety of economic costs both to the individual and to society (Welsh 2003). Scott and colleagues (2001) provided costs data on children with conduct disorder who were followed up into adulthood when many of them showed antisocial behaviour. By the age of 28 years they had cost society approximately ten times as much as their non-antisocial counterparts.

There are, however, several reasons for thinking that the savings that might come from preventing personality disorders would be less than anticipated. First, reducing the incidence of a disorder does not necessarily mean that the costs of treating it become less. The rising costs of health and social care mean that even if a smaller number of people develop a problem they can cost more to treat. For example, rates of heart disease have gone down over the past 20 years in the UK, but the number of bypass operations has greatly increased and heart surgeons are busier than ever. Even if preventive programmes reduced the number of people with personality disorder, those that remain could be very expensive to treat.

Second, the idea that reducing the incidence of a disorder leads to a reduction in treatment costs assumes that we live in an ideal world in which demands for care accurately reflect needs, which are themselves closely linked to service provision and costs. However, in the world in which most of us actually work there is only a weak relationship between costs of mental healthcare and the mental health needs of young people. The money that is spent on the care of antisocial young people is influenced by many other factors, such as the attitudes of politicians and the public towards mental and behavioural disorder, newspaper reports, the location of existing services, government policies and, perhaps most importantly, the organisation and attitudes of agencies who fund services. Research on juvenile offenders in secure care (Kroll *et al.* 2002), many of whom will go on to develop antisocial personality, has shown that service provision is only partly related to need. The secure system meets some of the needs of juveniles who have committed serious offences very well, such as their need for educational services. However, services for other needs are very patchy, being excellent in some geographical areas and virtually absent in others. It is unlikely therefore that changes in the incidence of mental health problems would lead automatically to changes in spending. The main argument for preventing personality disorder, therefore, is as much humanitarian as it is economic. Personality disorder causes great suffering to many individuals, their families and to society (Harrington and Bailey 2003).

Life after care and/or detention

It is sobering to note that the environments to which seriously violent young people return after periods in detention or in secure accommodation remain depressingly constant and are a reminder of the importance of education, housing and employment opportunities for those who are disadvantaged (Little and Bullock 2004). A positive situation between the ages of 18 and 21 is no indication of 'a life happy thereafter'. Many young people have stored up problems of health or isolation that revisit them later and many are settled in happy domestic relationships that come under strain in subsequent years. Most of the grave offenders have been law abiding but still have to be considered a long-term risk to the public.

The relative lack of scientific and practice knowledge about what happens to disordered young people between the ages of 18 and 30 is striking. In the past, researchers and professionals have tended to view young adults as merely adolescents writ large, focusing on unfinished tasks such as educational underachievement and failing to look to the future and encourage what will help them as adults, such as late entry into continuing education or social skills to stay in work. Little and Bullock (2004) ask for more evidence to be extracted on how careers develop, whether or not protective factors continue to operate and how long the effects of treatment last. They say that only by looking at what happens in the very long term can we know whether the cautious optimism resulting from achievements to date is well founded.

Challenges for research, policy and practice

Having recently completed a review of the research literature in the field of young offenders and mental health (Bailey 2003), it is possible to see how far we have travelled over the past 20 years. Certainly we have a rapidly developing knowledge base about the life routes of these young people. It remains to be seen, however, whether the increasingly promising findings from evaluations of prevention, early intervention and treatment programmes delivered to children and adolescents in the context of families, communities and institutions can reduce the burden on adult mental health, social care and criminal justice services. A further challenge is how best to engage children and families that are hostile or difficult to reach. Further chapters in this book start to address some of these questions from a range of professional and international perspectives.

Key longitudinal studies continue also to inform what programmes should be taken forward and what this means to society in financial and human costs (Farrington 2002; Moffitt et al. 2002). The ongoing Dunedin and New Zealand Study of young people, led by Moffitt and her colleagues (2002), is testing and refining a developmental taxonomy of antisocial behaviour and making challenging recommendations about interventions for all aggressive children and adolescent offenders. Smith and McVie (2003) are engaged in the early stages of an innovative longitudinal study in Edinburgh that concentrates on transitions and personal transformations during adolescence, integrating explanations at the levels of the individual and the social ecology.

The search for the Holy Grail of what turns a child with difficulties into an adult with psychopathy continues, as does the search for the most promising early interventions. The assessment of psychopathy in children and adolescents is a very important area of research and is still in its infancy. There seems to be reasonable evidence that juvenile psychopathy shows similar correlates (e.g. aggression, neurocognitive deficits, substance misuse) to adult psychopathy. Our knowledge about the nature, stability and consequences of juvenile psychopathy, however, is still very limited. There have been no published longitudinal studies of the stability of psychopathy as assessed by any of the current measures and it remains unclear to what degree the antisocial behavioural items that contribute to the psychopathy label change over time, given what we know about adolescent-limited antisocial behaviours. The limited data on the psychometric properties of current instruments, particularly information on recommended or specific cut-off scores for prototypical psychopathy, suggest that it is premature to assign this label to younger cohorts. For this reason many researchers in this field refer to juveniles with 'psychopathic characteristics' rather than using the term 'psychopathy'. However, these instruments do include items we know to be associated with high-risk behaviours, and they can inform clinical assessments of risk and treatment planning.

At present, there is no general agreement on whether or not psychopathy exists in childhood and adolescence. A consensus is likely to be reached only when we have longitudinal studies demonstrating the stability of psychopathic traits over the lifespan and evidence that the same aetiological factors contribute to this disorder at all ages. As there is significant overlap between the behavioural aspects of juvenile psychopathy and ADHD and between the callous-unemotional dimension of psychopathy and autistic spectrum disorders, future work needs to disentangle these constructs from a phenomenological and aetiological perspective. As yet, there are few treatment outcome studies in juveniles with psychopathic traits, although the limited data suggest that these traits might be a moderator of outcome. Most clinicians view youth psychopathy as a potentially treatable disorder, and there is some evidence that identification of psychopathic traits in young people has a number of benefits, which include:

- identifying high-risk offenders

- reducing misclassifications that have negative ramifications for children and adolescents

- improving and optimising treatment planning for young people with psychopathic traits, who may require more intensive and risk-focused therapeutic approaches (Dolan 2004).

Reflected in recent research conducted by Little and Bullock (2004) around specific interventions, the literature suggests that the most promising interventions need to be multimodal, intensive, well structured and lengthy, and include multisystemic therapy, functional family therapy, treatment foster care, multimodal cognitive behavioural packages and some therapeutic communities.

Research needs to cover detailed assessments of the characteristics of the individual at the outset of an intervention and at long-term follow-up of a treatment series if it is to detect the stage at which additional intervention is required and the effects of additional top-up interventions. Other necessary conditions for improving mental health services for young offenders are clear definitions in research of risk and protective factors, detailed descriptions of interventions, methods of identifying high-risk adolescents and ways of ensuring that troubled adolescents are perceived as a priority rather than a last resort (Bailey 2002). This should include not only interventions directly with adolescents to reduce reoffending, in the context of evidence-based provision, but also research into policy development.

References

Apfel, R. and Bennet, S. (eds) (1996) *Minefields in their Hearts: The Mental Health of Children in War and Communal Violence*. New Haven: Yale University Press.

Bailey, S. (1992) 'Delinquency in context.' *Current Opinion in Psychiatry 5*, 778.

Bailey, S. (1996) 'Adolescents who murder.' *Journal of Adolescence 19*, 19–39.

Bailey, S. (1997a) 'Adolescent offenders.' *Current Opinion in Psychiatry 10*, 445–453.

Bailey, S. (1997b) 'Sadistic and violent acts in the young.' *Child Psychology and Psychiatry Review 2*, 3, 92–102.

Bailey, S. (1999) 'The interface between mental health, criminal justice and forensic mental health services for children and adolescents.' *Current Opinion in Psychiatry 12*, 425–432.

Bailey, S. (2002) 'Violent children – a framework for assessment.' *Advances in Psychiatry Treatment 8*, 97–106.

Bailey, S. (2003) 'Young offenders and mental health.' *Current Opinions in Psychiatry 16*, 581–591.

Bailey, S. and Dolan, M. (2004) 'Violence.' In S. Bailey and M. Dolan *Adolescent Forensic Psychiatry*. London: Arnold, pp.213–227.

Bailey, S. and Whittle, N.J. (2004) 'Young people: Victims of violence.' *Current Opinion in Psychiatry 17*, 263–268.

Barkley, R.A. (1990) *Attention Deficit Hyperactivity Disorder: A Handbook for Diagnosis and Treatment*. New York: Guilford Press.

Barkley, R.A. (1997) *Defiant Children: A Clinician's Manual for Assessment and Parent Training*, 2nd edn. New York: Guilford Press.

Bjerregaard, B. and Smith, C. (1993) 'Gender differences in gang participation, delinquency and substance use.' *Journal of Quantitative Criminology 9*, 329–355.

Block, R. and Block, C.R. (1993) *Street Gang Crime in Chicago: Research in Brief*. Washington, DC: US Department of Justice, Office of Justice Programs, National Institute of Justice.

Block, C.R., Christakos, A., Jacob, A. and Przybylski, R. (1996) *Street Gangs and Crime: Patterns and Trends in Chicago*. Chicago, IL: Illinois Criminal Justice Information Authority.

Borum, R., Bartel, P. and Forth, A. (2002) *Manual for the Structured Assessment of Violence Risk in Youth (SAVRY)*. Tampa, FL: University of South Florida.

Boswell, G. (1995) *Violent Victims. The Prevalence of Abuse and Loss in the Lives of Section 53 Offenders*. London: Prince's Trust.

Bullock, R., Little, M. and Millham, S. (1998) *Secure Treatment Outcomes: The Care Careers of Very Difficult Adolescents*. Aldershot: Ashgate.

Caspi, A. (2000) 'The child is father of the man: Personality continuities from childhood to adulthood.' *Journal of Personality and Social Psychology 78*, 1, 158–172.

Chicchetti, D. and Newcombe, B. (1997) 'Special issue: Conceptual and scientific underpinnings of research in developmental psychopathology.' *Developmental Psychopathology 9*, 189–472.

Chitsabesan, P., Kroll, L., Bailey, S. *et al.* (2005) 'National study of mental health provision for young offenders. Part I: The mental health needs of young offenders in custody and in the community.' *British Journal of Psychiatry 188*, 534–540.

Coid, J. (2003) 'Formulating strategies for the primary prevention of adult antisocial behaviour: "High risk" or "population" strategies?' In D.P. Farrington and J.W. Coid (eds) *Early Prevention of Adult Antisocial Behaviour*. Cambridge: Cambridge University Press, pp.32–78.

Curry, G.D. and Decker, S.H. (1998) *Confronting Gangs: Crime and Community.* Los Angeles, CA: Roxbury.

Decker, S.H. and Van Winkle, B. (1996) *Life in the Gang: Family, Friends and Violence.* New York: Cambridge University Press.

Dolan, M. (2004) 'Psychopathic personality in young people.' *Advances in Psychiatric Treatment 10,* 466–473.

Dolan, M., Holloway, J., Bailey, S. and Kroll, L. (1996) 'The psychosocial characteristics of juvenile sexual offenders referred to an adolescent forensic service in the UK.' *Medicine, Science and the Law 36,* 343–351.

Douglas, S.L. and O'Shaker, M. (1995) *Mindhunter.* New York: Schriber.

Esbensen, F. and Huizinga, D. (1993) 'Gangs, drugs, and delinquency in a survey of urban youth.' *Criminology 31,* 565–589.

Esbensen, F. and Osgood, D.W. (1997) *National Evaluation of GREAT Research in Brief.* Washington, DC: US Department of Justice, Office of Justice Programs, National Institute of Justice.

Farrington, D.P. (1995) 'The development of offending and antisocial behaviour from childhood: Key findings from the Cambridge study in delinquent development.' *Journal of Child Psychology and Psychiatry 36,* 929–964.

Farrington, D.P. (2002) 'Criminology.' *Criminal Behaviour and Mental Health 12,* 4, S10–S16.

Farrington, D.P. (2003) 'British randomized experiments on crime and justice.' *Annals of the American Academy of Political and Social Science 589,* 150–167.

Garbarino, J. (1995) *Raising Children in a Socially Toxic Environment.* San Francisco: Jossey-Bass.

Garbarino, J. (2001) 'An ecological perspective on the effects of violence on children.' *Journal of Community Psychology 29,* 3, 361–378.

Garbarino, J. and Kostelny, K. (1996) 'The impact of political violence on the behavioural problems of Palestine children.' *Child Development 67,* 33–45.

Gilligan, J. (1996) *Violence: Our Deadly Epidemic and its Causes.* New York: Gosset/Putman.

Gordon, R.M. (1994) 'Incarcerating gang members in British Columbia: Preliminary study.' Unpublished study, Ministry of the Attorney General. Victoria, BC.

Hagell, A. (2004) *The Mental Health of Young Offenders.* A report commissioned by the Mental Health Foundation.

Hagell, A. and Shaw, C. (1996) *Opportunity and Disadvantage at Age 16.* London: Policy Studies Institute.

Hare, R.D. (1991) *The Hare Psychopathy Checklist – Revised.* Toronto: Multi Health Systems.

Harrington, R. and Bailey, S. (2003) *The Scope for Preventing Personality Disorder by Intervening in Adolescence.* NHS National Programme on Forensic Mental Health Research and Development Expert Paper.

Harrington, R., Fudge, H., Rutter, M. *et al.* (1991) 'Adult outcomes of childhood and adolescent depression: II. Links with antisocial disorders.' *Journal of the American Academy of Child and Adolescent Psychiatry 30,* 3, 434–439.

Harrington, R.C., Kroll, L., Rothwell, J., McCarthy, K., Bradley, D. and Bailey, S. (2005) 'Psychosocial needs of boys in secure care for serious or persistent offending.' *Journal of Child Psychology and Psychiatry 46,* 8, 859–866.

Hill, K.G., Hawkins, J.D., Catalano, R.F. *et al.* (1996) 'The longitudinal dynamics of gang membership and problem behaviour: A replication and extension of the Denver and Rochester gang studies in Seattle.' Paper presented at the annual meeting of the American Society of Criminology, Chicago, Illinois.

Horowitz, R. (1983) *Honor and the American Dream: Culture and Identity in a Chicano Community.* New Brunswick, NJ: Rutgers University Press.

Howell, J.C. (1998) 'Promising programs for youth gang violence prevention and intervention.' In R. Loeber and D.P. Farrington (eds) *Serious and Violent Juvenile Offenders: Risk Factors and Successful Interventions.* Thousand Oaks, CA: Sage, pp.284–312.

Kasen, S., Cohen, P., Skodol, A.E., Johnson, J.G., Smailes, E. and Brook, J.S. (2001) 'Childhood depression and adult personality disorder: Alternative pathways of continuity.' *Archives of General Psychiatry 58,* 3, 231–236.

Klinteberg, B., Andersson, T., Magnusson, D. and Stattin, H. (1993) 'Hyperactive behavior in childhood as related to subsequent alcohol problems and violent offending: A longitudinal study of male subjects.' *Personality and Individual Differences 15,* 4, 381–388.

Kosterman, R., Hawkins, J.D., Hill, K.G. *et al.* (1996) 'The developmental dynamics of gang initiation: When and why young people join gangs.' Paper presented at the annual meeting of the American Society of Criminology, Chicago, Illinois.

Kotlowitz, A. (ed) (1991) *There Are No Children Here.* New York: Doubleday.

Kroll, L., Woodham, A., Rothwell, J. *et al.* (1999) 'Reliability of the Salford Needs Assessment Schedule for Adolescents.' *Psychological Medicine 29,* 891–902.

Kroll, L., Rothwell, J., Bradley, D., Shah, P., Bailey, S. and Harrington, R. (2002) 'Mental health needs of boys in secure care for serious or persistent offending: A prospective, longitudinal study.' *The Lancet 359,* 9322, 1975–1979.

Liebling, A. (1993) 'Suicides in young prisoners: A summary.' *Death Studies 17,* 5, 381–409.

Lipsey, M.W. and Derzon, J.H. (1998) 'Predictors of violent or serious delinquency in adolescence and early adulthood: A synthesis of longitudinal research.' In R. Loeber and D.P. Farrington (eds) *Serious and Violent Juvenile Offenders: Risk Factors and Successful Interventions.* Thousand Oaks, CA: Sage, pp.86–105.

Little, M. (2002) *Prediction: Perspectives on Diagnosis, Prognosis and Interventions for Children in Need.* Dartington: Warren House Press.

Little, M. and Bullock, R. (2004) 'Administrative frameworks and services for very difficult adolescents in England.' In S. Bailey and M. Dolan (eds) *Adolescent Forensic Psychiatry.* London: Arnold, pp.336–344.

Loeber, R. and Hay, D.F. (1994) 'Developmental approaches to aggression and conduct problems.' In M. Rutter and D.F. Hay (eds) *Development Through Life: A Handbook for Clinicians.* Boston: Blackwell Scientific, pp.288–516.

Loeber, R., Burke, J.D. and Lahey, B.B. (2002a) 'What are adolescent antecedents to antisocial personality disorder?' *Criminal Behaviour and Mental Health 12,* 1, 24–36.

Loeber, R., Stouthamer-Loeber, M., Farrington, D.P., Lahey, B.B., Keenan, K. and White, H.R. (2002b) 'Editorial introduction: Three longitudinal studies of children's development in Pittsburgh: The Developmental Trends Study, the Pittsburgh Youth Study, and the Pittsburgh Girls Study.' *Criminal Behaviour and Mental Health 12,* 1, 1–23.

Loeber, R., Green, S.M. and Lahey, B.B. (2003) 'Risk factors for antisocial personality.' In D.P. Farrington and J.W. Coid (eds) *Early Prevention of Adult Antisocial Behaviour.* Cambridge: Cambridge University Press, pp.79–108.

Lynam, D. (1996) 'Early identification of chronic offenders: who is the fledgling psychopath?' *Psychologist Bulletin 120,* 209–234.

Miller, W.B. (1974) 'American youth gangs: past and present.' In A. Blumberg (ed) *Current Perspectives on Criminal Behaviour.* New York: Knopf, pp.410–420.

Miller, W.B. (1992) *Crime by Youth Gangs and Groups in the United States.* Washington, DC: US Department of Justice, Office of Justice Programs, Office of Juvenile Justice and Delinquency Prevention.

Moffitt, T.E. (1993) 'The neuropsychology of conduct disorder.' *Development and Psychopathology 5,* 135–151.

Moffitt, T.E. and Caspi, A. (2003) 'Preventing the inter-generational continuity of antisocial behaviour: Implications of partner violence.' In D.P. Farrington and J.W. Coid (eds) *Early Prevention of Adult Antisocial Behaviour.* Cambridge: Cambridge University Press, pp.109–129.

Moffitt, T.E, Caspi, A., Harrington, H. and Milne, B.J. (2002) 'Males on the life-course-persistent and adolescence-limited antisocial pathways: Follow-up at age 26 years.' *Development and Psychopathology 14,* 1, 179–207.

Osofsky, J. (1995) 'The effects of exposure to violence on young children.' *American Psychologist 50,* 782–788.

Pynoos, R. and Nader, K. (1988) 'Psychological first aid and treatment approach to children exposed to community violence: Research implications.' *Journal of Traumatic Stress 1,* 445–473.

Robins, L. and Rutter, M. (eds) (1990) *Straight and Devious Pathways from Childhood to Adulthood.* Cambridge: Cambridge University Press.

Rutter, M., Giller, H. and Hagell, A. (eds) (1998) *Antisocial Behavior by Young People.* New York: Cambridge University Press.

Sanders, W. (1994) *Gangbangs and Drive-bys: Grounded Culture and Juvenile Gang Violence.* New York: Cambridge University Press.

Scott, S., Knapp, M., Henderson, J. and Maughan, B. (2001) 'Financial cost of social exclusion: Follow up study of antisocial children into adulthood.' *British Medical Journal 323,* 191–197.

Smith, C.A. and Farrington, D.P. (2004) 'Continuities in antisocial behavior and parenting across three generations.' *Journal of Child Psychology and Psychiatry 45,* 2, 230–247.

Smith, D.J. and McVie, S. (2003) 'Theory and method in the Edinburgh Study of Youth Transitions and Crime.' *British Journal of Criminology 43,* 1, 169–195.

Spergel, I.A. (1995) *The Youth Gang Problem.* New York: Oxford University Press.

Thornberry, T.P. (1998) 'Membership in youth gangs and involvement in serious and violent offending.' In R. Loeber and D.P. Farrington (eds) *Serious and Violent Offenders: Risk Factors and Successful Interventions.* Thousand Oaks, CA: Sage, pp.147–166.

Thornberry, T.P., Huizinga, D. and Loeber, R. (1995) 'The prevention of serious delinquency and violence: Implications from the program of research on the causes and correlates of delinquency.' In J.C. Howell, J.D. Hawkins and J.J. Wilson (eds) *A Sourcebook: Serious, Violent and Chronic Juvenile Offenders.* Thousand Oaks, CA: Sage, pp.213–237.

Torgersen, S., Kringlen, E. and Cramer, V. (2001) 'The prevalence of personality disorders in a community sample.' *Archives of General Psychiatry 58,* 6, 590–596.

Welsh, B.C. (2003) 'Economic costs and benefits of primary prevention of delinquency and later offending: A review of the research.' In D.P. Farrington and J.W. Coid (eds) *Early Prevention of Adult Antisocial Behaviour.* Cambridge: Cambridge University Press, pp.318–355.

Widom, C.S. (1989) 'The cycle of violence.' *Science 244,* 160–166.

Youth Justice Board (YJB) (2003) www.youth-justice-board.org.uk

3

Risk factors for serious and violent antisocial behaviour in children and youth

Friedrich Lösel and Doris Bender

Introduction

Many countries are experiencing strong concerns about seriously aggressive and violent children and youth. They cause a lot of problems for parents, relatives, teachers, peers, neighbours, social services and – in the long run – themselves as well. The most serious cases of physical injury or even death of others gain intensive coverage in the mass media, and many people want to know why children grow up and act in this way. The present chapter tries to answer this question. Specifically, we shall summarise the literature on empirically founded risk factors for the development of persistent antisocial and violent behaviour in children. Before we can do this, however, we need briefly to address some basic issues regarding the definition and development of this target group. The second part and core of the chapter presents the main risk factors within an integrated bio-psychosocial perspective. The third part then goes on to address structured instruments for risk assessment and management. The chapter closes with a brief discussion of protective factors and interventions that may help to reduce the impact of developmental risks (see also Chapter 6 in this volume).

Although some risk assessment instruments will be discussed, the chapter does not aim to review this literature comprehensively. Instead, it focuses on the foundations of such tools; that is, on the available empirical knowledge about a broad range of risk factors. This should enable practitioners to make adequate assessments and develop effective modes of risk communication and management in their own field. Tiffin and Richardson (Appendix 1) also discuss some tools to help practitioners. A realistic framework must take into account the basic limits of prediction and behavioural control in everyday life. These are related to the developmental principles of continuity and flexibility. Bearing these in mind should help to avoid the negative effects of undue pessimism and stigmatisation when working with such difficult children.

Basic developmental issues in antisocial behaviour

Although there are similarities in the backgrounds and behaviour of many seriously aggressive children, they do not form a homogeneous group. They also do not stand out completely from other groups of aggressive and delinquent young people. Even studies of young murderers show that these have much in common with youth exhibiting less serious aggression (Lempp 1977; Traverso and Bianchi 2002). Despite the lack of a clear taxonomy, approximately half of the youngsters who have committed a violent offence are also 'chronic' delinquents (Loeber, Farrington and Waschbusch 1998b). These individuals show early-starting, relatively persistent, and serious antisocial behaviour in various forms (e.g. Moffitt 1993; Patterson *et al.* 1998). This developmental pathway can be distinguished from the much more prevalent adolescent-limited antisocial behaviour that leads to the typical age curve of criminality with its increase in adolescence and decline in early adulthood (Farrington 1989; Loeber *et al.* 1998a). The adolescence-limited pathway is a typical youth transition problem. The serious and persistent group, in contrast, not only carry on offending into adulthood but also have already exhibited frequent aggression, delinquency and other conduct problems during childhood (e.g. Farrington and Loeber 2001; Patterson *et al.* 1998). More than 5 per cent of boys follow this pathway (Moffitt and Caspi 2001; Moffitt *et al.* 1996); while girls have a lower prevalence rate of serious antisociality (Loeber *et al.* 1998a; Moffitt *et al.* 2001). Individuals on this pathway are clearly overrepresented among serious and violent offenders. In adolescence and adulthood, more than one half of the offences in each age cohort can be attributed to this group (Loeber *et al.* 1998a; Wolfgang, Figlio and Sellin 1972). Moreover, such early-starting antisocial behaviour is also a strong risk marker for other psychiatric and social problems in adulthood (Robins and Price 1991).

Naturally, a differentiation into two types does not cover the whole range of antisocial developments in real life. For example, Nagin and Land (1993) found a third group of less serious low-level chronics. Loeber and Hay (1994) suggest three pathways that differ in their behaviour:

- directly aggressive behaviour such as bullying, hitting, fighting or cruelty to animals leading to later assault, rape or manslaughter (*overt antisocial behaviour*)

- more indirect forms of antisocial behaviour such as shoplifting, frequent lying, vandalism or fire setting leading to burglary, fraud or serious theft (*covert antisocial behaviour*)

- stubborn behaviour, defiance or disobedience leading to truancy, running away or staying out late (*authority conflict*).

On all three pathways, the proportion of youngsters exhibiting such problem behaviour decreases with age, whereas the severity of the problem behaviour increases. Some children exhibit problem behaviour in all three areas (*versatile antisocial behaviour*), and these form the core group on the early-starting, serious and persistent pathway.

Although there is strong empirical support for this type of development, one should not overestimate the continuity of problem behaviour (Lösel and Bender 2003; Tremblay 2000). About one half of children with severe conduct disorders and intensive aggression in childhood do not progress to serious criminal behaviour in adolescence (e.g. Moffitt *et al.* 1996; Patterson *et al.* 1998; Robins 1978). This is partly due to natural developmental changes, protective mechanisms and social interventions in the life course (Laub and Sampson 2003; Lösel and Bender 2003). When addressing risk factors, we must also take into account other principles of developmental psychopathology: problem behaviour rarely has a single cause or origin. It results from multiple bio-psychosocial influences. Even well-designed studies cannot always demontrate clear causal relationships, but only risk factors that enhance the probability of a negative outcome. Specific behavioural outcomes may result from different risks (equifinality), but the same risk factors may lead to different outcomes (multifinality). Factors relevant for the onset of antisocial development may differ from those influencing its persistence or aggravation. Moreover, difficult children are not only a more or less passive object of biosocial influences but – with increasing age – also active constructors of their own development (e.g. through their choice of peers and social contexts). Finally, whether an individual exhibits violent or other problem behaviour at a specific time and in a specific context depends not only on these long-term influences and psychological dispositions but also on situational factors. The situational risks of aggressive behaviour are a product of both objective characteristics and their subjective interpretations.

Risk factors for serious antisociality

Adolescents with early, serious and persistent antisocial behaviour typically reveal multiple bio-psychosocial risks that have been accumulating since childhood (Farrington and Loeber 2001; Hawkins *et al.* 1998; Loeber 1982; Lynam 1996). The accumulation of such factors consolidates and aggravates problem behaviour like a chain reaction (Lösel 2001; Lösel and Bender 2003). The high-risk chain reactions can best be understood within a theoretical framework of biosocial vulnerability, social learning and neuropsychological development (Bandura 1979; Lösel and Bender 2003; Moffitt 1993). Table 3.1 gives an overview of factors that longitudinal research has shown to represent a risk in this process. Such single factors mostly have very small or small effects (correlations between $r = 0.10$ and 0.20). It is an accumulation of problems in various domains that is accompanied by a strong increase in the probability that serious problem behaviour will emerge (Farrington 1997a; Loeber et al. in press; Lösel and Bliesener 2003). This dosage–response relationship appears to be robust across both genders. We shall now address the various risk domains in more detail.

Table 3.1 Risk factors for the development of serious antisocial behaviour

Areas of risk	PB	EP	MC	AD	Effect
Biological/biosocial risks					
Male gender	X	X	X	X	***
Genetic disposition (hereditary factors)	X	X	X	X	***
Prenatal risks/pregnancy complications	X	X	X	X	*
Perinatal problems	X	X	X	X	*
Low level of physiological arousal	X	X	X	X	***
Neurotransmitter dysfunction	X	X	X	X	**
Hormonal factors		X	X	X	*
Early puberty (particularly in girls)				X	*
Family risks					
Poverty/low SES/living on welfare	X	X	X	X	***
Low parental education	X	X	X	X	**
Ethnic background (in some countries)	X	X	X	X	***
Teenage motherhood	X	X	X	X	**
Single parenthood	X	X	X	X	*
Large family size	X	X	X	X	*
Divorce/separation		X	X	X	*
Frequent change of caregiver		X	X	X	**
Parental unemployment	X	X	X	X	*
Parental criminality	X	X	X	X	***
Parental substance abuse	X	X	X	X	**
Parental mental disorder	X	X	X	X	*
Disharmony and conflict between parents		X	X	X	**
Child neglect/lack of parental warmth		X	X	X	***

Continued on next page

Table 3.1 continued

Areas of risk	PB	EP	MC	AD	Effect
Family risks					
Child abuse		X	X	X	***
Physical punishment		X	X	X	**
Inadequate supervision and discipline			X	X	***
High family stress		X	X	X	**
Lack of social support/social isolation		X	X	X	**
Parental attitudes that encourage deviance			X	X	**
Sibling delinquency			X	X	**
Early child personality and behavioural risks					
Low intelligence	X	X	X	X	**
Language problems		X	X	X	*
Poor executive functioning		X	X	X	***
Developmental delays		X	X	X	*
Difficult temperament/negative emotionality	X	X	X	X	***
Impulsivity		X	X	X	***
Attention deficit hyperactivity disorder		X	X	X	***
Risk taking and need for stimulation		X	X	X	**
Lack of guilt		X	X	X	***
Callousness/lack of empathy		X	X	X	***
Attachment deficits		X	X	X	***
Early onset of antisocial behaviour		X	X	X	***
Problem behaviour in multiple contexts		X	X	X	***
School-related risks					
Achievement problems			X	X	***
Low motivation/commitment to the school			X	X	**
Truancy			X	X	**
School dropout/frequent change of school			X	X	**
Poor school-leaving qualifications				X	***
Low parental interest in school			X	X	**
Unfavourable school and classroom climate			X	X	*
High proportion of antisocial students			X	X	**
Peer group risks					
Peer rejection		X	X	X	*
Few prosocial contacts		X	X	X	**
Affiliation with delinquent cliques			X	X	***
Gang membership				X	***

Area of risk	PB	EP	MC	AD	Effect
Risks in social cognitions and attitudes					
Aggression-prone social information processing		X	X	X	***
Deficits in coping and social problem solving			X	X	***
Unrealistic self-esteem			X	X	*
Deviant attitudes/identification with deviant subcultures			X	X	***
Lifestyle risks					
Unstructured leisure-time activities			X	X	**
High consumption of violence in the mass media		X	X	X	**
Alcohol abuse			X	X	***
Use of illegal drugs				X	***
Drug dealing				X	***
Carrying of weapons				X	***
Other health risk behaviour				X	**
Difficulties with vocational training/unemployment				X	**
Community/neighbourhood risks					
Concentration of poverty/problem families			X	X	**
Disorganised neighbourhood			X	X	*
Easy access to weapons			X	X	*
Context of violence and drugs			X	X	**

Presence of risk factors: PB = Prenatal/Birth; EP = Early Childhood/Preschool (age 0–5 years); MC = Middle Childhood (age 6–12 years); AD = Adolescence (age 13–18 years)

Approximate effect size ratings: * Very small effect and/or not yet well replicated; ** Small effect and replicated; *** Up to medium effect and replicated

Biological and biosocial factors

Although biological influences are often neglected in theories of antisocial behaviour, they form a basis of vulnerability (Raine 1993; Rowe 1994). Genetic factors obviously play an important role. In most cultures, males face a higher risk for serious aggression and only a part of this risk can be attributed to social learning (Hyde 1984; Miles and Carey 1997; Moffitt *et al.* 2001). Even within the same sex, genetic factors have a substantial impact on the degree of antisocial behaviour (Harris 1995; Mason and Frick 1994). They are responsible for significant differences in temperament and in cognitive functions that, in turn, relate to aggression and delinquency (Plomin 1994; Raine 1997). Approximately 40 per cent of the inter-individual differences in stable antisocial behaviour can probably be traced back to genetic factors. Nonetheless, the genotype marks out only the boundaries delineating the breadth of possible behaviour (the phenotype). How this is actually shaped in individual development depends on the environment and nature–nurture interaction. For example, genetic components of social family factors can operate in various ways: (a) children may inherit environments along with genes from their parents; (b) parents may react to genetically influenced child traits; (c) older children may seek out environmental niches suited to their own genotype (Pike et al. 1996).

Environmental influences can already be found during pregnancy. Neuropsychological development can be impaired through a mother's alcoholism (foetal alcohol syndrome; Conry and Fast 2000; Steinhausen, Willms and Spohr 1993). Pregnant mothers who smoke expose their offspring to a prenatal intoxication that has an impact on the infant's neurobiology and future anti- social behaviour (Fergusson, Woodward and Horwood 1998; Koglin 2003). However, such an effect is related to a greater or lesser degree with family risks. For example, mothers who smoke during pregnancy more often have a low socio-economic status (SES), are less well educated and otherwise more at risk for deficits in parenting (Koglin 2003; Raine 1993).

Birth complications and a postnatal lack of emotional affection, stimulation or poor nutrition are further biological risks (Hodgins, Kratzer and McNeil 2002; Koglin 2003; Raine, Brennan and Mednick 1994). Here as well, it does not seem to be isolated effects that are significant, but, above all, combinations with social factors. For example, pregnancy and birth complications impact on a child's social behaviour when they are accompanied by social risks such as parental rejection, poverty or family instability (Brennan, Mednick and Raine 1997). Vice versa, social risks such as experiencing little affection also relate to biological factors (Plomin 1994). For example, a deprived relation to the primary caregiver can impair an infant's brain development and attachment behaviour (Kraemer 1997).

Biological predispositions are also involved when some children react more impulsively than others and are less able to learn from negative experiences. Antisocial children have, for example, lower pulse rates, reduced psycho-galvanic responses and slower electroencephalograms (e.g. Farrington 1997b; Raine 1993). Low arousal manifests in a greater need for stimulation (sensation seeking, thirst for adventure), less fear of punishment and poorer avoidance learning (Eysenck 1977; Zuckerman 1994).

Another risk may be related to the androgen hormone testosterone. Enhanced testosterone levels seem to be both causal and consequential factors of human aggression (Archer 1991). Although relations between aggression and testosterone have been investigated more thoroughly in adults, we may expect an impact at least from puberty onwards (Tremblay *et al.* 1997). Early puberty is in itself a risk factor, particularly for girls (Stattin and Magnusson 1990). Due to their physical precosity, these girls have more contacts to deviant boys and groups; however, they also grow out of their behavioural problems earlier. The stress hormone cortisol plays a further role in biological vulnerability and may interact with testosterone in adolescence (Tremblay *et al.* 1997). Whereas anxious and withdrawn children have higher cortisol levels, the relation to antisocial behaviour is more complex (Lahey *et al.* 1999). In our own research (Lösel *et al.* 2004), for example, we found particularly high salivary concentrations of cortisol in children who were both anxious and aggressive. In contrast, they were relatively low in the more proactively aggressive and 'cooler' children.

There is still little available research on the relation between antisocial behaviour of young people and hormonal or neurotransmitter activity (Susman and Ponirakis 1997; Tremblay *et al.* 1997). For example, some studies suggest that reduced levels or imbalances in the neurotransmitter serotonin play a role in antisocial behaviour (af Klinteberg 1998, 2002; Schalling *et al.* 1988; Virkkunen *et al.* 1994). However, here as well genetic dispositions seem to interact with social influences. Caspi *et al.* (2002) found that specific genetic factors involved in decomposing serotonin in the monoamine oxidase (MAO) relate strongly to antisocial behaviour when a child had also experienced serious abuse in the family. Research on such nature–nurture interactions may open up new opportunities for measures of prevention that fit with the specific vulnerabilities of the child.

Family characteristics and upbringing

Although the impact of the family on the development of antisocial behaviour has sometimes been questioned (e.g. Harris 1995), this area of risk factors is well confirmed in longitudinal research (e.g. Loeber and Farrington 1998, 2001). Families of children who develop serious antisocial behaviour have to cope with significantly more structural problems and multiple deprivations than comparison groups. They reveal more poverty and low SES, teenage motherhood, single parenthood and low parental education (Farrington 1998; Fergusson and Woodward 1999; Hawkins *et al.* 1998). The families more often live on social welfare, are relatively large, belong to deprived minorities and have to cope with unemployment, social isolation or other stressors (Elliott, Huizinga and Menard 1989; Farrington 1989; Hill *et al.* 1994). Parents exhibit more antisocial behavior, substance abuse and other mental disorders (Farrington *et al.* 1990; Hawkins *et al.* 1998; Tremblay *et al.* 2004). Most of these factors are also risks for child maltreatment and abuse (Jeyarajah-Dent 1998; Hagell 1998).

The more proximal problems in family interaction and childrearing are particularly crucial. There is often disharmony and conflict between the parents of aggressive children and, as a consequence, more separation, divorce and change of caregivers over time (Elliott 1994; Hawkins *et al.* 1998). The parents do not treat their children lovingly and empathically (Kolvin *et al.* 1990; McCord 1979). They use more physical punishment and are either rigidly strict, too lax or inconsistent in their discipline (Farrington 1992, 1998; Frick 1998; Lösel and Bliesener 2003; Loeber and Stouthamer-Loeber 1998; McCord 1979; Patterson, Reid and Dishion 1992). Of course, extreme deficits in childrearing are more important than minor differences in degree. For example, child abuse and neglect are particularly strong risk factors for anti-social child behaviour (Bender and Lösel 2005). However, the 'cycle of violence' is not closed (Oliver 1993; Widom 1989). 'Only' approximately one-third of children from abusing families develop serious aggression, and aggressive children also come from families without domestic violence.

From the perspective of social learning theory, the above-mentioned features of family upbringing serve as models for aggressive behaviour and reinforce it. This leads to the acquisition of cognitive schemes that favour aggression (Crick and Dodge 1994; Huesmann 1997; Lösel *et al.* in press). When external controls are either lacking or too rigid, deficits in self-control will develop or increase (Lösel, Toman and Wüstendörfer 1976). When parents are low in childrearing competence, their response to early behaviour problems in their child will tend to be rejecting, impatient, aggressive or inconsistent (Patterson *et al.* 1992; Rutter 1990). The child will then behave accordingly, and coercive interactions will emerge (Patterson *et al.* 1992). In such a family climate, there is also a greater risk that children will not develop sound emotional attachments (Ainsworth 1991). Avoidant, fearful, compulsive or dis-organised attachment behaviour may be more frequent (Fagot and Pears 1996), providing unfavourable preconditions for later social relationships and coping (Cassidy *et al.* 1996).

Most individual family characteristics explain only a small amount of variance in child problem behaviour and many correlate with each other (see Hawkins *et al.* 1998; Lipsey and Derzon 1998; Lösel 2002). However, their cumulative impact forms a multi-problem milieu with a clear increase in risk.

Early child personality and behaviour problems

Social and biological influences contribute to temperament characteristics and cognitive functions in a child that increase the risk of antisocial behaviour. These include impulsiveness, hyperactivity, attention problems, emotional instability, developmental delays, language deficits and relatively low overall intelligence (Farrington 1992, 1998; Hawkins *et al.* 1998; Lipsey and Derzon 1998; Moffitt 1993; Rutter, Giller and Hagell 1998). Neuropsychological dispositions lead to problems in the executive brain functions responsible for abstract thinking, goal-directed actions and self-control (Moffitt and Henry 1991; Séguin et al. 2004). Nonetheless, many at-risk children do not have major functional impairments or diminished abilities, and the typical differences in intelligence between antisocial and well-adjusted groups average out at only a few IQ points (Rutter et al. 1998). Attention deficit hyperactivity disorder (ADHD) also shows only moderate correlations with antisocial behaviour (Loeber et al. 1998a). There are various facets of this syndrome, and both types of externalising problems should not be seen too much as combined (Séguin et al. 2004). The child's predispositions once again have to be viewed within the context of their interaction with factors in the social milieu. Whereas, for example, parents can often cope with a child's difficult temperament, learning problems and minor antisocial behaviour, the negative cycles in childrearing described above emerge more readily when parents have individual and social problems of their own (Rutter 1990).

It is also necessary to assume not only cumulative risks but also different patterns depending on a child's individual personality. For example, Frick (1998) found that the typical deficits in socialisation and cognitive functioning form just one of the pathways to deviance. There is also a second path for a smaller group of children who are particularly callous, non-emphatic and otherwise prone to psychopathic personality disorder in adulthood (Lynam 1996). Some other aggressive individuals seem to be less impulsive, hyperactive and poorly socialised but more inhibited and withdrawn. Such 'over-controlled hostility' probably involves a more neurotic personality constellation (see Blackburn 1993; White and Heilbrun 1995). It triggers violence only when escalating conflicts lead to strong affect. These may well be those severe cases of violent outbursts in which no clear signs of aggressiveness have been noticed before by the social environment.

School-related risks

School-related risks for serious antisocial development are partially individual child factors and partially social context factors. The problematic cognitive competencies, hyperactivity and impulsivity sketched above are unfavourable preconditions for a successful school career. Correspondingly, there is an enhanced risk of low achievement, repetition of classes and early school dropout (Hawkins et al. 1998; McCord and Ensminger 1997; Moffitt et al. 1996). In addition, and partially in interaction with achievement problems, such children also have poor bonds to their school. Low motivation, poor relations to teachers and truancy are significant predictors of antisocial behaviour (Hawkins et al. 1998). Further school-related risks derive from parents' attitudes and behaviour. Parents of children who develop antisocial behaviour have low school-oriented aspirations and values and show little interest in their child's school life (Farrington 1992; Stouthamer-Loeber *et al.* 1993).

However, school-oriented risks for antisocial behaviour are not just 'imported' from individual and family characteristics. They are also due to the school itself. Contrary to popular stereotypes, the average size of classes, the sizes of schools or their architecture have little impact (Lösel and Bliesener 2003; Olweus 1993). It is factors related to the life and climate in the school and classroom that are more important. Schools with deficits in organisation and educational structure (i.e. low emphasis on school values, inconsistent teacher behaviour, many conflicts, low participation and responsibility) enhance the risk for antisocial behaviour (e.g. Gottfredson 2001; Lösel and Bliesener 2003; Mortimore 1995; Rutter *et al.* 1979). A further risk factor is a concentration of aggressive and delinquent children in schools and classes (e.g. Kellam *et al.* 1998). If a large proportion of children have similar behaviour problems, this may impact negatively on the school climate and enhance the risk of negative learning processes.

Peer group

The peer group is a particularly important source of risk for antisocial behaviour (Harris 1995; Lösel 2003a; Thornberry 1998). As with other risk factors, the literature suggests some change of relevant factors over time as well as relations to other areas of influence. Younger children who exhibit aggressive behaviour are often rejected by their more normal age-mates (Cairns and Cairns 1991; Parker *et al.* 1995; Patterson *et al.* 1992). Partially as a consequence of such rejection and partially due to other factors, these deviant children frequently join cliques in which aggressive and delinquent activities prevail (Elliott 2004; Reiss and Farrington 1991; Thornberry 1998; Tremblay *et al.* 1995). Such peers serve as models and additionally reinforce aggression, delinquency, substance abuse, drug dealing, deviant attitudes and a risky lifestyle focusing on immediate need gratification (Jessor, Donovan and Costa 1992; Lösel and Bliesener 1998; Tremblay *et al.* 1995). A further enhancement of risk occurs when youngsters affiliate with organised youth gangs (Thornberry 1998). Criminal youth gangs are a long-term issue in North America that has become increasingly topical in recent times (Klein 1995). In Europe, this issue is closely related to problems of migration and ethnic conflict (BMI and BMJ 2001).

Youngsters who join criminal cliques not only select this social context but are also influenced by it. They already show a personal disposition towards aggressive and delinquent behaviour and are less well integrated into other groups (Lösel 2003b; Thornberry 1998; Tremblay *et al.* 1995). In addition, the deviant group has a reinforcing effect, leading to an increasing severity of offences – particularly in gangs. Adolescents more readily join gangs when they come from families with multiple stressors and childrearing deficits, have problems at school, exhibit early antisocial behaviour, are rejected by other peers, live in disorganised and deprived residential areas and have contacts to persons with similar difficulties (Thornberry 1998). Once again, it becomes clear that risk factors in various domains should not be viewed in isolation.

Social cognitions and attitudes

Experiences of violence in the family, the peer group, school and in the mass media contribute to the development of perceptions and thinking patterns that encourage aggressive behaviour (Crick and Dodge 1994; Huesmann 1997; Lösel et al. in press). Already at preschool age, aggressive children exhibit schemes and scripts in their social information processing that differ significantly from their non-deviant peers. For example, they more frequently interpret the intentions of interaction partners as being hostile; they find it harder to view motives and feelings from the other person's perspective; they choose more egocentric goals; they have more aggressive reaction patterns stored in their memory; they evaluate the consequences of aggressive behaviour more positively; and they possess fewer skills for engaging in non-aggressive interaction (e.g. Crick and Dodge 1994; Lösel and Bliesener 2003). This type of information processing makes aggression a subjectively consequent reaction to their environment.

Schemes of social information processing can also serve as an 'interface' between a strong consumption of violence in the mass media and aggressive behaviour. Research has shown that mass media have a unfavourable influence when children are already predisposed to aggression or emotionally deprived (Bushman 1995; Huesmann and Miller 1994). Obviously, there are some serious single cases in which children or adolescents may have imitated serious acts of violence from videos or other mass media directly (Glogauer 1993). However, the broader effects and the breeding ground for acts of violence come from a habituation to violent acts, the internalisation of dehumanisation, and a consolidation of aggression-prone cognitive schemes (Huesmann and Miller 1994; Selg 1990). Given such potentials, children are more easily predisposed to react more aggressively when faced with difficult situations.

Through their social experiences and self-reinforcing cognitive processes, antisocial young persons acquire attitudes and values that encourage their deviant behaviour. For example, they tolerate more deviance than others, evaluate aggression more positively, place more value on autonomy, put less emphasis on traditional achievement norms and have more negative attitudes towards established institutions (Gottfredson and Hirschi 1990; Jessor et al. 1992; Lösel and Bliesener 2003). Group processes encourage such attitudes. Adolescents who join delinquent cliques or gangs increasingly develop a subcultural identification (Thornberry 1998). Of course, deviant attitudes in adolescents should not always be viewed as negative, because they are typical for the phase of separating from the family and developing one's own identity. Less aggressive adolescents are also torn between the influences of the parental home and the peer group (Lösel and Bliesener 2003). Nonetheless, critical thresholds are crossed if adolescents identify exclusively with deviant groups and subcultures.

The relation between self-evaluation and antisocial behaviour is also relatively complex. Deviant attitudes and behaviours can be an attempt to increase self-esteem. However, in contrast to widespread opinions, there is no consistent empirical relationship between low self-esteem and antisocial behaviour (Lösel and Schmucker 2004). Although some aggressive children suffer from problems of self-worth, another subgroup does not possess a negative but an unrealistically high self-image (Baumeister, Smart and Boden 1996). Insulting this fragile self-image may well contribute to aggression-prone information processing and violent reactions.

Deviant lifestyle

Deviant cliques and subcultures encourage unstructured leisure-time activities, alcohol and drug abuse, risk taking in road traffic, risky sexual behaviour and other health risks related to antisocial behaviour. In many deviant young persons, this leads to the emergence of a broad syndrome of adolescent problem behaviour (Jessor et al. 1992; Junger, Terlouw and van der Heijden 1995; Lösel and Bliesener 1998). In a moderate form, this is also typical for normal youth, and the different problem behaviours do not necessarily coincide. However, in most high-intensity cases, antisocial behaviour goes along with substance abuse (Lösel and Bliesener 1998). This in turn increases the risk of committing serious offences under the influence of drugs or alcohol as well as the threat of poor achievement at school or work. As criminality progresses, this is joined by social stigmatisation and exclusion, which further reduce social opportunities and strengthen the negative momentum of a criminal career (Hermann and Kerner 1988).

During late adolescence and early adulthood, many persistently antisocial individuals have difficulties with their work and employment. They more frequently fail to commence vocational training or drop out of it (Göppinger 1997; Sampson and Laub 1993). With relatively poor educational qualifications, and at times even basic deficits in reading, writing, and arithmetic skills, they have fewer chances on the labour market. Should they manage to start a career, this often develops a negative trajectory with fluctuating unqualified short-term jobs and periods of unemployment. There are some cases in which delinquency follows on from unemployment; but most cases tend to reveal the opposite causal direction (Farrington 2000). Hence, unemployment should always be viewed within the context of a young person's motivation. This is illustrated by the low success rates of job creation schemes for antisocial juveniles (Lipsey and Wilson 1998). Being able to hold down a job seems to be more decisive. Naturally, the problem of negative work careers is enhanced when national or regional unemployment rates are also high (Sherman *et al.* 1997).

If a young person has gone through such a prototypical trajectory of long-term and serious antisocial behaviour, problems may often continue into adulthood. Although criminal careers tend to fade out as time goes by, other difficulties persist (e.g. alcoholism, chronic unemployment, psychiatric problems, and violence in the family; Farrington 1989). Such lifestyles and the inheritance of genetic information are, in turn, a risk for the next generation. However, here as well, the cycle is not closed (Bender and Lösel 2005).

Risk factors in the neighbourhood and community

The risks in the individual, family, school and peer group interact with those in the broader social context. These particularly include socially disintegrated and deprived neighbourhoods (see Catalano *et al.* 1998; Eisner 2001). Such neighbourhoods contain a high rate of poverty; an accumulation of persons on welfare; high levels of violence, alcoholism and drug use; and easy access to weapons (Sampson and Lauritsen 1994; Thornberry 1998). In these contexts, it is easy to find models for aggression, violence, delinquency and substance abuse. Although it is easy to disentangle family and person characteristics from those of the neighbourhood, both independent effects and interactions have been described (Oberwittler *et al.* 2001; Wikström and Loeber 2000). Interestingly, intact family relations can act as a buffer against the negative effects of a violent environment (Richters and Martinez 1993), and a favourable environment may lower the risks from a difficult family background (Kupersmidt, Burchinal and Patterson 1995). However, a negative environment seems to encourage antisocial behaviour, particularly in young persons with no massive familial and personal risks who develop more behaviour problems in adolescence than in childhood (Wikström and Loeber 2000). For children who already come from very deprived families and exhibit early antisocial behaviour, the additional influence of the neighbourhood environment seems to be less important.

Structured risk assessment instruments

The factors summarised above have been used to develop structured risk assessment instruments that aim to increase the validity of clinical prediction. These scales typically contain a number of risk items selected from reviews of research, crime theories and clinical considerations (Farrington and Tarling 1985; Le Blanc 1998). Items are summed to form a total risk score and may also reveal specific risk patterns (e.g. mainly family or child factors). Such instruments are used for screening, in-depth assessment and related risk management (e.g. for decisions on the child's placement or specific interventions). They can also be applied in differentiated evaluations of intervention programs. Instruments vary with respect to the age and gender of their clients, problem intensity in the target groups, theoretical and empirical foundations, the number and domains of risks included, scoring procedures, time required for assessment, information sources, institutional contexts of administration and other issues (e.g. Hoge and Andrews 1996; Le Blanc 2002). Although many instruments have been designed for application in the juvenile justice system (e.g. Achenbach 1998; Barnoski 2002; Borum, Bartel and Forth 2002; Hoge, Andrews and Leschied 1996), an increasing number are available for earlier assessment in the community and in clinical contexts (Augimeri et al. 2001; Beuhring 2002; Corrado 2002; Doreleijers et al. 2000). Some instruments focus on specific areas of risk. For example, more than 50 years ago Glueck and Glueck (1950) had already developed short scales for screening family risks. Other scales such as the child and youth versions of the Psychopathy Checklist – Revised (Hare 2001) focus on individual characteristics of young people (Forth, Kosson and Hare 2002; Frick, Bodin and Barry 2000). Most instruments contain factors from various areas of risk (e.g. individual, family, neighbourhood).

Risk assessment instruments need to comply with a number of methodological and practical criteria. Item content and scoring must be clearly explicated in order to meet standards of objectivity and reliability. Systematic training should precede the application of a complex scale. Instruments must maintain a balance between broadness of information and economy. When screening large groups, it is best to apply a stepwise gating procedure (Loeber, Dishion and Patterson 1984). Items should refer to multiple contexts of behaviour and use multiple sources of independent information (Achenbach, McConaughy and Howell 1987; Lösel et al. 2005). They should tap not only static risks but also dynamic factors that can be changed by interventions. Information on risks should be complemented by data on protective factors and strengths; however, this is rarely the case (e.g. Borum et al. 2002). Although scales need to be sufficiently specific to the target child's age and gender, they should also enable systematic comparisons across groups and time. In many countries, cultural differences will need to be taken into account (Cooke and Michie 2002). Legal and ethical aspects also need to be integrated in order to avoid stigmatisation, violations of data protection and other problems (Le Blanc 1998). Last but not least, instruments need to be backed up with ongoing research on their validity. In the following, we shall sketch two examples of risk assessment devices that are both scientifically founded and clinically relevant. Several other tools that may be of particular use to practitioners are discussed in Tiffin and Richardson (Appendix 1).

The Early Assessment Risk List

The Early Assessment Risk List for Boys (EARL-20B, Version 2; Augimeri *et al.* 2001) was developed in the Under 12 Outreach Project (ORP) of the Earlscourt Child and Family Centre in Toronto, Canada (Howell 2001). The programme contains various components for early antisocial children and their families. The EARL-20B was developed, tested and revised to meet the need for early detection and differentiated placement of at-risk children within this framework. Because some risk factors are not equally relevant for both genders, a specific instrument was created for girls (EARL-21G; Levene *et al.* 2001). Both scales were derived from the empirical literature and clinical experience on aggression and violence in children under 12 years of age. They focus on risk factors between ages 6 and 12. However, attempts have also been made to extend the assessment to younger and older age groups. The structure of the instrument is similar to other well-known risk assessment devices from this research group that address violent offenders (HCR-20; Webster *et al.* 1997) and sexually violent offenders (SVR-20; Boer *et al.* 1997). To attain transparency and objectivity, each item is defined precisely and scored on a three-point scale. As Table 3.2 shows, items are structured into three domains: family, child and responsivity. Various pilot studies suggest that the scale is both reliable and valid (Webster *et al.* 2002). However, more long-term and large-scale evaluations are still needed.

The Krakow Instrument of Risk Assessment

This tool has been developed at the Simon Fraser University, Vancouver, Canada (Corrado 2002; Odgers, Vincent and Corrado 2002). It is an outcome of a NATO Advanced Research Workshop held at Krakow, Poland. The instrument covers a particularly broad range of risks. Its items are derived from empirical studies and clinical experience. A specific feature of this tool is that it differentiates between the developmental stages of the respective child and thus has different scales covering Conception–Birth, Early Childhood (age 0–5), Middle Childhood (age 5–12), and Adolescence (age 13–18). The assessment of middle childhood, for example, covers those risk factors that were already present at birth and during early childhood plus factors that emerged later. Sometimes, the content of an item varies with age (e.g. biological parents at birth and caregiver later). Items are well described and coded on a three-point severity rating. Furthermore, each item requires notes on the kind of information or data sources on which the specific rating is based. A second coding addresses the most critical items in each case. The most critical issues for each child are those that must be targeted for the highest intensity of intervention. Risk items are grouped into five areas: environmental, individual, family, interventions and externalising behaviour. Table 3.3 summarises the contents of the tool for different child ages.

Table 3.2 Items in the Revised Early Assessment Risk List for Boys (EARL-20B; Augimeri et al. 2001)

Family (F) items	Child (C) items	Responsivity (R) items
F1 Household circumstances	C1 Developmental problems	R1 Family responsivity
F2 Caregiver continuity	C2 Onset of behavioural difficulties	R2 Child responsivity
F3 Supports	C3 Abuse/neglect/trauma	
F4 Stressors	C4 Hyperactivity/impulsivity/attention deficits	
F5 Parenting style	C5 Likeability	
F6 Antisocial values and conduct	C6 Peer socialisation	
	C7 Academic performance	
	C8 Neighbourhood	
	C9 Authority contact	
	C10 Antisocial attitudes	
	C11 Antisocial behaviour	
	C12 Coping abilities	

Because the Krakow Instrument is relatively new, its predictive validity needs further investigation. Preliminary data from our own developmental and prevention study on kindergarten children (Lösel et al. 2004) have revealed significant correlations between both the Pre-Perinatal Score and the Early Childhood Score and antisocial behaviour several years later. Correlations for the Early Childhood Scale were higher, ranging from approximately 0.20 to 0.40 (depending on the length of follow-up and outcome criterion).

Such effect sizes are rather typical. With the exception of previous antisocial behaviour, most correlations between single predictors and outcome are small ($r = 0.10$ to 0.20; Lösel 2002). Nearly all predictors are more or less interrelated, and the low base rate of serious cases sets a further limit for prediction. As a consequence, a correlation of 0.40 to 0.50 or approximately 20 per cent explained variance is a typical upper threshold in the early prediction of antisocial behaviour and violence. Such effect sizes are by no means trivial because they confirm that more than 80 per cent of cases can be predicted correctly (Hawkins et al. 1998; Lipsey and Derzon 1998). Although there remains a substantial proportion of false positives and false negatives, careful early risk assessment is the cornerstone for a differentiated risk management through measures of prevention and intervention.

Table 3.3 Contents of the Krakow Risk Assessment Instrument (Corrado 2002; Odgers *et al.* 2002)

Environmental

E1 Obstetrical complications (PP→)
E2 Maternal substance use in pregnancy (PP→)
E3 Community disorganisation (PP→)
E4 Family socio-economic status (PP→)
E5 Residential mobility (EC→)
E6 Exposure to violence (EC→)
E7 Peer socialisation (EC→)
E8 School environment (EC→)
Other E (optional) (PP→)

Individual

I1 Birth deficiencies (PP→)
I2 Parental history of mental illness (PP→)
I3 Executive dysfunction (EC→)
I4 Chronic under-arousal (EC→)
I5 Cognitive delays/disorders (EC→)
I6 Personality traits/disorders (EC→)
I7 Other mental illnesses (EC→)
I8 Antisocial attitudes (EC→)
I9 Poor coping abilities (EC→)
I10 School functioning (EC→)
Other I (optional) (PP→)

Family

F1 Teenage pregnancy (PP→)
F2 Maternal/parental coping ability (PP→)
F3 Parental antisocial practices/attitudes (PP→)
F4 Family supports (PP→)
F5 Family conflict/domestic violence (PP→)
F6 Sibling delinquency (EC→)
F7 Ineffective parenting (EC→)
F8 Early caregiver disruption and attachment (EC→)
Other F (opt.) Parental education and IQ (PP→)
Family structure/single parent family (PP→)

Interventions

IV1 Previous interventions (specify) (PP→)
IV2 Accessibility to interventions (PP→)
IV3 Family responsivity to intervention (PP→)
IV4 Child responsivity to intervention (EC→)
Other IV considerations (optional) (PP→)

Externalising behaviour

EB1 General behavioural problems (EC→)
EB2 Violence and aggression (EC→)
EB3 Substance use (MC→)
EB4 General offending (MC→)
EB5 Considerations (optional) (EC→)

PP→ = Pre-/Perinatal and later; EC→ = Early Childhood and later; MC→ = Middle Childhood and later

Protective factors and interventions

Naturally, all the links in the above-mentioned chain of development do not need to be present in the single case. Nonetheless, their accumulation is accompanied by a marked increase in the risk of a serious and long-term negative development (Farrington 1997a; Hawkins *et al.* 1998; Lösel and Bliesener 2003). Vice versa, positive characteristics or experiences in some domains may disrupt a negative chain reaction. Although this may be an outcome of deliberate interventions, it also occurs within the natural context of development. When protective factors are available to young people, they may show positive social development despite high risk of antisocial behaviour, or they may abandon their problem behaviour after a difficult phase. The mechanisms underlying such trajectories are less well investigated than the risks (e.g. Lösel and Bliesener 1994; Sampson and Laub 2003; Werner and Smith 1992). It is also more difficult to implement adequate research designs in this field (Lösel and Bender 2003; Luthar, Cicchetti and Becker 2000). Of course, one can assume that the opposite to the risk value of the variables listed in Table 3.1 may promote positive development. However, truly protective effects need to compensate a given high-risk constellation (moderator approach; Rutter 1985). The available research suggests a number of factors that may protect from the risks of antisocial behaviour. Table 3.4 reports a selection of such personal and social resources that have already been proven or may be promising (for a detailed review see Lösel and Bender 2003).

Table 3.4 Multilevel examples for protective factors against serious antisocial behaviour (Lösel and Bender 2003)

Biological/biosocial	Non-deviant close relatives; no genetic vulnerabilities; high arousal; normal neurological and hormonal functioning
Pre- and perinatal	Non-alcoholic mother; no maternal smoking during pregnancy; no birth complications
Child personality	Easy temperament; inhibition; ego-resiliency; intelligence; verbal skills; planning for the future; self-control; social problem-solving skills; victim awareness, secure attachment; feelings of guilt; school and work motivation; special interests or hobbies; resistance to drugs
Cognitions/attitudes	Non-hostile attributions; non-aggressive response schemes; negative evaluation of aggression; self-efficacy in prosocial behaviour; non-deviant beliefs; realistic self-esteem; sense of coherence
Family	No poverty; income stability; harmony; acceptance; good supervision; consistency; positive role models; continuity of caretaking; no disadvantage; availability of social support
School	Achievement and bonding; low rate of aggressive students; climate of acceptance, structure, and supervision
Peer group	Non-delinquent peers; support from close, prosocial friends
Community	Non-deprived, integrated and non-violent neighbourhood; availability of professional help
Situational	Target hardening; victim assertiveness; social control
Legal	Effective firearm and drug control; effective criminal justice interventions
Cultural	Low violence; tradition of moral values; shame- and guilt-orientation; low exposure to violence in the media

As with risks, protective factors also reveal cumulative effects (Stattin, Romelsjö and Stenbacka 1997). Depending on their specific combination with other characteristics, some factors may also serve both a risk and a protective function. For example, Bender and Lösel (1997) found that although satisfaction with social support protected high-risk youth with low antisociality from a negative development, it increased problem behaviour in those juveniles who were already deviant. When looking at the interplay of risk and protective factors, it is always necessary to phrase one's questions in a differentiated way and ask 'risk of what and protection against what?' For example, anxiety and social withdrawal are protective factors against antisocial development, but they may enhance the risk for depression and other internalising problems.

Because protective effects become increasingly rare the greater and more permanent the individual disorder and social disorganisation, professional prevention and intervention programmes need to compensate for deficits in natural resources. Various reviews have shown that early developmental prevention and intervention can effectively counter antisocial behaviour (e.g. Farrington and Welsh 2003; Kazdin 1998; Lösel 2005; Lösel and Beelmann, 2003, 2005; Tremblay and Japel 2003; Utting 2003; see also Chapter 9 of this volume). However, overall effects are only small to medium and outcomes vary greatly. Because of the many different risk factors, multimodal programmes that address various areas of risk are most promising. In the field of child skills training, for example, we found the largest effects for social-cognitive programmes addressing both cognitive and behavioural skills in non-aggressive social problem solving (Lösel and Beelmann 2005). Relatively successful family-oriented prevention programmes contain combinations of parent trainings and child trainings (Conduct Problems Prevention Research Group 2002; Tremblay et al. 1995), multitargeted early home visits for single mothers (Olds et al. 1998), intensive preschool programmes for children and related parent counselling (Schweinhart, Barnes and Weikart 1993) or multisystemic therapy (Henggeler et al. 1998). Both child- and family-oriented programmes reveal larger effects when they address children who already show behaviour problems (indicated prevention). The age of children does not relate significantly to outcome (Farrington and Welsh 2003; Lösel and Beelmann 2003). This is encouraging because it indicates that it may be neither too early nor too late to promote protective mechanisms.

Hence, the literature on young offender treatment also demonstrates the inappropriateness of the 'nothing works' doctrine (Lipsey and Wilson 1998; Lösel 1995; McGuire 2002). Theoretically well-founded, structured cognitive-behavioural, social-therapeutic, multimodal and family-oriented programmes are particularly promising. The contents of effective treatment and prevention seem to be rather similar (Lösel 2005). Therefore, instead of prevention versus treatment, we need integrated approaches to what works during different phases of development and at different degrees of deviance. This is in line with the discovery of a broad range of risk factors emerging at various ages in a child's development.

Conclusion

Many violent and otherwise seriously antisocial youngsters show early-starting and persistent problem behaviour. Numerous factors enhance the risk of such a development and facilitate chain reactions leading towards chronic problems. Particularly important are biological vulnerabilities; temperament characteristics, neuropsychological deficits, and early problem behaviour in the child; structural problems, economic disadvantage, multiple stressors, disharmony, abuse, neglect, and poor parenting in the family; school failure, truancy, and a problematic school context; affiliation with deviant peer groups or gangs; aggression-prone schemes of social information processing and deviant attitudes; an antisocial lifestyle; and deprived and violent neighbourhoods. Although most single factors only reveal a small effect, their accumulation strongly increases the risk of serious problems. Natural protective factors or professional interventions can interrupt such chain reactions by reducing specific risks or compensating for their impact. Systematic and clinically relevant instruments may help to improve the practice of risk assessment and management. Prevention and intervention should use such information on the overall risk as well as on specific patterns of risks, needs and protective potentials in each individual case.

Acknowledgement

Work on this chapter was supported by grants from the Oak Foundation and the German Ministry for Family Affairs, Seniors, Woman, and Youth.

References

Achenbach, T.M. (1998) 'Diagnosis, assessment, taxonomy, and case formulations.' In T.H. Ollendick and M. Hersen (eds) *Handbook of Child Psychology*. New York: Plenum Press.

Achenbach, T.M., McConaughy, S.H. and Howell, C.T. (1987) 'Child/adolescent behavioral and emotional problems: Implications of cross-informant correlations for situational specificity.' *Psychological Bulletin 101*, 213–232.

Ainsworth, M.D.S. (1991) 'Attachments and other affectional bonds across the life cycle.' In C.M. Parkes, J. Stevenson-Hinde and P. Marris (eds) *Attachment Across the Life Cycle*. London: Routledge.

Archer, J. (1991) 'The influence of testosterone on human aggression.' *British Journal of Psychology 82*, 1–28.

Augimeri, L.K., Koegl, C.J., Webster, C.D. and Levene, K.S. (2001) *Early Assessment Risk List for Boys (EARL-20B), Version 2*. Toronto: Earlscourt Child and Family Centre.

Bandura, A. (1979) 'The social learning perspective: Mechanisms of aggression.' In H. Toch (ed) *Psychology of Crime and Criminal Justice*. New York: Holt, Rinehart and Winston.

Barnoski, R. (2002) 'Monitoring vital signs: Integrating a standardized assessment into Washington State's Juvenile Justice System.' In R. Corrado, R. Roesch, S. Hart and

J. Gierowski (eds) *Multi-Problem Violent Youth: A Foundation for Comparative Research on Needs, Interventions and Outcomes.* Amsterdam: IOS Press/NATO Science Series.

Baumeister, R.F., Smart, L. and Boden, J.M. (1996) 'Relation of threatened egotism to violence and aggression: The dark side of high self-esteem.' *Psychological Review 103*, 5–33.

Bender, D. and Lösel, F. (1997) 'Protective and risk effects of peer relations and social support on antisocial behavior in adolescents from multi-problem milieus.' *Journal of Adolescence 20*, 260–271.

Bender, D. and Lösel, F. (2005) 'Risikofaktoren, Schutzfaktoren und Resilienz bei Misshandlung und Vernachlässigung' [Risk factors, protective factors and resilience in child abuse and neglect]. In U.T. Egle, S.O. Hoffmann and P. Joraschky (eds) *Sexueller Missbrauch, Misshandlung, Vernachlässigung [Sexual Abuse, Physical Abuse, and Neglect]*, 3rd edn. Stuttgart: Schattauer.

Beuhring, T. (2002) 'The Risk Factor Profile Instrument: Identifying children at risk for serious and violent delinquency.' In R. Corrado, R. Roesch, S. Hart and J. Gierowski (eds) *Multi-Problem Violent Youth.* Amsterdam: IOS Press/NATO Science Series.

Blackburn, R. (1993) *The Psychology of Criminal Conduct.* Chichester: Wiley.

BMI and BMJ (eds) (2001) *Erster Periodischer Sicherheitsbericht [First Periodic Report on Public Safety].* Berlin: Bundesministerium des Innern und Bundesministerium der Justiz.

Boer, D.P., Hart, S.D., Kropp, P.R. and Webster, C. (1997) *Manual for the Sexual Violence Risk-20. Professional Guidelines for Assessing Risk of Sexual Violence.* Burnaby, Canada: Mental Health, Law, and Policy Institute, Simon Fraser University.

Borum, R., Bartel, P. and Forth, A. (2002) *Manual for the Structured Assessment of Violence Risk in Youth (SAVRY).* Tampa, FL: University of South Florida.

Brennan, P.A., Mednick, S.A. and Raine, A. (1997) 'Biosocial interactions and violence: A focus on perinatal factors.' In A. Raine, P.A. Brennan, D.P. Farrington and S.A. Mednick (eds) *Biosocial Bases of Violence.* New York: Plenum Press.

Bushman, B.J. (1995) 'Moderating role of trait aggressiveness in the effect of violent media on aggression.' *Journal of Personality and Social Psychology 69*, 950–960.

Cairns, R.B. and Cairns, B.D. (1991) 'Social cognition and social networks: A developmental perspective.' In D.J. Pepler and K.H. Rubin (eds) *The Development and Treatment of Childhood Aggression.* Hillsdale, NJ: Erlbaum.

Caspi, A., McClay, J., Moffitt, T.E. *et al.* (2002) 'Role of genotype in the cycle of violence in maltreated children.' *Science 297*, 851–854.

Cassidy, J., Scolton, K.L., Kirsh, S.J. and Parke, R.D. (1996) 'Attachments and representations of peer relationships.' *Developmental Psychology 32*, 892–904.

Catalano, R.F., Arthur, M.W., Hawkins, J.D., Berglund, L. and Olson, J.L. (1998) 'Comprehensive community and school-based interventions to prevent antisocial behavior.' In R. Loeber and D.P. Farrington (eds) *Serious and Violent Juvenile Offenders: Risk Factors and Successful Interventions.* Thousand Oaks, CA: Sage.

Conduct Problems Prevention Research Group (2002) 'Evaluation of the first three years of the fast track prevention trial with children at high-risk for adolescent conduct problems.' *Journal of Abnormal Child Psychology 30*, 1–17.

Conry, J. and Fast, D.K (2000) *Fetal Alcohol Syndrome and the Criminal Justice System.* Vancouver: Law Foundation of British Columbia.

Cooke, D.J. and Michie, C. (2002) 'Towards valid cross-cultural measures of risk.' In R. Corrado, R. Roesch, S. Hart and J. Gierowski (eds) *Multi-Problem Violent Youth.* Amsterdam: IOS Press/NATO Science Series.

Corrado, R. (2002) 'An introduction to the risk/needs case management instrument for children and youth at risk for violence: The Cracow Instrument.' In R. Corrado, R. Roesch, S. Hart and J. Gierowski (eds) *Multi-Problem Violent Youth: A Foundation for Comparative Research on Needs, Interventions and Outcomes.* Amsterdam: IOS Press/NATO Science Series.

Crick, N.R. and Dodge, K.A. (1994) 'A review and reformulation of social information-processing mechanisms in children's social adjustment.' *Psychological Bulletin 115,* 74–101.

Doreleijers, Th. A.H., Moser, F., Thijs, P., van Engeland, H. and Beyaert, F.H.M. (2000) 'Forensic assessment of juvenile delinquents: Prevalence of psychopathology and decision-making at court in the Netherlands.' *Journal of Adolescence 23,* 263–275.

Eisner, M. (2001) 'Kriminalität in der Stadt – Ist Desintegration das Problem?' [Crime in the city: Is disintegration the problem?] In J.M. Jehle (ed) *Raum und Kriminaliät [Space and Crime].* Mönchengladbach: Forum Verlag.

Elliott, D.S. (1994) 'Serious violent offenders: Onset, development course, and termination.' *Criminology 32,* 1–21.

Elliott, D.S., Huizinga, D. and Menard, S. (1989) *Multiple Problem Youth: Delinquency, Substance Use, and Mental Health Problems.* New York: Springer.

Eysenck, H.J. (1977) *Crime and Personality.* St Albans: Paladin Frogmore.

Fagot, B.I. and Pears, K.C. (1996) 'Changes in attachment during the third year: Consequences and predictions.' *Development and Psychopathology 8,* 325–344.

Farrington, D.P. (1989) 'Long-term prediction of offending and other life outcomes.' In H. Wegener, F. Lösel and J. Haisch (eds) *Criminal Behavior and the Justice System: Psychological Perspectives.* New York: Springer.

Farrington, D.P. (1992) 'Psychological contributions to the explanation, prevention, and treatment of offending.' In F. Lösel, D. Bender and T. Bliesener (eds) *Psychology and Law: International Perspectives.* Berlin: De Gruyter.

Farrington, D.P. (1997a) 'Early predictions of violent and nonviolent youthful offending.' *European Journal on Criminal Policy and Research 5,* 51–66.

Farrington, D.P. (1997b) 'The relationship between low resting heart rate and violence.' In A. Raine, P.A. Brennan, D.P. Farrington and S.A. Mednick (eds) *Biosocial Bases of Violence.* New York: Plenum Press/NATO ASI Series.

Farrington, D.P. (1998) 'Predictors, causes, and correlates of male youth violence.' In M. Tonry and M.H. Moore (eds) *Youth Violence. Crime and Justice,* Vol. 24. Chicago: University of Chicago Press.

Farrington, D.P. (2000) 'Explaining and preventing crime: The globalization of knowledge.' *Criminology 38,* 801–824.

Farrington, D.P. (2005) 'The integrated cognitive antisocial potential (ICAP) theory.' In D.P. Farrington (ed) *Integrated Developmental and Life-Course Theories of Offending.* New Brunswick, NJ: Transaction Publishers.

Farrington, D.P. and Loeber, R. (2001) 'Summary of key conclusions.' In R. Loeber and D.P. Farrington (eds) *Child Delinquents.* Thousand Oaks, CA: Sage.

Farrington, D.P. and Tarling, R. (eds) (1985) *Prediction in Criminology.* Albany, NY: State University of New York Press.

Farrington, D.P. and Welsh, B.C. (2003) 'Family-based prevention of offending: A meta-analysis.' *Australian and New Zealand Journal of Criminology 36,* 127–151.

Farrington, D.P, Loeber, R., Elliot, D.S., Hawkins, J.D., Kandel, D.B., Klein, M.W., McCord, J., Rowe, D.C. and Tremblay, R.E. (1990) 'Advancing knowledge about the onset of delinquency and crime.' In B. Lahey and A.E. Kadzin (eds) *Advances in Clinical Child Psychology*, Vol. 5. New York: Plenum, pp.283–342

Fergusson, D.M. and Woodward, L.J. (1999) 'Maternal age and educational and psychosocial outcomes.' *Journal of Child Psychology and Psychiatry 40*, 479–489.

Fergusson, D.M., Woodward, L.J. and Horwood, L.J. (1998) 'Maternal smoking during pregnancy and psychiatric adjustment in late adolescence.' *Archives of General Psychiatry 55*, 71–77.

Forth, A., Kosson, D. and Hare, R.D. (2002) *The Hare Psychopathy Checklist: Youth Version (PCL-YV)*. Toronto: Multi-Health Systems.

Frick, P.J. (1998) *Conduct Disorders and Severe Antisocial Behavior*. New York: Plenum Press.

Frick, P.J., Bodin, S. and Barry, C. (2000) 'Psychopathic traits and conduct problems in community and clinic-referred samples of children: Further development of the psychopathy screening device.' *Psychological Assessment 12*, 382–393.

Glogauer, W. (1993) *Kriminalisierung von Kindern und Jugendlichen durch Medien [The Mass Media and Crime in Children and Youth]*. Baden-Baden: Nomos.

Glueck, S. and Glueck, E. (1950) *Unraveling Juvenile Delinquency*. Cambridge, MA: Harvard University Press.

Göppinger, H. (1997) *Kriminologie [Criminology]*, 5th edn. München: Beck.

Gottfredson, D. (2001) *Schools and Delinquency*. Cambridge: Cambridge University Press.

Gottfredson, M. and Hirschi, T.M. (1990) *A General Theory of Crime*. Stanford, CA: Stanford University Press.

Hagell, A. (1998) *Dangerous Care*. London: Policy Studies Institute.

Hare, R.D. (2001) 'Psychopaths and their nature: Some implications for understanding human predatory violence.' In A. Raine and J. Sanmartin (eds) *Violence and Psychopathy*. New York: Kluwer Academic/Plenum Publishers.

Harris, J.R. (1995) 'Where is the child's environment? A group socialization theory of development.' *Psychological Review 102*, 458–489.

Hawkins, J.D., Herrenkohl, T., Farrington, D.P., Brewer, D., Catalano, R.F. and Harachi, T.W. (1998) 'A review of predictors of youth violence.' In R. Loeber and D.P. Farrington (eds) *Serious and Violent Juvenile Offenders: Risk Factors and Successful Interventions*. Thousand Oaks, CA: Sage.

Henggeler, S.W., Schoenwald, S.K., Borduin, C.M., Rowland, M.D. and Cunningham, P.B. (1998) *Multisystemic Treatment of Antisocial Behaviour in Children and Adolescents: Treatment Manuals for Practitioners*. New York: Guilford Press.

Hermann, D. and Kerner, H.J. (1988) 'Die Eigendynamik der Rückfallkriminalität' [The dynamics of reoffending]. *Kölner Zeitschrift für Soziologie und Sozialpsychologie 40*, 485–504.

Hill, H.M., Soriano, F.L., Chen, S.A. and LaFramboise, T.D. (1994) 'Sociocultural factors in the etiology and prevention of violence among ethnic minority youth.' In L.D. Eron and J.H. Gentry (eds) *Reason to Hope: A Psychosocial Perspective on Violence and Youth*. Washington, DC: American Psychological Association.

Hodgins, S., Kratzer, L. and McNeil, T.F. (2002) 'Are pre and perinatal factors related to the development of criminal offending?' In R.R. Corrado, R. Roesch, S.D. Hart and J.K. Gierowski (eds) *Multi-Problem Violent Youth*. Amsterdam: IOS Press/NATO Science Series.

Hoge, R.D. and Andrews, D.A. (1996) *Assessing the Youthful Offender: Issues and Techniques*. New York: Plenum Press.

Hoge, R.D., Andrews, D.A. and Leschied, A.W. (1996) 'An investigation of risk and protective factors in a sample of youthful offenders.' *Journal of Child Psychology and Psychiatry and Allied Disciplines 37*, 419–424.

Howell, J.C. (2001) 'Juvenile justice programs and strategies.' In R. Loeber and D.P. Farrington (eds) *Child Delinquents.* Thousand Oaks, CA: Sage.

Huesmann, L.R. (1997) 'Observational learning of violent behavior: Social and biosocial processes.' In A. Raine, D.P. Farrington, P. Brennan and S.A. Mednick (eds) *Biosocial Bases of Violence.* New York: Plenum Press.

Huesmann, L.R. and Miller, L.S. (1994) 'Long-term effects of repeated exposure to media violence in childhood.' In L.R. Huesmann (ed) *Aggressive Behavior: Current Perspectives.* New York: Plenum.

Hyde, J.S. (1984) 'How large are gender differences in aggression? A developmental meta-analysis.' *Developmental Psychology 20*, 722–736.

Jeyarajah-Dent, R. (1998) *Dangerous Care: Working to Protect Children.* London: Bridge Child Care Development Service.

Jessor, R., Donovan, J.E. and Costa, F.M. (1992) *Beyond Adolescence: Problem Behavior and Young Adult Development.* Cambridge: Cambridge University Press.

Junger, M., Terlouw, G.J. and van der Heijden, P.G.M. (1995) 'Crime, accidents, and social support.' *Criminal Behaviour and Mental Health 5*, 386–410.

Kazdin, A.E. (1998) 'Psychosocial treatments for conduct disorder in children.' In P.E. Nathan and J.M. Gorman (eds) *A Guide to Treatments that Work.* New York: Oxford University Press.

Kellam, S.G., Ling, X., Merisca, R., Brown, C.H. and Ialongo, N. (1998) 'The effect of the level of aggression in the first grade classroom on the course and malleability of aggressive behavior into middle school.' *Development and Psychopathology 10*, 165–185.

Klein, M.W. (1995) *The American Street Gang: Its Nature, Prevalence and Control.* New York: Oxford University Press.

af Klinteberg, B. (1998) 'Biology and personality: Findings from a longitudinal project.' In D.J. Cooke, A.E. Forth and R.D. Hare (eds) *Psychopathy: Theory, Research and Implications for Society.* Dordrecht, NL: Kluwer.

af Klinteberg, B. (2002) 'Underlying vulnerability influencing outcome factors/behaviours in psychosocial disturbances.' In R. Corrado, R. Roesch, S. Hart and J. Gierowski (eds) *Multi-Problem Violent Youth: A Foundation for Comparative Research on Needs, Interventions and Outcomes.* Amsterdam: IOS Press/ NATO Science Series.

Koglin, U. (2003) 'Die Soziale und Emotionale Entwicklung von Kindern mit Biologischen Risiken' [Social and Emotional Development of Children with Biological Risks]. Doctoral Dissertation. University of Erlangen-Nuremberg: Institute of Psychology.

Kolvin, I., Miller, F.J.W., Scott, D. McI., Gatzanis, S.R.M. and Fleeting, M. (1990) *Continuities of Deprivation? The Newcastle 1000 Family Study.* Aldershot: Avebury.

Kraemer, G.W. (1997) 'Social attachment, brain function, aggression, and violence.' In A. Raine, P.A. Brennan, D.P. Farrington and S.A. Mednick (eds) *Biosocial Bases of Violence.* New York: Plenum Press.

Kupersmidt, J.B., Burchinal, M. and Patterson, C.J. (1995) 'Developmental patterns of childhood peer relations as predictors of externalizing behavior problems.' *Development and Psychopathology 7*, 825–843.

Lahey, B.B., Miller, T.L., Gordon, R.A. and Riley, A.W. (1999) 'Developmental epidemiology of the disruptive behavior disorders.' In H.C. Quay and A.E. Hogan (eds) *Handbook of Disruptive Behavior Disorders.* New York: Kluwer Academic/Plenum.

Laub, J.H. and Sampson, R.J. (2003) *Shared Beginnings, Divergent Lives: Delinquent Boys to Age 70*. Cambridge, MA: Harvard University Press.

Le Blanc, M. (1998) 'Screening of serious and violent juvenile offenders.' In R. Loeber and D.P. Farrington (eds) *Serious and Violent Juvenile Offenders*. Thousand Oaks, CA: Sage.

Le Blanc, M. (2002) 'Review of clinical assessment strategies and instruments for adolescent offenders.' In R. Corrado, R. Roesch, S. Hart and J. Gierowski (eds) *Multi-Problem Violent Youth*. Amsterdam: IOS Press/NATO Science Series.

Lempp, R. (1977) *Jugendliche Mörder [Juvenile Murderers]*. Bern: Huber.

Levene, K.S., Augimeri, L.K., Pepler, D., Walsh, M., Webster, C.D. and Koegl, C.J. (2001) *Early Assessment Risk List for Girls, Version 1 (EARL-21G)*. Toronto: Earlscourt Child and Family Centre.

Lipsey, M.W. and Derzon, J.H. (1998) 'Predictors of violent or serious delinquency in adolescence and early adulthood.' In R. Loeber and D.P. Farrington (eds) *Serious and Violent Juvenile Offenders: Risk Factors and Successful Interventions*. Thousand Oaks, CA: Sage.

Lipsey, M.W. and Wilson, D.B. (1998) 'Effective intervention for serious juvenile offenders: A synthesis of research.' In R. Loeber and D.P. Farrington (eds) *Serious and Violent Juvenile Offenders*. Thousand Oaks, CA: Sage.

Loeber, R. (1982) 'The stability of antisocial and delinquent child behavior.' *Child Development 53*, 1431–1446.

Loeber, R. and Farrington, D.P. (eds) (1998) *Serious and Violent Juvenile Offenders: Risk Factors and Successful Interventions*. Thousand Oaks, CA: Sage.

Loeber, R. and Farrington, D.P. (eds) (2001) *Child Delinquents: Development, Intervention and Service Needs*. Thousand Oaks, CA: Sage.

Loeber, R. and Hay, D.H. (1994) 'Developmental approaches to aggression and conduct problems.' In M. Rutter and D.H. Hay (eds) *Development Through Life: A Handbook for Clinicians*. Oxford: Blackwell.

Loeber, R. and Stouthamer-Loeber, M. (1998) 'Development of juvenile aggression and violence: Some common misconceptions and controversies.' *American Psychologist 53*, 242–259.

Loeber, R., Dishion, T.J. and Patterson, G.R. (1984) 'Multiple gating: A multistage assessment procedure for identifying youths at risk for delinquency.' *Journal of Research in Crime and Delinquency 21*, 7–32.

Loeber, R., Farrington, D.P., Stouthamer-Loeber, M. and van Kammen, W.B. (1998a) *Antisocial Behavior and Mental Health Problems*. Mahwah, NJ: Lawrence Erlbaum.

Loeber, R., Farrington, D.P. and Waschbusch, D.A. (1998b) 'Serious and violent juvenile offenders.' In R. Loeber and D.P. Farrington (eds) *Serious and Violent Juvenile Offenders*. Thousand Oaks, CA: Sage.

Loeber, R., Homish, D.L., Wei, E.H. *et al.* (2005) 'The prediction of violence and homicide in young males.' *Journal of Consulting and Clinical Psychology 73*, 1074–1088.

Lösel, F. (1995) 'The efficacy of correctional treatment: A review and synthesis of meta-evaluations.' In J. McGuire (ed) *What Works: Reducing Reoffending. Guidelines From Research and Practice*. Chichester: Wiley.

Lösel, F. (2001) 'Nonviolence: Protective factors.' In N.J. Smelser and P.B. Baltes (eds) *International Encyclopedia of the Social and Behavioral Sciences*. Oxford: Pergamon Press.

Lösel, F. (2002) 'Risk/need assessment and prevention of antisocial development in young people.' In R.R. Corrado, R. Roesch, S.D. Hart and J.K. Gierowski (eds) *Multi-Problem Violent Youth*. Amsterdam: IOS Press/NATO Science Series.

Lösel, F. (2003a) 'The development of delinquent behavior.' In D. Carson and R. Bull (eds) *Handbook of Psychology in Legal Contexts*, 2nd edn. Chichester: Wiley.

Lösel, F. (2003b) 'Gruppendelikte' [Group offending]. In R. Lempp, G. Schütze and G. Köhnken (eds) *Forensische Psychiatrie und Psychologie des Kindes- und Jugendalters [Forensic Psychiatry and Psychology in Childhood and Adolescence]*, 2nd edn. Darmstadt: Steinkopff.

Lösel, F. (2005) 'Evaluating developmental prevention of antisocial behavior: An example and a brief review.' In A. Cerederecka, T. Jaskiewicz-Obdydzinska, R. Roesch and J. Wojcikiewicz (eds) *Forensic Psychology and Law*. Krakow: Forensic Research Publishers.

Lösel, F. and Beelmann, A. (2003) 'Effects of child skills training in preventing antisocial behavior: A systematic review of randomized evaluations.' *Annals of the American Academy of Political and Social Science 587*, 84–109.

Lösel, F. and Beelmann, A. (2005) 'Social problem solving programs for preventing antisocial behavior in children and youth.' In M. McMurran and J. McGuire (eds) *Social Problem Solving and Offending: Evidence and Evolution*. Chichester: Wiley.

Lösel, F. and Bender, D. (2003) 'Resilience and protective factors.' In D. P. Farrington and J. Coid (eds) *Prevention of Adult Antisocial Behavior*. Cambridge: Cambridge University Press.

Lösel, F. and Bliesener, T. (1994) 'Some high-risk adolescents do not develop conduct problems: A study of protective factors.' *International Journal of Behavioral Development 17*, 753–777.

Lösel, F. and Bliesener, T. (1998) 'Zum Einfluss des Familienklimas und der Gleichaltrigengruppe auf den Zusammenhang zwischen Substanzengebrauch und antisozialem Verhalten von Jugendlichen' [The impact of family climate and peer group on the relation between substance use and antisocial behaviour in youth]. *Kindheit und Entwicklung 7*, 208–220.

Lösel, F. and Bliesener, T. (2003) *Aggression und Delinquenz unter Jugendlichen: Untersuchungen von kognitiven und sozialen Bedingungen [Aggression and Delinquency in Adolescence: Studies on Cognitive and Social Origins]*. Neuwied: Luchterhand.

Lösel, F. and Schmucker, M. (2004) 'Persönlichkeit und Kriminalität' [Personality and criminal behavior]. In K. Pawlik (ed) *Persönlichkeitspsychologie [Personality Psychology]*, Vol. 5. Göttingen: Hogrefe.

Lösel, F., Toman, W. and Wüstendörfer, W. (1976) 'Eine Untersuchung zum perzipierten elterlichen Erziehungsstil bei jugendlichen Delinquenten' [A study of perceived parental childrearing in juvenile delinquents]. *Zeitschrift für Experimentelle und Angewandte Psychologie 23*, 45–61.

Lösel, F., Selg, H., Müller-Luckmann, E. and Schneider, U. (1990) 'Ursachen, Prävention und Kontrolle von Gewalt aus psychologischer Sicht' [Origins, prevention, and control of violence from a psychological perspective]. In H.-D. Schwind and J. Baumann *et al.* (eds) *Ursachen, Prävention und Kontrolle von Gewalt. Analysen und Vorschläge der Unabhängigen Regierungskommission zur Verhinderung und Bekämpfung von Gewalt [Report of the German Federal Government's Commission on Origins, Prevention, and Control of Violence]*, Vol. 2. Berlin: Duncker and Humblot.

Lösel, F., Beelmann, A., Jaursch, S. and Stemmler, M. (2004) *Soziale Kompetenz für Kinder und Familien [Social Competence for Children and Families]*. Berlin: Bundesministerium für Familie, Senioren, Frauen und Jugend.

Lösel, F., Stemmler, M., Beelmann, A., and Jaursch, S. (2005) 'Aggressives Verhalten im Vorschulalter: Eine Untersuchung zum Problem verschiedener Informanten [Aggressive behaviour in preschool children: A study on the problem of different informants]. In I. Seiffge-Krenke (ed) *Aggressionsentwicklung zwischen Normalität und*

Pathologie [The Development of Aggression Between Normality and Pathology]. Göttingen: Vandenhoeck and Ruprecht.

Lösel, F., Bliesener, T. and Bender, D. (in press) 'Social information processing, experiences of aggression in social contexts, and aggressive behavior in adolescents.' *Criminal Justice and Behavior.*

Luthar, S.S., Cicchetti, D. and Becker, B. (2000) 'The construct of resilience: A critical evaluation and guidelines for future work.' *Child Development 71*, 543–562.

Lynam, D.R. (1996) 'Early identification of chronic offenders: Who is the fledgling psychopath?' *Psychological Bulletin 120*, 209–234.

McBurnett, K., Lahey, B.B. and Pathouz, P. (2000) 'Low salivary cortisol and persistent aggression in boys referred for disruptive behavior.' *Archives of General Psychiatry 57*, 38–43.

McCord, J. (1979) 'Some child-rearing antecedents of criminal behavior in adult men.' *Journal of Personality and Social Psychology 37*, 1477–1486.

McCord, J. and Ensminger, M.E. (1997) 'Multiple risks and comorbidity in an African-American population.' *Criminal Behaviour and Mental Health 7*, 339–352.

McGuire, J. (2002) 'Integrating findings from research reviews.' In J. McGuire (ed) *Offender Rehabilitation and Treatment: Effective Programs and Policies to Reduce Reoffending.* Chichester: Wiley.

Mason, D.A. and Frick, P.J. (1994) 'The heritability of antisocial behavior: A meta-analysis of twin and adoption studies.' *Journal of Psychopathology and Behavioral Assessment 16*, 301–323.

Miles, D.R. and Carey, G. (1997) 'Genetic and environmental architecture of human aggression.' *Journal of Personality and Social Psychology 72*, 207–217.

Moffitt, T.E. (1993) 'Adolescence-limited and life-course-persistent antisocial behavior: A developmental taxonomy.' *Psychological Review 100*, 674–701.

Moffitt, T.E. and Caspi, A. (2001) 'Childhood predictors differentiate life-course persistent and adolescence-limited pathways among males and females.' *Development and Psychopathology 13*, 355–375.

Moffitt, T.E. and Henry, B. (1991) 'Neuropsychological studies of juvenile delinquency and juvenile violence.' In J.S. Milner (ed.) *Neurospsychology of Aggression.* Boston: Kluwer.

Moffitt, T.E., Caspi, A., Dickson, N., Silva, P. and Stanton, W. (1996) 'Childhood-onset versus adolescent-onset antisocial conduct problems in males: Natural history from ages 3 to 18 years.' *Development and Psychopathology 8*, 399–424.

Moffitt, T.E., Caspi, A., Rutter, M. and Silva, P.A. (2001) *Sex Differences in Antisocial Behavior: Conduct Disorder, Delinquency, and Violence.* Cambridge: Cambridge University Press.

Mortimore, P. (1995) 'The positive effect of schooling.' In M. Rutter (ed) *Psychological Disturbances in Young People: Challenge for Prevention.* New York: Cambridge University Press.

Nagin, D.S. and Land, K.C. (1993) 'Age, criminal careers, and population heterogeneity: Specification and estimation of a nonparamateric, mixed Poisson model.' *Criminology 31*, 327–362.

Oberwittler, D., Blank, T., Köllisch, T. and Naplava, T. (2001) *Soziale Lebenslagen und Delinquenz von Jugendlichen [Social Conditions and Juvenile Delinquency].* Freiburg: Max-Planck-Institut für ausländisches und internationales Strafrecht.

Odgers, C., Vincent, G.M. and Corrado, R.R. (2002) 'A preliminary conceptual framework for the prevention and management of multi-problem youth.' In R.R. Corrado,

R. Roesch, S.D. Hart and J.K. Gierowski (eds) *Multi-Problem Violent Youth*. Amsterdam: IOS Press/NATO Science Series.

Olds, D.L., Henderson, C.R. jr., Cole, R., *et al.* (1998) 'Long-term effects of nurse home visitation on children's criminal and antisocial behavior: 15-year follow-up of a randomized controlled trial.' *Journal of the American Medical Association 280*, 1238–1244.

Oliver, J. (1993) 'Intergenerational transmission of child abuse: Rates, research, and clinical implications.' *American Journal of Psychiatry 150*, 1315–1324.

Olweus, D. (1993) *Bullying at School*. Oxford: Blackwell.

Parker, J.G., Rubin, K.H., Price, J.M. and DeRosier, M.E. (1995) 'Peer relationships, child development, and adaptation: A developmental psychopathology perspective.' In D. Cicchetti and D.J. Cohen (eds) *Developmental Psychpathology, Vol. 2: Risk, Disorder, and Adaptation*. New York: Wiley.

Patterson, G.R., Reid, J.B. and Dishion, T.J. (1992) *Antisocial Boys*. Eugene, OR: Oregon Social Learning Center.

Patterson, G.R., Forgatch, M.S., Yoerger, K.L. and Stoolmiller, M. (1998) 'Variables that initiate and maintain an early-onset trajectory for juvenile offending.' *Development and Psychopathology 10*, 531–547.

Pike, A., McGuire, S., Hetherington, E.M., Reiss, D. and Plomin, R. (1996) 'Family environment and adolescent depressive symptoms and antisocial behavior: A multivariate genetic analysis.' *Developmental Psychology 32*, 590–603.

Plomin, R. (1994) *Genetics and Experience*. Newbury Park: Sage.

Raine, A. (1993) *The Psychopathology of Crime: Criminal Behavior as a Clinical Disorder*. San Diego: Academic Press.

Raine, A. (1997) 'Antisocial behavior and psychopathology: A biosocial perspective and a prefrontal dysfunction hypothesis.' In D.M. Stoff, J. Breiling and J.D. Maser (eds) *Handbook of Antisocial Behavior*. New York: Wiley.

Raine, A., Brennan, P. and Mednick, S.A. (1994) 'Birth complications combined with early maternal rejection at age 1 year predispose to violent crime at age 18 years.' *Archives of General Psychiatry 94*, 984–988.

Reiss, A.J. and Farrington, D.P. (1991) 'Advancing knowledge about co-offending: Results from a prospective longitudinal survey of London males.' *Journal of Criminal Law and Criminology 82*, 360–395.

Richters, J.E. and Martinez, P.E. (1993) 'Violent communities, family choices, and children's chances: An algorithm for improving the odds.' *Development and Psychopathology 5*, 609–627.

Robins, L.J. (1978) 'Sturdy childhood predictors of adult antisocial behavior: Replications from longitudinal studies.' *Psychological Medicine 8*, 611–622.

Robins, L.N. and Price, R.K. (1991) 'Adult disorders predicted by childhood conduct problems: Results from the NIMH epidemiologic catchment area project.' *Psychiatry 54*, 116–132.

Rowe, D.C. (1994) *The Limits of Family Influence: Genes, Experience, and Behavior*. New York: Guilford Press.

Rutter, M. (1985) 'Resilience in the face of adversity. Protective factors and resistance to psychiatric disorder.' *British Journal of Psychiatry 147*, 598–611.

Rutter, M. (1990) 'Psychosocial resilience and protective mechanisms.' In J. Rolf, A. Masten, D. Cicchetti, K. Nuechterlein and S. Weintraub (eds) *Risk and Protective Factors in the Development of Psychopathology*. New York: Cambridge University Press.

Rutter, M., Maughan, B., Mortimer, P. and Ouston, P. (1979) *Fifteen Thousand Hours. Secondary Schools and their Effects on Children*. Somerset: Open Books.

Rutter, M., Giller, H. and Hagell, A. (1998) *Antisocial Behavior by Young People*. Cambridge: Cambridge University Press.

Sampson, R.J. and Laub, J.H. (1993) *Crime in the Making: Pathways and Turning Points Through Life*. Cambridge, MA: Harvard University Press.

Sampson, R.J. and Laub, J.H. (2003) 'Life-course desisters? Trajectories of crime among delinquent boys followed to age 70.' *Criminology 41*, 319–339.

Sampson, R. and Lauritsen, J. (1994) 'Violent victimization and offending: Individual-, situational-, and community-level risk factors.' In A.J. Reiss and J.A. Roth (eds) *Understanding and Preventing Violence, Vol. 3: Social Influences*. Washington, DC: National Academy Press.

Schalling, D., Edman, G., Åsberg, M. and Oreland, L. (1988) 'Platelet MAO activity associated with impulsivity and aggressivity.' *Personality and Individual Differences 9*, 597–605.

Schweinhart, L.L., Barnes, H.V. and Weikart, D.P. (1993) *Significant Benefits: The High/Scope Perry Preschool Study through age 27*. Ypsilanti, MI: High/Scope Press.

Séguin, J.R., Nagin, D., Assaad, J.-M. and Tremblay, R. (2004) 'Cognitive-neuropsychological function in chronic physical aggression and hyperactivity.' *Journal of Abnormal Psychology 113*, 603–613.

Selg, H. (1990) 'Gewaltdarstellungen in Medien und ihre Auswirkungen auf Kinder und Jugendliche' [Violence in the media and their impact on children and youth]. *Zeitschrift für Kinder- und Jugendpsychiatrie 13*, 152–156.

Sherman, L.W., Gottfredson, D., MacKenzie, D., Eck, J., Reuter, P. and Bushway, S. (1997) *Preventing Crime: What Works, What Doesn't, What's Promising*. Washington, DC: US Department of Justice.

Stattin, H. and Magnusson, D. (1990) *Pubertal Maturation in Female Development*. Hillsdale, NJ: Erlbaum.

Stattin, H., Romelsjö, A. and Stenbacka, M. (1997) 'Personal resources as modifiers of the risk for future criminality.' *British Journal of Criminology 37*, 198–223.

Steinhausen, H.-Ch., Willms, J. and Spohr, H. (1993) 'Long-term psychopathological and cognitive outcome of children with fetal alcohol syndrome.' *Journal of the Academy of Child and Adolescent Psychiatry 32*, 990–994.

Stouthamer-Loeber, M., Loeber, R., Farrington, D.P., Zhang, Q., van Kammen, W. and Maguin, E. (1993) 'The double edge of protective and risk factors for delinquency: Interrelations and developmental patterns.' *Development and Psychopathology 5*, 683–701.

Susman, E.J. and Ponirakis, A. (1997) 'Hormones-context interactions and antisocial behavior in youth.' In A. Raine, P.A. Brennan, D.P. Farrington and S.A. Mednick (eds) *Biosocial Bases of Violence*. New York: Plenum.

Thornberry, T.P. (1998) 'Membership in youth gangs and involvement in serious and violent offending.' In R. Loeber and D.P. Farrington (eds) *Serious and Violent Juvenile Offenders: Risk Factors and Successful Interventions*. Thousand Oaks, CA: Sage.

Traverso, G.B. and Bianchi, M. (2002) 'Adolescent murderers: A Genoa sample.' In R. Corrado, R. Roesch, S. Hart and J. Gierowski (eds) *Multi-problem Violent Youth*. Amsterdam: IOS Press/NATO Science Series.

Tremblay, R.E. (2000) 'The development of aggressive behavior during childhood: What have we learned in the past century?' *International Journal of Behavioral Development 24*, 129–141.

Tremblay, R.E. and Japel, C. (2003) 'Prevention during pregnancy, infancy, and the preschool years.' In D.P. Farrington and J.W. Coid (eds) *Early Prevention of Adult Antisocial Behaviour.* Cambridge: Cambridge University Press.

Tremblay, R.E., Masse, L.C., Vitaro, F. and Dobkin, P.L. (1995) 'The impact of friends' deviant behavior on early onset of delinquency: Longitudinal data from 6 to 13 years of age.' *Development and Psychopathology 7,* 649–667.

Tremblay, R.E., Schaal, B., Boulerice, B., Arseneault, L., Soussignan, R. and Perusse, D. (1997) 'Male physical aggression, social dominance and testosterone levels at puberty.' In A. Raine, D.P. Farrington, P. Brennan and S.A Mednick (eds) *Biosocial Bases of Violence.* New York: Plenum.

Tremblay, R.E., Nagin, D.S., Séguin, J.R. *et al.* (2004) 'Physical aggression during early childhood: Trajectories and predictors.' *Pediatrics 114,* 43–45.

Utting, D. (2003) 'Prevention through family and parenting programmes.' In D.P. Farrington and J.W. Coid (eds) *Early Prevention of Adult Antisocial Behaviour.* Cambridge: Cambridge University Press.

Virkkunen, M., Kallio, E., Rawlings, R., Tokala, R., Poland, R.E., Guidotti, A. *et al.* (1994) 'Personality profiles and state aggressiveness in Finnish alcoholic violent offenders, fire setters, and healthy volunteers.' *Archives of General Psychiatry 51,* 28–33.

Webster, C.D., Douglas, K.S., Eaves, D. and Hart, S.D. (1997) *HCR-20: Assessing Risk for Violence, Version 2.* Burnaby, BC: Mental Health, Law and Policy Institute; Simon Fraser University.

Webster, C.D., Augimeri, L.K. and Koegl, C.J. (2002) 'The Under 12 Outreach Project for antisocial boys: A research based clinical program.' In R.R. Corado, R. Roesch, S.D. Hart and J.K. Gierowski (eds) *Multi-problem Violent Youth.* IOS Press/Nato Science Series, pp.207–218.

Werner, E.E. and Smith, R.S. (1992) *Overcoming the Odds.* Ithaca: Cornell University Press.

White, A.J. and Heilbrun, K. (1995) 'The classification of overcontrolled hostility: Comparison of two diagnostic methods.' *Criminal Behaviour and Mental Health 5,* 106–123.

Widom, C.S. (1989) 'Does violence beget violence? A critical examination of the literature.' *Psychological Bulletin 106,* 3–28.

Wikström, P.-O. and Loeber, R. (2000) 'Do disadvantaged neighbourhoods cause well-adjusted children to become adolescent delinquents? A study of male juvenile serious offending, risk and protective factors, and neighbourhood context.' *Criminology 38,* 1109–1142.

Wolfgang, M.E., Figlio, R.M. and Sellin, T. (1972) *Delinquency in a Birth Cohort.* Chicago, IL: Chicago University Press.

Zuckerman, M. (1994) *The Psychology of Sensation Seeking.* Cambridge: Cambridge University Press.

4

Children with sexually abusive behaviour – a special subgroup

Eileen Vizard

Introduction

The existence of children who sexually abuse other children is now acknowledged in clinical practice in the UK, North America and other countries. However, the clinical characteristics of these children presenting to agencies at different stages of their development are still not well known by practitioners and early identification of children with sexually abusive behaviour is not occurring consistently. There is still a low awareness of the fact that around 30 per cent of all sexual abuse of children is perpetrated by other children and young people under 21 years of age. Treatment outcome studies now indicate that good results with adolescent sex offenders can be obtained with carefully designed, multisystemic treatment interventions which are also cost effective. Longitudinal follow-up studies are needed to test developmental models, recidivism rates and treatment outcome. The evidence base and clinical experience with this group strongly supports the need for coherent government policies in relation to young sexual abusers. The objectives for this chapter are to describe the main characteristics of these children from the existing evidence base, to discuss the implications of these characteristics in terms of clinical need, to present the limited information available on outcomes and finally to discuss policy implications.

Who are the children who sexually abuse?

Definitions

There is a wide range of labels for children with sexual behaviour problems (Araji 1997; Cantwell 1995) because the children concerned may range from early childhood through to late adolescence and the sexual behaviour problems may range from relatively minor incidents of indecent touching to serious cases of rape or buggery. This has led to persistent definitional difficulties in the UK and North America (Calder 2004; Johnston and Doonan 2004). The point has been made recently that it is the *behaviour*, not the child, that should be labelled (Calder 2004). The need for a new diagnostic category of Sexual Behaviour Disorder of Childhood in DSM-IV (American Psychiatric Association 1994) has been suggested (Vizard 2004) since this might improve early identification of the problem.

Prevalence and incidence

In England and Wales children under 10 years old cannot be prosecuted; hence sexually abusive behaviour by younger children is not included in official statistics. However, recorded crime statistics for those cautioned or convicted show that 20 per cent of all sexual offences are committed by juveniles under 18 years old.

Other sources of data such as retrospective victim surveys present a different picture in relation to prevalence with much higher rates of sexual abuse by children and adolescents reported across a wide variety of countries and contexts. For instance, the estimated prevalence of sexually abusive behaviour by children and young people ranges from 30 to 50 per cent of all sexual abuse of children (Davis and Leitenberg 1987; Horne *et al.* 1991; Halperin *et al.* 1996; Kelly, Regan and Burton 1991; Vizard, Monck and Misch 1995).

Two conclusions can be drawn from these somewhat opposing sets of data. First, the recorded crime statistics for sexual offences by juveniles are recognised to be an underestimate of the extent of the problem in the same way that this is known for adult sex offenders. Second, there is a substantial amount of sexual abuse by children and adolescents disclosed in retrospective studies and the majority of this alleged abuse does not reach the court setting. In summary, a significant minority of the sexual abuse of children is perpetrated by other children and young people and most of this behaviour is not reflected in recorded crime statistics.

Characteristics of children who sexually abuse

There is mixed evidence on whether or not child sexual abusers form a discrete enough group to allow us to conclude that there is anything particularly distinctive about them. Thus four recent UK studies (Bladon *et al.* 2005 [n = 141]; Dolan *et al.* 1996 [n = 121]; Manocha and Mezey 1998 [n = 51]; Richardson *et al.* 1995 [n = 100]) showed broadly similar background and offence specific characteristics amongst young sexual abusers presenting to specialist forensic services. However, these findings were in contrast to those of an Eire (O'Halloran *et al.* 2002 [n = 27]) and a UK community-based study (Taylor 2003 [n = 227]) of young sexual abusers which did not show the same complex characteristics and where the samples were less disturbed and showed less recidivism.

A similar mixed picture emerges from the North American literature where juvenile sexual abusers emerge as a heterogeneous group in terms of types of offences and the range of victims. The typical profile of the adolescent sex offender as described in the North American literature is that of a 14- to 15-year-old male with learning difficulties (Awad and Saunders 1991; Bagley 1992), from a dysfunctional family home (Becker, Cunningham-Rathner and Kaplan 1986) where he has witnessed domestic violence (Ford and Linney 1995; Lewis, Shankok and Pincus 1979; Smith 1988) and often, but not always, experienced sexual abuse (Bagley 1992; Groth 1979; Langevin, Wright and Handy 1989) where multiple experiences of sexual and physical abuse may put him at risk of becoming a sexual abuser (Freeman-Longo 1985) and where child molester juveniles as opposed to rapist juveniles have been more frequently sexually victimised (Ford and Linney 1995; Seghorn, Prentky and Boucher 1987).

In the UK, the average age of the samples for four studies (Bladon *et al.* 2005; Dolan *et al.* 1996; Manocha and Mezey 1998; Richardson *et al.* 1995) was 14.9 years old. Only three UK studies included sexually abusive girls and in these the vast majority were males (Bladon *et al.* 2005, 92.2%; Manocha and Mezey 1998, 96.1%; Taylor 2003, 92%). The ethnicity of these UK samples (not recorded in Bladon *et al.* 2005 and O'Halloran *et al.* 2002) ranged between 93.3 per cent Caucasian (Dolan *et al.* 1996) and 76 per cent (but data missing in 15% of cases, Taylor 2003). However, Groth's (1977) research in the USA indicated that white males tended to victimise younger white females whereas juveniles who raped adult victims were likely to be black males engaging in interracial assault.

Many children and young people with sexually harmful behaviour present with other emotional and behavioural problems to mental health agencies. The proportion of children previously referred to child mental health services ranged from 37.3 per cent to 72 per cent of cases (Dolan *et al.* 1996; Manocha and Mezey 1998; Richardson *et al.* 1995; Taylor 2003) and it was noted that those children seen in specialist services (Bladon *et al.* 2005; Dolan *et al.* 1996; Manocha and Mezey 1998; Richardson *et al.* 1995) had higher rates of psychopathology than those seen in community services (O'Halloran 2002; Taylor 2003). In Bladon *et al.*'s 2005 study, just over half (54.6%) had an average of two Axis I DSM-II psychiatric disorders which included post-traumatic stress disorder (PTSD) and reactive attachment disorder of childhood, noted on clinical assessment in a specialist centre.

Studies in the UK and in North America consistently report links between sexually abusive behaviour by children, learning difficulties and school-based behavioural problems with an average of 35 per cent having learning difficulties and an average of 41 per cent having been statemented under section 5 of the Education Act 1981. Truancy was noted in 44 per cent (Dolan *et al.* 1996), 13.7 per cent (Manocha and Mezey 1998) 59 per cent (Richardson *et al.* 1995) and 20 per cent of cases (Taylor 2003), confirming the impression of pervasive school-based problems.

Comorbidity or co-occurrence of more than one psychiatric disorder is the norm in referred non-sexual, delinquent populations (Moffitt 2001; Rutter, Giller and Hagell 1998) and sexually delinquent populations (Bladon *et al.* 2005; Epps 1991). Bladon *et al.*'s (2005) study of children (n = 141) referred to a specialist forensic child and adolescent mental health service (CAMHS) showing sexually harmful behaviour. An average of four Axis 1 DSM-IV psychiatric disorders were noted, of which the most common were childhood onset, severe conduct disorder, post-traumatic stress disorder, paedophilia (over 16 years old) and reactive attachment disorder of childhood. In addition, Bladon *et al.* (2005) also found that 62 per cent of the population had a learning disability and 20 per cent had chronic physical illness.

The co-occurrence of psychiatric disorders such as reactive attachment disorder with developmental disorders such as learning disability, in the presence of domestic violence and family dysfunction, may well predispose to poor attachment relationships, coercive interpersonal styles and later sexually abusive behaviours, as indicated in work with adult sex offenders (Marshall and Barbaree 1990; Ward and Siegert 2002) where poor childhood attachments have been widely reported.

In the clinical sample of offending children referred to the UK-based Young Abusers Project (YAP), diagnostic queries about the possibility of pervasive developmental disorders (PDDs), autism or Asperger's have come in consistently over the last 13 years. Although only a very small number of the YAP sample fulfil formal criteria for autism or Asperger's, a number of children are known to have a PDD or to be within the autistic spectrum. Many of these children have significant histories of developmental delay, neurocognitive difficulties, learning disability and physical developmental problems, notably lack insight, show remorseless violence or are sexual offenders who may present with bizarre behaviour that often raises the question of mental illness, fitness to plead, etc. Social and cognitive processing deficits may be relevant for offenders with autistic spectrum disorders and also for some serious sexual offenders within this spectrum whose attitudes towards their offending are characterised by a lack of empathy for their victims which goes beyond the usual processes of denial. Theory of Mind was proposed (Baron-Cohen, Leslie and Frith 1985) as a deficit in autistic individuals which prevented the mentalising of another person's state of mind, i.e. a type of 'mind blindness' (Baron-Cohen 1990). Lack of theory of mind and insensitivity to social norms may contribute to the range of sexual deviations (Tantam 2003) in some cases of Asperger's Syndrome. These behaviours include fetishism, addiction to internet child pornography, targeting younger children for inappropriate friendships and stalking behaviour with an obsessional and sometimes violent quality.

Rates of sexual victimisation varied across the UK studies (Bladon *et al.* 2005, 71.6%); Dolan *et al.* 1996, 25.5%; Manocha and Mezey 1998, 29.4%; Richardson *et al.* 1995, 41%). There was also a variation in rates of physical abuse experienced and the percentage witnessing or experiencing domestic violence (Bladon *et al.* 2005, 51.8% physical abuse; Dolan *et al.* 1996, 30% physical abuse; Manocha and Mezey 1998, 23.5% and 37.3%; Richardson *et al.* 1995, 55% and 53% physical abuse). In a study of 37 younger children between three and seven years old with sexual behaviour problems Silovsky and Niec (2002) found that 38 per cent had been sexually abused, 47 per cent had been physically abused and 58 per cent had witnessed domestic violence.

Family backgrounds

Most UK studies of sexually abusive children show high levels of family dysfunction (Dolan *et al.* 1996; Manocha and Mezey 1998; Richardson *et al.* 1995). Seriously discordant intrafamilial relationships were described in 33.3 per cent of cases and parents were described as 'rejecting', 'uncaring', 'unloving' and 'disinterested' in 29.4 per cent of cases (Manocha and Mezey 1998). Bladon *et al.*'s 2005 study noted that 90.1 per cent of the sample had problems with their primary support group and that 65.2 per cent had other problems related to their social environment. Many abusive adolescents came from homes where parents had separated or divorced (Manocha and Mezey 1998, 50%; Richardson *et al.* 1995, 58%). Experiences of loss of a parent were also noted in Manocha and Mezey's (1998) study in which 13.7 per cent of the sample had lost one biological parent through death, the majority of which (71.4%) were deaths of the father.

Parental criminality is noted in several studies (Dolan *et al.* 1996, 19.6% of fathers and 5.3% of mothers; Manocha and Mezey 1998, 27.5% of mothers and fathers; Richardson *et al.* 1995, 26% of fathers and 13% of mothers). A climate of violence within the home was prevalent in many cases. Parental violence towards children was noted in 55 per cent (Richardson *et al.* 1995) and 23.5 per cent (Manocha and Mezey 1998), and 30 per cent of Dolan *et al.*'s 1996 sample had been subject to physical abuse but the perpetrators were not noted. Violence between siblings was also a feature (Richardson *et al.* 1995, 28%; Manocha and Mezey 1998, 9.8%).

From this home context, it is not surprising that most studies showed histories of local authority involvement including reception into care with rates ranging from 39 per cent (Bladon *et al.* 2005) to 71 per cent (Richardson *et al.* 1995). Overall, this small sample of younger children had suffered a wide range of psychosocial adversity.

Risk factors

Risk factors for the development of sexually abusive behaviour in sexually victimised adolescent boys were identified in a cross-sectional study which compared victimised boys who had sexually abused with victimised boys who had not sexually abused (Skuse *et al.* 1998). In this study (Skuse *et al.* 1998) witnessing domestic violence discriminated abusing boys from the comparison group. In a subsequent longitudinal study (7 to 19 years' duration) of n = 224 male victims of sexual abuse (Salter *et al.* 2003), it was concluded that most male victims of childhood sexual abuse do not become paedophiles. However, childhood risk factors for later sexual offending included material neglect, lack of supervision, sexual abuse by a female and witnessing serious intrafamilial violence (Salter *et al.* 2003).

In a review of risk factors for sexual assault recidivism for adolescent sexual offenders, Worling (2002) describes 'well supported' risk factors. These risk factors include deviant sexual interests, attitudes supportive of sexual offending, numerous past sexual offences, selection of a stranger victim, lack of intimate peer relationships or social isolation, high stress family environment, problematic parent–offender relationships or parental rejection and incomplete offence-specific treatment. 'Possible' risk factors include selection of a male victim, threats of or use of excessive violence/weapons during sexual violence and interpersonal aggression. Worling (2002) notes that 'unlikely' risk factors include denial of the sexual offence, lack of victim empathy, history of non-sexual crimes, penetrative sexual assaults on victims and the offender's own history of child sexual abuse, since there is little convincing research to support these presumed risk factors.

Links with emerging personality disorder

A robust evidence base exists to support the notion of persistence of non-sexual severe, childhood onset conduct disorder into adult antisocial personality disorder and criminality (Farrington 1995; Moffitt *et al.* 1996; Robins 1978). Moffitt *et al.*'s 1996 model proposes an early onset conduct disordered group with delinquent behaviour which persists into adult life, 'life course persistent', and an adolescent onset group whose behaviour desists in adult life, 'adolescence limited'. In relation to possible developmental trajectories towards adult sexual offending, little longitudinal research has been done in the UK or North America to test for the existence of these pathways and to map their course into adult life. However, Silovsky and Niec (2002) noted that in those cases of young children who do progress from sexual behaviour problems in childhood to sexual offending in later life 'the causes and developmental trajectories of sexual behaviour problems are likely to involve multiple complex pathways' (p.194).

A personality-based typology of juvenile sexual offenders has been explored (Worling 2001) based on links between antisocial personality and criminality and the fact that juvenile sexual offenders have high rates of non-sexual offending in adult life. Worling (2001) identified four groups of juvenile sexual abusers: antisocial/impulsive; unusual/isolated; over-controlled/reserved and confident/aggressive. The antisocial/impulsive and the unusual/isolated groups were the most pathological and were more likely to have been charged with a subsequent violent (sexual or non-sexual) or non-violent offence after a six-year follow-up. The author (Worling 2001) concludes that personality factors may be used to predict risk of violent or non-violent recidivism for adolescent male sexual offenders.

Links with psychopathy

An association between sex offenders and psychopathy traits is possible because some differences between sex offenders relate to clinical features of psychopathy, for example, empathy, use of violence, variety of victims. This seems to be borne out in studies which show that psychopaths, as defined by the PCL-R (Psychopathy Check List – Revised), make up about 10 to 15 per cent of child molesters, 40 to 50 per cent of rapists and mixed offenders are estimated to be psychopaths (Brown and Forth 1997; Firestone *et al.* 2000; Porter *et al.* 2000; Prentky and Knight 1991; Quinsey, Rice and Harris 1995) and 35 per cent of a sample of adult sex offenders were high scoring (>30 PCL score) psychopaths (Brown and Forth 1997). In Gretton *et al.*'s studies (2001, 2005) of juvenile sexual abusers, 13 per cent were high-scoring psychopaths.

Associations have been demonstrated between adult and juvenile sex offenders and psychopathy traits which, in sex offenders, are associated with an increased risk of violent and non-violent offending but no increased risk for sexual offending. The strongest associations are with rapists and versatile offenders who commit sexual offences as part of a wide repertoire.

The case for a paraphilic (disorder of sexual preference) personality disorder in adult life has also been discussed and it has been noted that 'inappropriate sexuality in paraphilic personality disorder is usually of early onset' (MacHovec 1999, p.29). The issue of sexual deviance may be relevant since a meta-analysis of factors predicting adult sex offender relapse (Hanson and Bussiere 1998) concluded that clear evidence of sexual deviancy was one of a number of consistent predictors.

Antisocial behaviour

It is important to look at the issue of antisocial behaviour as it relates to children and adolescents with sexually abusive behaviour because a consistent characteristic of this group is the co-occurrence of conduct disorder in sexually abusive children and antisocial personality disorder in older young people (Bladon *et al.* 2005; Dolan *et al.* 1996; Manocha and Mezey 1998; Richardson *et al.* 1995) and antisocial outcomes in later life (Gretton *et al.* 2005; Langstrom and Grann 2002; Nisbet, Wilson and Smallbone 2004; Rubenstein *et al.* 1993; Sipe, Jensen and Everett 1998; Worling and Curwen 2000).

In Richardson *et al.*'s (1995) study, 60 per cent were involved in multiple antisocial activities, predominantly crimes against the person, and 69 per cent of the sample had chronic histories of physical aggression towards others. In Dolan *et al.*'s (1996) study, 42 per cent had previous convictions for non-sexual offences and 17.6 per cent had previous violent offence convictions. In Manocha and Mezey's (1998) study, 21.5 per cent had been arrested for a non-sexual offence (usually stealing) of whom only 9.8 per cent were subsequently convicted.

This pattern of concurrent antisocial behaviour is reflected in the North American literature where a prior history of non-sexual offences in about half of all juvenile sexual offenders has been noted as well as different types of sexual offences (Awad and Saunders 1991; Bagley 1992; Becker *et al.* 1986; Ford and Linney 1995).

With these histories, the fact that many young people met the criteria, or had many of the components of conduct disorder, is not surprising (Bagley 1992; Becker *et al.* 1986; Kavoussi, Kaplan and Becker 1988). In Richardson *et al.*'s (1995) study, 68 per cent met the criteria for DSM-III-R Conduct Disorder. Dolan *et al.* (1996) showed that the majority of the referrals were conduct disordered. In Manocha and Mezey's (1998) study 43.1 per cent were reported as having marked problems in relation to conduct and Bladon *et al.*'s (2005) study noted that 60.3 per cent fulfilled criteria for DSM-III conduct disorder of which 42.6 per cent were childhood onset, severe type. In Bladon *et al.*'s (2005) study further indications of antisocial and conduct disordered behaviour were noted in that 23.4 per cent engaged in fire setting, 19.1 per cent had been seriously cruel to animals and 7.1 per cent had sexually abused an animal. Higher levels of firesetting than non-sexual delinquent controls have been noted in populations of young sex offenders (Bagley 1992; Ford and Linney 1995).

Developmental trajectories towards sexually abusive behaviour

In reviewing the issue of developmental trajectories in children with sexually abusive behaviour, Vizard (2006) notes that although there are few longitudinal studies looking at adult outcomes, it is nevertheless well known that many adult sex offenders start their sexually abusive behaviour in adolescence or earlier.

However, in relation to the age of onset of sexually abusive behaviour, only one UK study (Richardson *et al.* 1995) engages with this issue. In Richardson *et al.*'s (1995) study of n = 100 adolescents between 11 and 18 years, the difference between the mean age at referral (15.0) and the mean documented age for onset of sexually abusive behaviour (13.9) gave a mean difference of 1.9 years as an indicator of duration of a sexually abusive 'career'. The youngest documented onset of sexually abusive behaviour in Richardson *et al.*'s (1995) sample was 12.75 years.

Taylor's (2003) paper showed that those children under ten years were responsible for 34 per cent of sexual incidents but no information is given about sexual or non-sexual offending prior to the study and there were no sexual offences recorded for the 109 cases which had reached their seventeenth birthday. Taylor (2003) notes that about one-quarter of the sample seemed to be developing criminal lifestyles.

In Dolan *et al.*'s (1996) study 28 per cent (n = 34) of the sample were 're-peaters' of earlier sexual offences at the time of referral and 85 per cent of this group committed similar offences to their sexual offence at referral. In Richardson *et al.*'s (1995) study it is noted that 55 per cent were involved in property offending. The numbers with non-sexual offending convictions were not given but 69 of the sample had chronic histories of physical aggression towards either parents, teachers or peers. The study (Richardson *et al.* 1995) showed that 40 adolescents had one previous and/or current conviction for a sexual offence of which 16 had been convicted for more than one sexual offence. Richardson *et al.* (1995, p.202) note:

> The results of the present study indicate a group of adolescents may be at high risk of following a course of chronic sexual offending into adulthood, by virtue of the early onset age of their sexually abusive behaviour, a sexually abusive career of almost two years, and the number of abusive acts and victims involved.

In a current study underway in the Young Abusers Project (Vizard *et al.* in press) the average age of onset of sexually abusive behaviour in a cohort of n = 280 children was 9.5 years old with a subgroup of children who showed sexually inappropriate behaviour at much younger ages. However, longitudinal outcome data for this cohort is needed to track persistence and desistance from sexually abusive behaviour in adult life.

In summary, a review of recent UK studies on the characteristics of children and young people with sexually harmful behaviour shows that they are a heterogeneous group in terms of their offending and that they have similar characteristics to those of their non-sexually delinquent peers. These findings are reflected in the North American literature (Allan *et al.* 2002; Ford and Linney 1995).

However, the research evidence also points towards a potential subgroup of young people who appear to start offending both sexually and non-sexually from an unknown early age, probably under ten years old, who have experienced multiple risk factors associated with delinquency, whose behaviour is linked with violence towards others and who may be on a career path towards later offending. It is possible that subgroups of such sexually abusive young people are on differing developmental trajectories towards adult outcomes. Overall, on the basis of limited follow-up data into early adult life, sexually abusive children and young people appear to reoffend non-sexually far more frequently than they sexually reoffend.

Limitations of research studies

An important limitation of most of the research reported here is the lack of any control or comparison group with which to anchor the results. Most studies of referred populations of all types show high levels of disturbance (otherwise they would not be referred), but having said that, data on 'normal' populations are lacking for many delinquency studies. This is particularly true in the field of sexually abusive behaviour by young people where there are real difficulties in undertaking ethically sound and appropriate research studies into what constitutes 'normal' behaviour (Vizard 2004; Vizard et al. 1995).

Other limitations of the UK and Eire studies include the fact that data were predominantly derived retrospectively from files or by completion of a psychometric assessment pack (O'Halloran et al. 2002). Only two studies (Bladon et al. 2005; Richardson et al. 1995) conducted clinical assessments and as a result psychiatric disorders and emotional disturbance were diagnosed differently or not at all across the studies. Furthermore, the absence of an adequate follow-up period meant that adult outcomes were not known. Questions left unanswered by these studies include the age of onset of sexually and non-sexually abusive behaviours, including the nature of any specific developmental antecedents to these behaviours and any developmental trajectories linking early onset sexual or non-sexual behaviours with later adult outcomes. Furthermore, the absence of a clinical assessment in most studies means that descriptions are limited to statistics about the behaviours perpetrated so that a clear picture of the nature of these young people and the way in which they resemble and differ from each other is yet to emerge from the literature.

Recidivism

A number of studies (Gretton et al. 2005; Langstrom and Grann 2002; Nisbet et al. 2004; Rubenstein et al. 1993; Sipe et al. 1998; Worling and Curwen 2000) have looked at the adult recidivism of convicted juvenile sexual abusers with follow-up periods of 2 to 14 years. The rates of sexual recidivism ranged from 9 per cent to 37 per cent but the rates of non-sexual recidivism were significantly higher and ranged from 37 per cent to 89 per cent across all the studies. An important aspect of this evidence base is the strong association between non-sexual recidivism in adult life and juvenile sexually abusive behaviour in adolescence.

Treatment outcome

Common sense and clinical experience suggest that the earliest possible interventions with young over-sexualised children, before their patterns of sexually aggressive behaviours become entrenched, are likely to be most effective. However, there is a dearth of longitudinal follow-up studies looking at treatment outcomes with this younger group of children.

Outcomes may be measured by looking at recidivism, treatment outcome or other measures. At present, there are no longitudinal outcome studies of children and adolescents with sexually abusive behaviour which have measured other outcomes such as adult adjustment, attitudinal change or parenting.

Ten years ago, in a review of 21 treatment outcome studies (Vizard *et al.* 1995) with recidivism as an outcome measure, low sexual reoffending rates and higher non-sexual reoffending rates were noted. Recidivism as a sole outcome measure for treatment is unlikely to be reliable since persistent sexual behaviour problems in children under the age of criminal responsibility will not appear in crime statistics and conviction statistics for sex offenders of all ages are notoriously unreliable for a variety of reasons including failure to report victimisation experiences, failure to proceed with charges and a high rate of trial failures.

Other factors appear to be highly relevant to treatment outcomes with juvenile sexual abusers such as good interprofessional communication and a systemic context for treatment to occur. For instance, Multi Systemic Therapy (MST) is a complex intervention into the lives of delinquent youth which provides 24-hour, home-based support for the young person and his family, educational input, social skills training and offence specific work, all delivered by highly trained and registered MST therapists. The ethos behind MST recognises that, with complex multidetermined problems, a complex multilayered professional response is needed.

In a very small study (n = 16) of Multi Systemic Therapy (MST) versus individual counselling for juvenile sexual abusers (Borduin *et al.* 1990), sexual recidivism and non-sexual recidivism rates for the MST group (12.5% and 25%) were notably better at three-year follow-up than the individual counselling group (75% and 50%). However, in a more recent study (Borduin and Schaeffer 2002), with a follow-up of eight years into adult life, a larger group (n = 48) of adolescent sex offenders was allocated randomly to MST or to the usual services. Outcomes were tracked with a range of measures and MST was found to be more effective than usual services, e.g. by decreasing youth criminal offending (self-reported); increasing family cohesion and adaptability; decreasing violence toward peers by aggressive offenders and improving youth grades in school. At eight years follow-up, MST was also more effective than usual services in reducing sexual recidivism (12.5% for MST vs. 41.7% for usual services); preventing other criminal offending (29.2% vs. 62.5%); and decreasing days incarcerated during adulthood (by 62%). Furthermore, MST claimed to be over four times cheaper and more cost effective to deliver than the usual services (Borduin and Schaeffer 2002). These treatment outcome results for MST are encouraging, but the results should be interpreted with caution since the sample sizes remain small and the study needs to be repeated in other settings. A 'transportability' study of the effectiveness of MST in real world settings is underway in 41 MST sites in the USA and Canada (Schoenwald *et al.* 2003).

Other forms of treatment intervention aim to tackle the mindset of the sexually abusive young person. For instance, cognitive behavioural therapy (CBT) is a treatment intervention which works with the young person to change his distorted thinking processes (cognitive distortions) and to provide him with alternative, acceptable ways of thinking which do not result in illegal behaviours. CBT with adult and juvenile sexual abusers remains the most commonly practised and popular form of treatment intervention in the UK and North America and it is also a core component of the overall MST approach.

New approaches to CBT with sexually abusing youth have recently been described within the context of relapse prevention (Steen 2005) and a more complex CBT intervention, Mode Deactivation Therapy (MDT), has been suggested for disturbed, sexually abusive young people with reactive conduct disorders or personality disorders (Apsche and Bailey 2005). CBT groupwork with sexually abusing children and young people is widely practised in the UK and the principles of this work are described by Print and O'Callaghan (1999).

However, other treatment approaches will take into account the living context of the young person and the need for his or her carers to be provided with support and explanation of the treatment process in order to maximise positive results. For instance, when children and young people who sexually abuse are still living at home or in contact with their parents, family work is usually needed. An approach to groupwork with parents of children with sexually abusive behaviour has been described (Hackett, Telford and Slack 2005). In the case of children and young people who are living in the care system, concurrent work for the professionals and carers looking after the sexually abusing child or young person has been strongly advocated (Griffin *et al.* 1997).

There are a significant number of mid-adolescent, recidivist, delinquent, sexually abusive youth who are too dangerous to other children and young people to be treated (with any treatment modality) alongside other young people. Many of these young people have been through the court system or they are currently facing charges. For these reasons, treatment of the sexually abusive young person needs to be undertaken within a closely supervised, intensive, community-based foster placement with specially trained foster carers who are experienced in dealing with young offenders, risk and dangerousness. This type of approach is known by various names such as Multidimensional Treatment Foster Care (MTFC, Chamberlein and Reid 1998) or forensic foster care (Yokely and Boettner 2002). Early results from small-scale studies with this type of intervention are reasonably encouraging.

Outcomes claimed for these approaches include significantly fewer subsequent criminal referrals and more incarcerated boys returning to live with relatives, compared with those who received group home care alone (Chamberlein and Reid 1998). In a seven-year study of forensic foster care at the Treatment for Appropriate Social Control (TASC), Yokely and Boettner (2002) describe a social responsibility model to teach recidivist youths 'pro-social skills and values that compete with antisocial behaviour' (p.309).

Dynamic psychotherapy aims to work at an unconscious level with the sexually abusive young person to explore and understand the reasons for his persistent behaviour. However, evidence-based treatment outcome studies have not yet been undertaken for dynamic therapy with juvenile sexual abusers. A clinical description of long-term dynamic therapy (Vizard and Usiskin 1999) with these children emphasises the need to establish a systemic child protection context for the safe delivery of such treatment. In summary the components of effective treatment interventions with children and young people who sexually abuse will include the following:

- A well planned, systemic, child protection orientated, treatment context in which therapy can occur.

- Treatment should be one of a number of positive interventions into the life of the young person and his or her family.

- All interventions should be part of an agreed inter-agency care plan for the young person.

- Offence-specific interventions, such as CBT, aimed at straightening out the distorted cognitions and self-justifications of sexually abusing young people should be the core of any intervention programme for this client group.

- Treatment programmes which focus solely on the victimisation of the young person are likely to be seriously counterproductive and to miss opportunities to challenge the young person on his or her offending behaviour.

- Interventions should occur at all possible levels including individual work with the young person, family work (where relevant), support for foster carers or for professional care staff and consultation to the professional network.

- Long-term follow-up by the same treatment delivery agency will reinforce messages learned from treatment for the young person and his carers, will reduce recidivism and will improve the long-term liaison of the agencies working together to support the young person.

Conclusions

The evidence base in the UK and North America suggests that children and young people presenting to services with sexually abusive behaviour have a wide range of other psychosocial, emotional and behavioural problems, usually including some form of childhood victimisation and learning disability in addition to sexually abusive behaviour. In relation to learning disability and psychiatric disturbance in sexually abusive children, full psychometric assessment of intellectual functioning (IQ) should be undertaken in all cases and particularly in cases involving young child defendants facing serious sexual charges in court. The reason for this stipulation is that a young person with a very low IQ (with or without psychiatric disturbance) may mean that the young person is not fit to plead to the charges and that the court case should not proceed. It is in such cases that a balance needs to be struck between the need for justice for any victim(s) and the rights of a possibly mentally impaired child defendant to be protected from the full rigours of the court context and to be provided with treatment.

It is clear that the great majority of children who are sexually abused themselves do not go on to sexually abuse others. Clinical experience with much younger, over-sexualised or sexually aggressive children suggests that early treatment intervention may move these children off a developmental trajectory towards adolescent or adult abusing behaviour. However, this assumption has not yet been tested in longitudinal treatment outcome studies.

Known adult outcomes for older children who are convicted of sexual offences include much higher rates of non-sexual, antisocial recidivism and lower rates of sexual recidivism. Personality typologies of children and young people with sexually abusive behaviour may predict the subgroup, possibly including those juveniles with psychopathic traits, who go on to violent reoffending, either sexual or non-sexual.

Given the complexity of psychopathology seen in referred populations of children with sexually abusive behaviour it is not surprising that treatment outcomes appear to be better for complex, multisystemic interventions which tackle all aspects of the young person's needs, including appropriate placements.

An evidence base exists to guide professionals in the early identification of children and young people with sexually abusive behaviour and in relation to best practice for treatment interventions. However, it is still not clear whether or not this group of children comprises a separate group of delinquents with different characteristics and differing developmental trajectories towards adult outcomes. In order to answer that particular question, there is no alternative to long-term, funded treatment outcome studies which will move beyond simple indicators of criminal recidivism and which will measure other outcomes such as social adjustment, parenting capacities and mental health in adult life. What is clear is that there has been a failure to identify and assess children with sexually abusive behaviour at an early enough point in the development of their behavioural disturbance to give effective interventions.

What is now needed are services to which such children can be referred for specialist assessment and treatment. These services will need to be staffed by professionals who are trained in child protection, child development and mental health and who can engage with this challenging and needy population, both as victims and perpetrators of abuse. Government policy should be developed to coordinate the development of such services at community, regional and national levels around the UK.

Cost benefit studies show huge financial savings from effective childhood interventions with antisocial and sexually abusive behaviour and this point should be made as clearly as possible to policymakers. Gaps in the evidence base include longitudinal treatment outcome studies with younger children, follow-up studies with convicted adolescent sexual abusers and the inclusion of questions about sexualised behaviour or sexually abusive behaviour in future lifespan studies with children. Finally, a long-term government research strategy should be developed in relation to children with sexually abusive behaviour.

References

Allan, A., Allan, M.M., Marshall, P. and Kraszlan, K. (2002) 'Juvenile sexual offenders compared to juvenile offenders in general in Western Australia.' *Psychiatry, Psychology and Law 9*, 2, 214–233.

American Psychiatric Association (1994) *Diagnostic and Statistical Manual of Mental Disorders – Fourth Edition (DSM-IV)*. Washington, DC: APA.

Apsche, J. and Bailey, S.R.W. (2005) 'Mode deactivation therapy: Cognitive-behavioural therapy for young people with reactive conduct disorders or personality disorders or traits who sexually abuse.' In M.C. Calder (ed) *Children and Young People who Sexually Abuse: New Theory, Research and Practice Developments*. Lyme Regis: Russell House, pp.253–315.

Araji, S.K. (1997) 'Identifying, labelling and explaining children's sexually aggressive behaviors.' In S.K. Araji (ed) *Sexually Aggressive Children. Coming to Understand Them*. London: Sage Publications, pp.1–46.

Awad, G.A. and Saunders, E.B. (1991) 'Male adolescent assaulters: Clinical observations.' *Journal of Interpersonal Violence 6*, 4, 446–460.

Bagley, C. (1992) 'Characteristics of 60 children with a history of sexual assault against others: Evidence from a comparative study.' *Journal of Forensic Psychiatry 3*, 2, 299–309.

Baron-Cohen, S. (1990) 'Autism: A specific cognitive disorder of "mind-blindness".' *International Review of Psychiatry 2*, 79–88.

Baron-Cohen, S., Leslie, A.M. and Frith, U. (1985) 'Does the autistic child have a "theory of mind"?' *Cognition 21*, 37–46.

Becker, J.V., Cunningham-Rathner, J. and Kaplan, M.S. (1986) 'Adolescent sexual offenders; demographics, criminal and sexual histories and recommendations for reducing future offences.' *Journal of Interpersonal Violence 1*, 431–445.

Bladon, E., Vizard, E., French, L. and Tranah, T. (2005) 'Young sexual abusers: A descriptive study of a UK sample of children showing sexually harmful behaviours.' *Journal of Forensic Psychiatry and Psychology 16*, 1, 109–126.

Borduin, C.M. and Schaeffer, C.M. (2002) 'Multisystemic treatment of juvenile sexual offenders: A progress report.' *Journal of Psychology and Human Sexuality 13*, 3, 25–42.

Borduin, C.M., Henggeler, S.W., Blaske, D.M. and Stein, R. (1990) 'Multisystemic treatment of adolescent sexual offenders.' *International Journal of Offender Therapy and Comparative Criminology 34*, 105–113.

Brown, S.L. and Forth, A.E. (1997) 'Psychopathy and sexual assault: Static risk factors, emotional precursors and rapist subtypes.' *Journal of Consulting and Clinical Psychology 65*, 845–857.

Calder, M.C. (2004) 'Introduction.' In M.C. Calder (ed) *Children and Young People who Sexually Abuse: New Theory, Research and Practice Developments*. Lyme Regis: Russell House, pp.1–3.

Cantwell, H.B. (1995) 'Sexually aggressive children and societal responses.' In M. Hunter (ed) *Child Survivors and Perpetrators of Sexual Abuse. Treatment Innovations*. London: Sage, pp.79–107.

Chamberlein, P. and Reid, J. (1998) 'Comparison of two community alternatives to incarceration for chronic juvenile abusers.' *Journal of Consulting and Clinical Psychology 66*, 4, 624–633.

Davis, G. and Leitenberg, H. (1987) 'Adolescent sex offenders.' *Psychological Bulletin 101*, 417–427.

Dolan, M., Holloway, J., Bailey, S. and Kroll, L. (1996) 'The psychosocial characteristics of juvenile sexual offenders referred to an adolescent forensic service in the UK.' *Medicine, Science and the Law 36*, 4, 343–352.

Epps, K. (1991) 'The residential treatment of adolescent sex offenders.' *Issues in Criminological and Legal Psychology 1*, 58–67.

Farrington, D.P. (1995) 'The development of offending and antisocial behaviour from childhood.' *Journal of Child Psychology and Psychiatry 36*, 929–964.

Firestone, P., Bradford, J.M., Greenberg, D.M. and Serran, G.A. (2000) 'The relationship of deviant sexual arousal and psychopathy in incest offenders, extra familial child molesters and rapists.' *Journal of the American Academy of Psychiatry and the Law 28*, 303–308.

Ford, M.E. and Linney, A.J.A. (1995) 'Comparative analysis of juvenile sexual offenders, violent nonsexual offenders and status offenders.' *Journal of Interpersonal Violence 10*, 56–70.

Freeman-Longo, R.E. (1985) 'The adolescent sexual offender: Background and research perspectives.' In E.M. Otey and G.D. Ryan (eds) *Adolescent Sex Offenders: Issues in Research and Treatment*. Rockville, MD: DHSS, pp.130–146.

Gretton, H.M., McBride, M., Hare, R.D., O'Shaughnessy, R. and Kumka, G. (2001) 'Psychopathy and recidivism in adolescent sex offenders.' *Criminal Justice and Behaviour 28*, 427–449.

Gretton, H.M., Catchpole, R.E., McBride, M., Hare, R.D. and Regan, K. (2005) 'The relationship between psychopathy, treatment completion and criminal outcome over ten years: A study of adolescent sex offenders.' In M.C. Calder (ed) *Children and Young People who Sexually Abuse: New Theory, Research and Practice Developments.* Lyme Regis: Russell House, pp.17–29.

Griffin, S., Williams, M., Hawkes, C. and Vizard, E. (1997) 'The professional carers group supporting group work with young sexual abusers.' *Child Abuse and Neglect 21,* 7, 681–690.

Groth, A.N. (1977) 'The adolescent sex offender and his prey.' *International Journal of Offender Therapy and Comparative Criminology 21,* 249–254.

Groth, A.N. (1979) 'Sexual trauma in the life histories of rapists and child molesters.' *Victimology: An International Journal 4,* 10–16.

Hackett, S., Telford, P. and Slack, K. (2005) 'Groupwork with parents of children who have sexually harmed others.' In M.C. Calder (ed) *Young People who Sexually Abuse. Building the Evidence Base.* Lyme Regis: Russell House, pp.150–160.

Halperin, D.S., Bouvier, P., Jaffe, P.D. *et al.* (1996) 'Prevalence of child sexual abuse among adolescents in Geneva: Results of a cross sectional survey.' *British Medical Journal 312,* 1326–1329.

Hanson, R.K. and Bussiere, M.T. (1998) 'Predicting relapse: A meta-analysis of sexual offender recidivism studies.' *Journal of Consulting and Clinical Psychology 66,* 348–362.

Horne, L., Glasgow, D., Cox, A. and Calam, R. (1991) 'Sexual abuse of children by children.' *Journal of Child Law 3,* 147–151.

Johnston, T.C. and Doonan, R. (2004) 'Children with sexual behaviour problems. What have we learned in the last two decades?' In M.C. Calder (ed) *Children and Young People who Sexually Abuse: New Theory, Research and Practice Developments.* Lyme Regis: Russell House, pp.30–56.

Kavoussi, R.J., Kaplan, M. and Becker, J.V. (1988) 'Psychiatric diagnoses in adolescent sex offenders.' *Journal of American Academy of Child and Adolescent Psychiatry 27,* 241–243.

Kelly, L., Regan, L. and Burton, S. (1991) *An Exploratory Study of the Prevalence of Sexual Abuse in a Sample of 16–21-year-olds.* Report for the ESRC Child Abuse Studies Unit, University of North London.

Langevin, R., Wright, P. and Handy, L. (1989) 'Characteristics of sex offenders who were sexually victimized as children.' *Annals of Sex Research 2,* 227–253.

Langstrom, N. and Grann, M. (2002) 'Risk for criminal recidivism among young sex offenders.' *Journal of Interpersonal Violence 15,* 855–871.

Lewis, D.O., Shankok, S.S. and Pincus, J.H. (1979) 'Juvenile male sexual assaulters.' *American Journal of Psychiatry 136,* 1194–1196.

MacHovec, F.J. (1999) 'The case for paraphilic personality disorder: Detection, diagnosis and treatment.' In M.C. Calder (ed) *Working with Young People who Sexually Abuse. New Pieces of the Jigsaw Puzzle.* London: Random House.

Manocha, K. and Mezey, G. (1998) 'British adolescents who sexually abuse: A descriptive study.' *Journal of Forensic Psychiatry 9,* 3, 588–608.

Marshall, W.L. and Barbaree, H.E. (1990) 'An integrated theory of the etiology of sexual offending.' In W.L. Marshall, D.R. Laws and H.E. Barbaree (eds) *Handbook of Sexual Assault: Issues, Theories, and Treatment of the Offender.* New York: Plenum Press, pp.257–275.

Moffitt, T.E. (2001) 'Life-course persistent and adolescence-limited antisocial behaviour among males and females.' In T.E. Moffitt, A. Caspi, M. Rutter and P.A. Silva (eds) *Sex Differences in Antisocial Behaviour. Conduct Disorder, Delinquency and Violence in the Dunedin Longitudinal Study*. Cambridge: Cambridge University Press.

Moffitt, T.E., Caspi, A., Dickson, N., Silva, P. and Stanton, W. (1996) 'Childhood-onset versus adolescent-onset antisocial conduct in males: Natural history from ages 3–18 years.' *Development and Psychopathology 8*, 399–424.

Nisbet, I.A., Wilson, P.H. and Smallbone, S.W. (2004) 'A prospective longitudinal study of sexual recidivism among adolescent sex offenders.' *Sexual Abuse: A Journal of Research and Treatment 16*, 3, 224–234.

O'Halloran, M., Carr, A., O'Reilly, G. *et al.* (2002) 'Psychological profiles of sexually abusive adolescents in Ireland.' *Child Abuse and Neglect 26*, 359–370.

Pierce, L.H. and Pierce, R.L. (1987) 'Incestuous victimization by juvenile sex offenders.' *Journal of Family Violence 2*, 351–364.

Porter, S., Fairweather, D., Drugge, J., Herve, H., Birt, A. and Boer, D.P. (2000) 'Profiles of psychopathy in incarcerated sexual offenders.' *Criminal Justice and Behaviour 27*, 216–233.

Prentky, R.A. and Knight, R.A. (1991) 'Identifying critical dimensions for discriminating among rapists.' *Journal of Consulting and Clinical Psychology 59*, 643–661.

Print, B. and O'Callaghan, D. (1999) 'Working in groups with young men who have sexually abused others.' In M. Erooga and H. Masson (eds) *Children and Young People who Sexually Abuse Others. Responses to an Emerging Problem*. London: Routledge.

Quinsey, V.L., Rice, M.E. and Harris, G.T. (1995) 'Actuarial prediction of sexual recidivism.' *Journal of Interpersonal Violence 10*, 85–105.

Richardson, G., Graham, F., Bhate, S.R. and Kelly, T.P. (1995) 'A British sample of sexually abusive adolescents: Abuser and abuse characteristics.' *Criminal Behaviour and Mental Health 5*, 187–208.

Robins, L.N. (1978) 'Sturdy predictors of adult antisocial behaviour: Replications from longitudinal studies.' *Psychological Medicine 8*, 611–622.

Rubenstein, M., Yeager, C.A., Goodstein, C. and Lewis, D.O. (1993) 'Sexually assaultive male juveniles: A follow up.' *American Journal of Psychiatry 150*, 2, 262–265.

Rutter, M., Giller, H. and Hagell, A. (1998) *Antisocial Behaviour by Young People*. Cambridge University Press.

Salter, D., McMillan, D., Richards, M. *et al.* (2003) 'Development of sexually abusive behaviour in sexually victimised males: A longitudinal study.' *Lancet 361*, 471–476.

Schoenwald, S.K., Sheidow, A.J., Letourneau, E.J. and Liao, J.G. (2003) 'Transportability of multisystemic therapy: Evidence for multilevel influences.' *Mental Health Services Research 5*, 223–239.

Seghorn, T.K., Prentky, R.A. and Boucher, R.J. (1987) 'Childhood sexual abuse in the lives of sexually aggressive offenders.' *Journal of American Academy of Child and Adolescent Psychiatry 26*, 262–267.

Silovsky, J.F. and Niec, L. (2002) 'Characteristics of young children with sexual behaviour problems: A pilot study.' *Child Maltreatment 7*, 3, 187–197.

Sipe, R., Jensen, E.L. and Everett, R.S. (1998) 'Adolescent sexual offenders grown up. Recidivism in young adulthood.' *Criminal Justice and Behavior 25*, 1, 109–124.

Skuse, D., Bentovim, A., Hodges, J. *et al.* (1998) 'Risk factors for development of sexually abusive behaviour in sexually victimised adolescent boys: Cross sectional study.' *British Medical Journal 317*, 7152, 175–179.

Smith, W.R. (1988) 'Delinquency and abuse among juvenile sexual offenders.' *Journal of Interpersonal Violence 3*, 400–413.

Steen, C. (2005) 'Cognitive-behavioural treatment under the relapse prevention umbrella.' In M.C. Calder (ed) *Children and Young People who Sexually Abuse: New Theory, Research and Practice Developments*. Lyme Regis: Russell House, pp.217–230.

Tantam, D. (2003) 'The challenge of adolescents and adults with Asperger Syndrome.' *Child and Adolescent Psychiatric Clinical Neuro-Anatomy 12*, 143–163.

Taylor, J. (2003) 'Children and young people accused of child sexual abuse: A study within a community.' *Journal of Sexual Aggression 9*, 1, 57–70.

Vizard, E. (2004) 'Sexually abusive behaviour by children and adolescents.' In S. Bailey and M. Dolan (eds) *Forensic Adolescent Psychiatry*. London: Arnold, pp.228–246.

Vizard, E. (2006) 'Sexually abusive behaviour by children and adolescents.' *Child and Adolescent Mental Health 11*, 1, 2–8.

Vizard, E. and Usiskin, J. (1999) 'Providing individual psychotherapy for young sexual abusers of children.' In M. Erooga and H. Masson (eds) *Children and Young People who Sexually Abuse Others. Responses to an Emerging Problem*. London: Routledge, pp.104–123.

Vizard, E., Monck, E. and Misch, P. (1995) 'Child and adolescent sex abuse perpetrators: A review of the research literature.' *Journal of Child Psychology and Psychiatry 36*, 5, 731–756.

Vizard, E., Hickey, N., French, L. and McCrory, E. (in press) 'Children and adolescents who present with sexually abusive behaviour: A UK descriptive study.' *Journal of Forensic Psychology and Psychiatry.*

Ward, T. and Siegert, R.J. (2002) 'Toward a comprehensive theory of child sexual abuse: A theory knitting perspective.' *Psychology, Crime and Law 8*, 319–351.

Worling, J. (2001) 'Personality-based typology of adolescent male sexual offenders: Differences in recidivism rates, victim selection characteristics and personal victimization histories.' *Sexual Abuse: A Journal of Research and Treatment 13*, 3.

Worling, J. (2002) 'Assessing risk of sexual assault recidivism with adolescent sexual offenders.' In M.C. Calder (ed) *Young People who Sexually Abuse. Building the Evidence Base for your Practice*. Lyme Regis: Russell House, pp.365–375.

Worling, J.R. and Curwen, T. (2000) 'Adolescent sexual offender recidivism: Success of specialized treatment and implications for risk prediction.' *Child Abuse and Neglect 24*, 965–982.

Yokely, J. and Boettner, S. (2002) 'Forensic foster care for young people who sexually abuse: Lessons from treatment.' In M.C. Calder (ed) *Young People who Sexually Abuse. Building the Evidence Base for Your Practice*. Lyme Regis: Russell House, pp.309–332.

5

Minors involved in murder and manslaughter

An exploration of the situation in the Netherlands

Paul Nieuwbeerta and Peter H. van der Laan

Introduction

The Dutch Central Bureau of Statistics produces annual statistics on juvenile suspects detained by the police. These figures, supplemented by the findings from periodic self-report studies, provide a good reflection of the development and nature of juvenile crime in the Netherlands. More detailed, complementary information on a wider range of variables within the young offenders' backgrounds, such as age, gender, ethnicity, co-offending and recidivism, can be sourced from the continuous stream of research studies that investigate specific aspects of juvenile crime. The same applies for considerations of the background and causes of juvenile crime.

Nonetheless, not every aspect of juvenile crime is known. For instance, we know little or nothing about the nature, causes or perpetrators of murder and manslaughter, the most serious forms of juvenile crime. This lack of knowledge is undoubtedly related to the fact that the extent of this phenomenon is limited and easily snowed under by less serious forms of juvenile crime. On the other hand, murder and manslaughter have a major and permanently life-changing impact on the victim's relatives and society, and in all probability a similar impact on the perpetrators themselves, their family and relations (Crespi and Rigazio-DiGili 1996). Perhaps even more so than with adult offenders, serious offences against the person perpetrated by juveniles raise fundamental questions about the background and causes of this type of violent crime, and how we should deal with them within the criminal justice system and within society generally.

The fact that comparatively few serious offences against the person are committed by minors has contributed to the situation that little research has been conducted into this phenomenon (Rutter, Giller and Hagell 1998). The little research done, mostly in the USA, usually involves case studies. The authors tend to work as forensic psychiatrists or psychologists, publishing about youths who have been referred to them for personality testing and case-handling advice, or for treatment (Dolan and Smith 2001; Heide 1992; Myers *et al.* 1995). It is unclear to what extent these youths are representative of the total group of youths who become involved in murder and manslaughter. It is equally unknown in what sense these youths are comparable with or different from other violent and non-violent juvenile delinquents. In research studies that do draw comparisons with other violent or non-violent offender groups, the numbers of offenders are generally small, and they are usually only compared in respect of a few factors such as psychopathological disorders or intelligence (Hays, Solway and Schreiner 1978; Myers and Scott 1998; Otnow Lewis *et al.* 1988; Zagar *et al.* 1990).

This contribution presents an initial exploration of murder and manslaughter in the Netherlands during the period 1992 to 2001, looking at murder and manslaughter cases in which legal minors were involved as principal offender or co-offender. Victims were actually killed in 84 cases, with some form of involvement by 105 minors. The data originate from the databank 'Murder and Manslaughter' compiled by Nieuwbeerta (2003; see also Leistra and Nieuwbeerta 2003), with supplementary information sourced from the criminal dossiers from the cases. The dossiers were consulted in 2003 and 2004.

The contribution consists of three parts. We begin with a short outline of the development of recorded juvenile crime in the Netherlands during the 1990s, focusing particularly on violent crime, so that murder and manslaughter can be located within this framework. We then describe the characteristics of known murder and manslaughter cases during the period 1992 to 2001, which involved legal minors as offenders. Finally, we explore the social and psychological background characteristics and risk factors of the juvenile perpetrators of murder and manslaughter.

Legal minors and violent crime

In 2001, the Dutch police recorded over 47,000 minor suspects aged between 12 and 17 years old inclusive (in addition to approximately 275,000 adults). These data are drawn from processing of official statistics (Van der Heide and Eggen 2003, 2004) Similar figures were recorded in preceding years. In the period 1992 to 1995, the figure was lower and fluctuated around 40,000. In 2002 and 2003 it was considerably higher, at 59,000, although it should be noted that this still forms a small proportion of the 1.18 million inhabitants aged between 12 and 17.[1] By far the most juvenile suspects were questioned in connection with a property crime or vandalism. Approximately a quarter, 10,596 juveniles to be precise, were questioned on suspicion of a violent crime (see Table 5.1). At 22 per cent, the share of violent crimes was twice as high in 2001 as it was in 1992 (4700 violent crimes). In 2001, 56 per cent of violent crimes involved an assault, 22 per cent involved robbery with violence and extortion, and 8 per cent involved a sex offence. The remaining 14 per cent (1450 youths) were questioned in connection with a more serious crime against the person, including serious threatening behaviour. The fact that so many youths were questioned on suspicion of a more serious crime against the person does not mean that in reality that many acts were committed, nor in any sense that there was evidence of mortal injury in all those cases. Attempts, for instance, are also included. Moreover, some cases go no further than a suspicion, or it is discovered that nothing actually happened. In a relatively small number of cases, youths are charged with a serious crime against the person. In 2001, 244 such charges were issued. In the process that follows, the public prosecutor may decide, perhaps for technical evidence reasons, to deviate from the police classification and to select a less serious or different type of offence. Moreover, the public prosecutor may decide not to prosecute, as happened in 32 cases of serious crimes against the person in 2001.

Table 5.1 Legal minors questioned by the police, by type of offence

Type	Number	%
Property crimes	22,775	48.3
Vandalism and disorderly conduct	10,966	23.3
Violent crimes	10,596	22.5
Assault	5986	12.7
Robbery with violence	2173	5.7
Serious crimes against the person	1450	3.1
Sex offences	821	1.7
Other offences	2775	5.9
Total	**47,112**	**100.0**

Ultimately, even fewer serious crimes against the person will actually be prosecuted. In 2001, the courts dealt with 133 cases in which a charge was made of (an attempted) serious crime against the person. A total of 122 guilty pronouncements were made; acquittal followed in eight cases. In many cases, the court does not accept the (primary) charge. A conviction may follow, but for a different, less serious crime of violence. This undoubtedly explains why in 2001 'only' 65 minors received unconditional youth detention because of (an attempted) serious crime against the person.[2, 3]

Given that serious crimes against the person also cover attempted murder and manslaughter, and serious threatening behaviour, the number of cases of murder and manslaughter that involved the actual death of the victim is much smaller. The following sections examine in more detail those cases in which the public prosecutor did indict the youth for murder or manslaughter, and a victim was killed.

Minors, murder and manslaughter

The data used to describe murder and manslaughter with the involvement of legal minors in the last ten years come from the databank 'Murder and Manslaughter 1992–2001', which contains information on all 2389 murders that took place during that period in the Netherlands. The information in the databank is based on material sourced from the Dutch Criminal Investigation Institute, the public prosecution service, extracts from criminal records and press reports from the Dutch press office ANP (for a detailed description, see Leistra and Nieuwbeerta 2003; Nieuwbeerta 2003). The data from the databank are supplemented with information from the dossiers of juvenile offenders who were involved in murder cases. This involved consultation of all the court dossiers at the different courts, in order to collect information about the case, and about background characteristics and risk factors.

As we have seen, in the period 1992 to 2001, 84 cases of murder and manslaughter took place, involving a total of 105 legal minors as principal offender or co-offender. 'Involvement' means that in the first instance the public prosecutor indicted the minors for murder or manslaughter. Murder is different from manslaughter in the sense that the perpetrator 'knew' in advance what he or she was going to do (i.e. kill someone); he or she had prepared themselves.[4] In both cases the intention (deliberately) is to kill, but in the case of murder this is more or less prepared beforehand (premeditated) whereas in the case of manslaughter it happens on the spur of the moment. In the following, for readability, we use the terms murder or murder case to cover manslaughter as well.

Murder cases that involved minors

Table 5.2 shows fluctuation in the number of cases that involved minors in the period 1992 to 2001. No clear rise or drop can be noted in this period, meaning that murder and manslaughter deviate from the general increase in violent crimes mentioned above. The murders vary by (presumed) motive and the relationship between the offender and the victim. With 28 cases, murder in the course of an argument forms the largest category (33%; see Table 5.3). The arguments may be initiated within the family, on a night out, or in criminal circles. They may be long-lasting or short-term conflicts, between acquaintances or strangers. Eleven cases took place on nights out, and could be regarded as a type of 'social' violence. In four cases, the argument was about money or goods. Alcohol and, to a lesser extent, drug use play a major role in

Table 5.2 Number of murder cases that involved legal minors and number of victims

Year	Number of cases	Number of victims
1992	10	10
1993	8	8
1994	7	7
1995	8	9
1996	14	15
1997	10	10
1998	7	7
1999	6	6
2000	11	11
2001	3	3
Total	**84**	**86**

murders in the course of an argument. In a number of cases, offenders, and occasionally victims too, were under the influence of drink or other substances. In a quarter of the cases, robbery was the motive for the murder. Around half of these involved robbery/burglary in a residence, whereby the resident was killed. In one case, the burglary of a residence resulted in two victims. Four acts of robbery took place in a shop or catering establishment, and one in a bank. Two victims were killed in separate muggings, and one taxi driver was murdered during a robbery.

A fifth of all murders that involved legal minors took place within the family. A parent was killed in seven cases, two of which were connected to a mental disorder suffered by the offender. Two others can be considered as a reaction to abuse within the family. In three cases, an honour killing was the motive for the murder. In the category 'other family', a brother or sister was the victim.

The fourth category concerns murder in the criminal world. Characteristic of these cases is that both offender and victim are involved in criminal practices, and that the murder is committed in light of such activities. These are assassinations, rip deals, murder in connection with money or goods (such as drugs or stolen goods), and murder in the course of argument between addicts. In a 'rip deal', the seller of goods (usually drugs) is killed to avoid having to pay for the goods. Eight cases fit within this category of murder in the criminal world. Four of these can be considered to be assassinations, one victim was murdered during an argument between addicts, and another victim was murdered in a rip deal.

Table 5.3 Murder cases by type

Type	Number	%
Argument	28	33
Robbery	21	25
Family	17	20
Partner	3	4
Child	2	2
Parent	7	8
Honour killing	3	4
Other family	2	2
Criminal	8	10
Sexual	8	10
Other	2	2
Total	**84**	**100**

Finally, sexual murders are classified as those preceded by (attempted) sexual assault, abuse or rape by a non-family member. In four of the eight cases, offender and victim knew each other. In two cases, the offenders were initially harassed by the victims, after which the offenders defended themselves with the outcome that the victims lost their lives.

Eighty-six victims died in the 84 cases. Two people were murdered in each of three cases, though these cases also involved more than one offender. All other cases involved a single victim. A quarter of the victims were women. A comparatively high number of these women were victims of murder within the family or of robbery with murder. Five of the eight victims of sexual murder were women.

The victims were on average 33 years old. The two youngest victims died respectively a few hours and two months after their birth (in part) through the actions of their underage mothers. The two oldest victims were both 68 years old, murdered when their homes were burgled. The average age of the victims was highest for robbery with murder, at 50 years old. Victims of murder in the course of an argument were on average the youngest, at 24 years old. Sexual murder involved both relatively young victims (four or five years old) and somewhat older victims. Expressed as the number per 100,000 inhabitants, the likelihood of becoming a victim of murder or manslaughter is highest for 16- to 20-year-olds. The likelihood for boys is 3.5 times higher than for girls. After the age of 30, this likelihood reduces significantly for men too.

Fifty-five per cent of the victims were born in the Netherlands.[5] The victims born outside the Netherlands were of Surinamese (8%) or North

African/Moroccan (11%) descent, came from elsewhere within or outside Europe (11%), or were of unknown origin (9%).

The ways in which the victims were killed vary from drowning and strangulation to hitting the victim with an axe. The weapon used most frequently was a stabbing or cutting weapon, followed by a firearm (see Table 5.4). Half or more of the offenders in cases of murder within the family, murder in the course of an argument and sexual murder killed their victims using a stabbing or cutting weapon. Murders in criminal circles more often involved the offender using a firearm (63%). A third of the victims of robbery with murder died through strangulation or asphyxiation, and a quarter through injury with a firearm.

Almost half of all victims (44%) were killed in a house, and nearly a third out on the street (29%). Only murder in the course of an argument happens in most cases out on the street. Half of all murders took place in the three major cities in the Netherlands: Amsterdam, The Hague and Rotterdam.

Table 5.4 Modus operandus

Method	Number of victims	%
Firearm	19	22
Stabbing or cutting weapon	39	46
Blunt instrument	8	9
Physical violence	7	8
Strangulation	12	14
Other	1	1
Total	**86**	**100**

Juvenile offenders

A total of 105 offenders were involved in 84 murders. Of these cases, 41 (49%) involved a single juvenile offender; the remaining cases involved between two and six offenders. Sixty-three adults took part in 30 cases, alongside one or more legal minors. Sexual murders were generally committed by a single offender. Murders in the criminal world involved on average the most offenders (over three).

Sixty per cent of the 105 youths were regarded as the principal offender, who took the initiative. Five youths were principal offenders but the initiative had come from someone else. A fifth of the youths were involved as a co-offender. They delivered the weapon, were present though did nothing, assaulted but did not kill the victim, or lured the victim to the place where the murder took place.

Just as other forms of violent crime, murder and manslaughter are mainly committed by boys. The offenders consisted of 94 boys (90%) and 11 girls (10%) (Table 5.5). Murder in the family is the only category in which comparatively many girls are involved as (co-)offenders (37%). Almost half of the juvenile offenders were 17 years old, and a quarter were 16 years old. One 12-year-old was involved in a murder, as were a 5-, 7-, 13- and 14-year-old (see Table 5.5).

Almost three-quarters of the juvenile offenders were born in the Netherlands. Since only a third of the offenders had parents who were both born in the Netherlands, two-thirds of the offenders can be considered to be of allochthonous descent.

Table 5.5 Age of legal minors involved in murder or manslaughter

Age	Boy	Girl	Total
12	1	–	1
13	5	–	5
14	7	–	7
15	16	3	19
16	22	2	24
17	43	6	49
Total	94	11	105

Court handling of murder and manslaughter cases

In principle, the Dutch criminal justice system does not distinguish between acts that criminal minors may be accused of, and those that may be attributed to adults. The formulation or description of the criminal act is no different. The system does apply a different set of criminal process regulations for youths aged between 12 and 17 years inclusive, and also sets different sanctions and maximum punishments to communal criminal justice (Doek and Vlaardingerbroek 2001). Youths aged between 12 and 15 years inclusive may be sentenced to youth detention to a maximum of one year. For youths of 16 and 17 years, the maximum detention period is two years. If the youth's personality development appears to be dysfunctional, the court may impose the criminal justice measure of placing the youth in a juvenile institution as a form of compulsory treatment. This measure is imposed for a two-year duration and can be extended twice at most. It can only be imposed if two behavioural specialists, including a psychiatrist, have carried out a personality test beforehand (reporting *Pro Justitia*). Personality tests will examine the youth's responsibility at the time of the offence, and advise on the sanction to be imposed (Duits *et al.* 2003). In special cases, adult criminal law can be applied to 16- and 17-year-olds; the decision to do this will often also be based on advice from behavioural specialists (Backer 2004). In these cases, imprisonment may be imposed rather than youth detention, or the youth may be admitted to a secure psychiatric unit rather than placed in a juvenile institution.

As far as we know, 97 youths were subjected to a personality test. Eighteen of those were declared not responsible for their actions, and another 18 were considered to have diminished responsibility. Varying advice was delivered on the type and duration of the punishment, but treatment in a closed setting was recommended in a quarter of the cases. The court accepted the recommendations made in the personality reports in half of the cases.

The public prosecutor indicted all 105 juvenile offenders for murder or manslaughter in the first instance. Ultimately, 30 youths were sentenced for murder, 40 for manslaughter, and 23 for other violent crimes against the person (assault leading to death). Three youths were acquitted on appeal, seven were discharged from any further prosecution, and the cases of two youths were dropped because of the circumstances leading to the offence.

The final verdict of 90 of the 93 youths who were sentenced is known. Forty-nine of them were placed in a juvenile institution; 22 of these youths received an imprisonment in addition (Table 5.6). The other 41 youths only received an imprisonment.[6] Treatment is ordered as part of a court measure comparatively more often in respect of murder than in respect of manslaughter and assault. The same applies when the youth concerned acted as the principal offender rather than co-offender.

Table 5.6 Distribution (in percentages) of sanctions and treatments imposed by conviction

Type of sanction	Murder	Manslaughter	Assault
Imprisonment	23	47	42
Imprisonment and treatment	43	18	6
Treatment	30	17	31
No sanction imposed	4	10	6
Unknown	–	–	9
Total	**100**	**100**	**100**
Number	**(30)**	**(40)**	**(23)**

Risk factors

According to a range of researchers, youths develop serious and violent delinquency during adolescence as a function of risk and protection factors, to which the youth is exposed during his or her development (Farrington 1998;

Loeber and Farrington 1998). These risk and protection factors are situated within different domains: the individual (the person of the youth), family/parenting, school, peer group and community (Hawkins *et al.* 1998). The probability of serious delinquent behaviour increases, not because of specific risk factors, but through an accumulation and combination of risk factors. The combinations may differ from person to person. This is true also of juvenile murderers (Heide 1999; Shumaker and Prinz 2000). In an overview of results from primarily US studies, Heide (1999) identifies risk factors for young murderers within four domains: (a) personality factors; (b) family factors; (c) environmental factors, which for this author also cover factors in the area of work, school and (criminal) friends; (d) factors associated with earlier delinquent behaviour. In other words, the broad groups of risk factors that are implicated do not differ from those for less serious antisocial behaviour.

Criminal dossiers were consulted to investigate the extent to which legal minors involved in murder or manslaughter in the Netherlands had been exposed to risk factors. In addition to the police charges, indictments by the public prosecutor and court verdicts, criminal dossiers also often contain the reports from personality testing. They therefore offer a good source of information on the youths' backgrounds and risk factors. At the time it was not possible to consult a detailed dossier for 21 of the 105 juveniles. Our findings therefore concern 84 youths.

Information was collected on individual factors, family factors, relationships, school and work, peers, home and neighbourhood factors, leisure time, delinquency and the criminal justice procedure. This chapter focuses on those factors that were studied in earlier Dutch research into risk factors associated with youths in judicial treatment institutions (Boendermaker 1993; Rietveld, Hilhorst and Van Dijk 2000).[7] The research group studied by Rietveld *et al.* (2000) comprised 102 youths from 11 to 19 years old inclusive, 36 of whom were placed in the institution under a criminal order and 66 of whom were placed under a civil order.[8] The comparison of minors involved in murder and manslaughter with youths in judicial treatment institutions should start to indicate the existence of any specific (combinations of) risk factors associated with young offenders of the most serious type of violence (see Table 5.7).

The presence of one or more personality disorders is reported in respect of 80 per cent of the youths involved in murder or manslaughter. A particularly high number of these risk factors are reported in respect of murder in the course of an argument and robbery with murder. By contrast, few are reported in respect of perpetrators of sexual murders. The risk factors reported frequently in the personality domain are weak regulation of aggression (44%) and difficulty processing emotions (30%). Developmental delays were evident among a quarter of the underage murderers. This factor was established considerably more frequently among other youths in judicial treatment centres (62%).

Table 5.7 Percentage of legal minors with a particular risk factor

Risk factor	Legal minors involved in murder or manslaughter (n = 84)	Legal minors in judicial juvenile institutions (n = 102)
Personality factors		
ADHD	5	22
Retarded moral development	33	49
Retarded social development	27	62
Weak regulation of aggression	44	34
Mood swings	19	10
Fear of failure	15	4
Difficulty processing emotions	30	30
Family factors		
Parents divorced	50	–
No contact with biological father	32	–
No contact with biological mother	14	–
Parental neglect	31	58
Physical abuse by parents	6	12
Parental addictions	24	15
Previous contact with support services	42	–
Previous child protection measures	29	–
Environmental factors		
Delinquent friends	55	–
Convicted friends	30	–
Use of soft drugs by friends	40	–
Use of hard drugs by friends	30	–
Substance use		
Alcohol use	57	35
Hard drug use	32	12
Soft drug use	52	48
Previous delinquent behaviour		
Previous convictions	55	74
More than 10 previous convictions	8	18
Previous convictions before age of 15	27	64

Risk factors connected with the family were also mentioned frequently. Over half of the youths come from a large family (four or more people living in the home). Half of the youths had experienced their parents' divorce, and a third had no contact with one of their biological parents. A range of parenting problems was signalled among the parents of most of the youths. The perpetrators of murder in the family had comparatively the most problems, ranging from a symbiotic relationship between child and parent(s), inadequate supervision by parents, harsh and inconsistent punishments, to the lack of a natural parental authority. A third of the youths had experienced physical abuse at the hands of their parents or others. In particular, the perpetrators of sexual murders and murders within the family had suffered this type of abuse relatively often. These youths had also relatively often witnessed domestic violence. Six minors mentioned criminal activity by their parents. Parental alcohol abuse was reported relatively frequently, particularly among the parents of youths involved in murders within the family and murders in the course of an argument. Parental drug abuse was reported by seven youths, and particularly by perpetrators of murders in the criminal world.

Over half of the underage murderers were attending school at the time of the crime. The school career of many youths was problematic, with difficulties generally beginning in secondary school. Comparatively the most school problems were signalled among minors involved in murder in the criminal world. They had to repeat a year most often, they played truant most often, and their average academic performance was unsatisfactory.

Over half of the juvenile murderers, and particularly youths involved in robbery with murder and murders in the criminal world, have delinquent friends. Half use soft drugs and a quarter use hard drugs (which also applies for their friends).

The history of a large number of the minors is characterised by a range of problem behaviours and contact with support services and child protection. In addition, over half of the youths had been sentenced for a previous offence. Again, youths involved in robbery with murder and murder in the criminal world stand out in a negative sense in respect of these points. These youths were moreover younger at the time of their first sentencing. For these youths, the murder tends to be a component of a criminal career that started at a relatively young age. Youths who killed someone in the family context, on the other hand, more often committed this murder as an independent act rather than as part of a career. Nonetheless, on average, minors involved in murder or manslaughter began their criminal activities at a later age than other minors taken into judicial juvenile institutions and fewer of them had previous convictions (see Table 5.7).

Concluding observations

This contribution has given an overview of murder and manslaughter with the involvement of minors, in the Netherlands during the period 1992 to 2001. At 84, the number of cases is very small in comparison with the total number of violent crime cases recorded by the police (over 10,000). On average, fewer than ten murder or manslaughter cases are recorded a year. No clear increase or decrease was evident during the 1990s. This contrasts with the increase in violent crime committed by youths that is repeatedly reported.

The handling of these cases (through prosecution and the imposition of sanctions) has a pronounced pedagogical flavour. In general, it may be stated that the approach to juvenile delinquency in the Netherlands is determined by a policy of minimal intervention, with a strongly pedagogical point of view. In other words, the emphasis is on restraint: only intervene if that is strictly necessary (for this, read: the likelihood of repeat offending is high) and preferably with no greater severity than needed. So the police will not always issue a charge, the public prosecutor may choose not to indict, and the court may prefer to impose a community sanction rather than an imprisonment or closed treatment. The system works like a sieve or funnel. At the same time, more than in the adult criminal justice system, the emphasis lies on education and treatment rather than on punishment. Although such a minimal intervention policy may seem contrary to expectations in respect of youths prosecuted for involvement in a murder or manslaughter, this is the practice in the Netherlands. Cases recorded by the police as murder or manslaughter in the first instance may not ultimately be presented to court as such. Moreover, the pedagogical nature of the punishments is recognisable in the fact that treatment is ordered in most cases, in the form of placement in a juvenile institution, sometimes in combination with imprisonment, rather than a straightforward youth detention or imprisonment. There are no indications of special policies for prosecuting or handling the cases of legal minors suspected of murder or manslaughter. The limited prevalence of this phenomenon is undoubtedly partly due to the fact that every case is judged on its own merits. Incidentally, this is also noted in the USA, where a considerably higher number of youths are sentenced for murder and manslaughter (Zimring 1998).

Youths who have been prosecuted for murder or manslaughter vary only slightly or not at all from other juvenile delinquents on points such as age, gender and ethnic background, and only to a limited extent on risk factors.[9] Murder and manslaughter are committed alone comparatively more often, and on average the perpetrators start their criminal activities at a later age and are much less likely to have previous convictions than (other) minors taken into judicial youth institutions (see Table 5.7). At the same time, it is clear that while the group of youths involved in murder and manslaughter may be small, it is anything but homogeneous. There is great variety in terms of motives, victims, modus operandi, etc. In simple terms, each case stands on its own. A murder in the criminal world is a totally different affair from the case of an underage mother guilty (along with others) of the death of her newly born child; and different again from the minor who kills a stepfather in response to his constant and serious abuse of the mother. Further research is needed to gain better insight into the potential categories of murder and manslaughter, and offender typologies. The question of the youth being the principal offender or a co-offender also warrants further research. Such research should also focus on differences between youths who are ultimately sentenced for murder, manslaughter or assault, and between youths who are sentenced or acquitted. That such differences are relevant is clear from the initial exploration of risk factors presented here, and from the way that cases are handled by the police and the justice system.

Notes

1. Police statistics say little about the real scale of juvenile crime. This is to do with the fact that not all crime is detected or brought to the attention of the police. By far not every crime that is reported is actually solved. The likelihood of the case being solved is higher for serious crimes (of violence), but is also dependent on the available police capacity and policy priorities. This explains the occasionally widely fluctuating numbers of suspects detained.

2. The average duration of the youth detention was 204 days, almost twice as high as the average.

3. One might expect that on a number of occasions, the 'placement in a juvenile institution' measure – a form of forced treatment – will have been imposed, but it is unclear how often this occurred.

4. Articles 287, 288, 289, 290 and 291 of the Dutch criminal code.

5. Very little or no data is available on the parents' countries of origin. The impression given of the victims' origins may therefore be somewhat distorted.

6. By way of comparison, in 2001 over 4800 youths received an imprisonment. Of those, 1600 were (partly) unconditional, in more than half of the cases because of a crime of violence (69% for violent robbery, 10% for assault and 8% for serious crimes against the person). The average duration of the youth detention imposed was 127 days. For serious crimes against the person, the average was 204 days. In 2001, 190 youths were placed in a juvenile institution.

7. The Dutch judicial treatment institutions are broadly comparable with secure training centres and secure accommodation under the responsibility of local authorities in the UK.

8. Civil law placement takes place within the framework of a supervision order or a guardianship measure, which is in some ways comparable with a UK care order.

9. US prospective research suggests that in terms of risk factors, although no qualitative differences may exist between youths who commit serious crimes against the person and youths who commit other violent offences, there may be quantitative differences: that is, the same type of risk factors but stronger and more frequently present (Loeber *et al.* in press).

References

Backer, H.S. (2004) 'Het advies toepassen meerderjarigenstrafrecht vanuit psychiatrisch perspectief.' *Tijdschrift voor Familie- en Jeugdrecht 26*, 40–45.

Boendermaker, L. (1993) *Jongeren in justitiële behandelinrichtingen.* Den Haag: Ministerie van Justitie, WODC.

Crespi, T.D. and Rigazio-DiGili, S.A. (1996) 'Adolescent homicide and family pathology: Implications for research and treatment with adolescents.' *Adolescence 31*, 353–366.

Doek, J.E. and Vlaardingerbroek, P. (2001) *Jeugdrecht en jeugdhulpverleningsrecht.* Den Haag: Elsevier.

Dolan, M. and Smith, C. (2001) 'Juvenile homicide offenders: 10 years' experience of an adolescent forensic psychiatry service.' *Journal of Forensic Psychiatry 12*, 313–329.

Duits, N., Harkink, J., Brink, W. van den and Doreleijers, Th.A.H. (2003) 'De relatie tussen advies uit de rapportage Pro Justitia van jeugdigen en het vonnis van de rechtbank.' *Tijdschrift voor Familie- en Jeugdrecht 25*, 157–163.

Farrington, D.P. (1998) 'Predictors, causes and correlates of male youth violence.' *Crime and Justice 24*, 421–475.

Hawkins, J.D.T., Herrenkohl, T., Farrington, D.P., Brewer, D., Catalano, R.F. and Harachi, T.W. (1998) 'A review of predictors of youth violence.' In R. Loeber and D.P. Farrington (eds) *Serious and Violent Juvenile Offenders.* Thousand Oaks: Sage.

Hays, J.R., Solway, K.S. and Schreiner, A.D. (1978) 'Intellectual characteristics of juvenile murderers versus status offenders.' *Psychological Reports 43*, 80–82.

Heide, K. (1992) *Why Kids Kill Parents.* Columbus: Ohio State University Press.

Heide, K.M. (1999) *Young Killers. The Challenge of Juvenile Homicide.* Thousand Oaks: Sage.

Heide, W. van der and Eggen, A.Th.J. (2004) *Criminaliteit en rechtshandhaving in cijfers. Tabellenboek met ontwikkelingen t/m 2003.* Den Haag: CBS/WODC.

Leistra, G. and Nieuwbeerta, P. (2003) *Moord en doodslag in Nederland.* Amsterdam: Prometheus.

Loeber, R. and Farrington, D.P. (eds) (1998) *Serious and Violent Juvenile Offenders: Risk Factors and Successful Interventions.* Thousand Oaks: Sage.

Loeber, R., Homish, D.L., Wei, E.H. *et al.* (2005) 'The prediction of violence and homicide in young males.' *Journal of Consulting and Clinical Psychology 73*, 1074–1088.

Myers, W.C. and Scott, K. (1998) 'Psychotic and conduct disorders symptoms in juvenile murderers.' *Homicide Studies 2*, 160–175.

Myers, W.C., Scott, K., Burgess, A.W. and Burgess, A.G. (1995) 'Psychopathology, biopsychological factors, crime characteristics and classification of 25 homicidal youths.' *Journal of the American Academy of Child and Adolescent Psychiatry 34*, 1483–1489.

Nieuwbeerta, P. (2003) *Moord en doodslag in Nederland 1992–2001 (Codeboek).* Leiden: NSCR.

Otnow Lewis, D., Lovely, R., Yeager, C. *et al.* (1988) 'Intrinsic and environmental characteristics of juvenile murderers.' *Journal of the American Academy of Child and Adolescent Psychiatry 27*, 582–587.

Rietveld, M., Hilhorst, N. and Dijk, B. van (2000) *Jeugdigen in justitiële behandelinrichtingen. Een analyse in het kader van de motie Duykers.* Amsterdam: DSP.

Rutter, M.H., Giller, H. and Hagell, A. (1998) *Antisocial Behavior by Young People.* Cambridge: Cambridge University Press.

Shumaker, D.M. and Prinz, R.J. (2000) 'Children who murder: A review.' *Clinical Child and Family Psychology Review 3*, 97–115.

Zagar, R., Arbit, J., Sylvies, R., Busch, K.G. and Hughes, J.R. (1990) 'Homicidal adolescents: A replication.' *Psychological Reports 67*, 1235–1242.

Zimring, F.E. (1998) *American Youth Violence.* Oxford: Oxford University Press.

Part 2

Outcomes and practical considerations

6

The placement, care and treatment of children and young people who commit serious acts of interpersonal violence or sexual offences

Ann Hagell and Patricia Moran

Introduction

In this chapter we move on from descriptions of the characteristics of children who pose serious risk to other children and discussion of what we know about what causes the development of serious antisocial behaviour in children, to a consideration of how we manage their placement, care and treatment. We draw here on two very distinct literatures. There is now a large, well-developed and robust body of research and writing on intervention strategies for children who are antisocial. A considerable amount of this evidence relates to children who are not as seriously disturbed and difficult as the group who has formed the focus of this project, but even so there is much to be gleaned that is of use and relevance. The bits we are most concerned with relate to intervening with children who are violent or who sexually offend. Most of this work comes from criminology, child psychology and child psychiatry, and much originates from the US and other countries. The conclusions are of international relevance. However, research and writing on the day-to-day management and care of these children is a different literature altogether, located within the disciplines of social care and public administration. This literature tends to be much more locally based, and also to be more variable in quality. Bringing the two literatures together is vital. Treatment does not take place in a vacuum, and the context in which it is delivered is very important. Conversely, managing care and placement is not enough without consideration of treatment.

We start this chapter by briefly reviewing the main conclusions of the intervention literature, and we then move on to the evidence on the management of the placements of these children.

General principles of what works with these groups of children

The 1970s and 1980s saw a particular low point in the world of youth violence prevention with the publication of several influential papers suggesting that in fact, after years of energy and effort, 'nothing works' (Martinson 1974). However, reanalyses of the information, and a resetting of our expectations of what was in fact possible (reduction in bad behaviour rather than elimination, for example), led to a series of new reviews that ended with a tone of cautious optimism (Farrington and Coid 2003; Harrington and Bailey 2003; Hedderman, Sugg and Vennard 1999; Howell et al. 1995; Lipsey and Wilson 1998; Loeber and Farrington 1998; McGuire 1995; Palmer 1994; Rutter, Giller and Hagell 1998). On the basis of an extensive review, Rutter et al. (1998), for example, concluded that there were clear grounds for thinking that antisocial behaviour was modifiable, but that researchers and practitioners also needed to be practical about what could be achieved given the multiplicity of causes and the complexity of human behaviour. Most analysts agree that the research evidence suggests that the typical effects on (for example) delinquency in successful interventions have been in the order of 12 per cent reduction in reoffending. Around this figure there is considerable variation, with some studies and some individuals reporting much better or much worse results (Lipsey 1995; Rutter et al. 1998).

Reviews have tended to be rather consistent in statements of the general principles of successful intervention. One such list, prepared for social care practitioners, is shown in Box 6.1.

Other things of importance include a matching of the level of need of the individual to the input provided by the programme, and multimodal delivery to reflect the wide range of complex needs often displayed. In addition, reviews have generally concluded that psychosocial treatments may work best if they contain cognitive-behavioural components (Rutter et al. 1998).

Looking specifically at prevention of the most serious types of antisocial behaviour – at the development of antisocial personality disorder, for example, or of serious, violent and chronic offenders – the messages essentially relate to the intensity and duration of the intervention, but there is nothing very specific about how the content should vary compared with interventions for less seriously antisocial young people. Two reviews on interventions for these particularly extreme young people concluded that effective programmes were longer; had greater attention to programme integrity; and used mental health personnel rather than youth justice personnel for their delivery (Lipsey and Wilson 1998; Brewer et al. 1995). They also concluded that what does not work is

> ## Box 6.1 The characteristics of successful programmes to change behaviour
>
> - They are based on a clear theoretical model of how they are intended to change behaviour.
> - There is a clear focus for all the activity involved in the programme. Everyone should know what it is hoped the outcome will be, and this should be specific and measurable (e.g. preventing the child from reoffending, improving child–parent communication).
> - They last for a reasonable length of time. A commonly used rule of thumb is that they should last at least six months in order to have a chance of impacting on behaviour.
> - They have reasonable frequent contact with the young people. Again, as a rule of thumb this is often suggested to be around twice a week although it depends very much on the type of work being done and the needs of the child.
> - The programme focuses on rewarding positive behaviour rather than on meting out punishment.
> - Following through the intervention with some aftercare also seems to be an important element.
>
> (Hagell 2003)

noncontingent, supportive mentoring or counselling relationships on their own (Brewer *et al.* 1995). However, so far the literature just seems to point to more intensive programmes, and programmes that address a wider range of needs. There are perhaps exceptions within the sexual abuse literature, where there are some suggestions of more specificity with respect to a particular subgroup (e.g. Erooga and Masson 1999). While we make limited reference to these studies in this chapter, a fuller review is provided by Vizard (Chapter 4, this volume).

There are other things that we do not know. We do not know how individual psychological treatments such as cognitive behavioural therapy (CBT) actually do compare with intensive multimodal interventions. We do not know what particular strategies are necessary to deal with young people who are resistant to treatment. Evidence of ways of preventing relapse or other complications such as suicidal behaviour is very limited (Harrington and Bailey 2003).

There are thus still some problems with the literature which mean that we cannot be absolutely prescriptive. We still need more random controlled trials so we can work out exactly what is the 'value added' component of any particular intervention, holding everything else constant. We need to do tests that will help us understand the actual mechanisms that translate the programme components into changes in behaviour. Despite cautious optimism, we do know that no one strategy will work for all children who need help, and all programmes will fail some children. However, in the section that follows we look in a little more detail at some of the more commonly used approaches.

Specific intervention approaches

A number of specific intervention approaches have been used to try to reduce serious interpersonal violence by adolescents. These range from programmes directed at the child's interpersonal skills; their relationship with their parents and their parents' parenting skills; multimodal and multisystemic programmes addressing a range of different areas of the child's life at the same time; specially supported types of out-of-family care; and residential and institutionally based programmes. Some of the main messages from evaluations of these approaches are summarised below.

Child- and parent-focused programmes

In terms of the content of interventions, results of a recent meta-analysis of randomised controlled trials (Lösel and Beelman 2003) found that child skills training, particularly well-structured cognitive behavioural programmes, were effective where prevention and early intervention of antisocial behaviour were concerned. These programmes typically focus on areas such as social skills and anger management. They are thought to be particularly effective when used in combination with other interventions such as parent training and also school-based intervention (e.g. Hawkins et al. 1999; Webster-Stratton and Hammond 1997).

In a review of family-based interventions aimed at delinquent and child behaviour problems across the spectrum from prevention to intervention with high-risk groups, Farrington and Welsh (2001) concluded that four categories of programmes were effective: home visitation; parent education plus day care/preschool; school-based child training plus parenting training; and, for higher risk individuals, Multi Systemic Therapy (MST; discussed below). However, the extent to which strategies work is very dependent on the age and developmental stage of the child; as difficult children move into being challenging adolescents, and the family becomes just one relatively limited part of social life, the behaviour becomes more entrenched and requires different strategies. Tiffin and Kaplan (2004) concluded that for older adolescents and those with more entrenched difficulties, parent training and child skills training may not be sufficient to reduce severe antisocial behaviour. More intensive multimodal and holistic interventions are required, allowing multiple risk factors to be addressed simultaneously in an integrated way.

Multimodal programmes

Multimodal programmes have traditionally formed part of the community-based interventions used with older young people who have committed serious violent or sexually abusive acts. In essence they involve tackling a specific problem by using a range of techniques at the same time. Vizard addresses various programmes in detail in Chapter 4 with respect to sexual abuse, but it is worth taking a brief look at the findings here. In addition to non-offence specific skills training, schemes for young people that have sexually abused, for example, typically include sex offence specific components in conjunction with family and individual therapy. Thus, Hunter and colleagues (2004) describe sex offender specific group therapy as usually involving some combination of social skills training, anger management, sex education, confrontation and correction of cognitive distortions, enhancing impulse control, victim empathy work, and teaching relapse prevention.

For adolescents who have sexually offended, some suggest that 'sex offence specific' work alongside work focusing on the offender's own personal history of abuse and victimisation is essential, while others challenge the view that these offenders are a special case requiring specialised intervention. However, results from the few robust evaluations of specialist interventions for young people who sexually offend suggest that such combined interventions can be effective, with typically recidivism rates of between 5 and 14 per cent following specialist intervention (Borduin et al. 1990). Worling and Curwen (2000), for example, reported on the evaluation of the Sexual Abuse, Family Education and Treatment (SAFE-T) programme, which involves concurrent group, individual and family therapy. It offers a combination of sexual offence specific cognitive-behavioural programmes as well as non-sexual offence specific programmes addressing social skills, body image, anger management, self-esteem, etc. As described earlier, at follow-up (on average six years later) recidivism rates for sexual offences among the intervention group were 5 per cent compared to 18 per cent for the comparison group who received 'treatment as usual'.

Multisystemic treatment

In the US there has been a shift over the last decade or so towards a firmer reflection of the 'ecology' of offending, with emphasis on the interdependent systems that produce and maintain offending, involving individual, familial, social and cultural influences. This shift has led to the development of 'wrap-around' services that address risks and enhance strengths at multiple levels; tackling a range of problems using a range of ways. Multi Systemic Therapy (MST) exemplifies this approach, and has a number of distinguishing features (Henggeler *et al.* 1998). First, interventions tackle all relevant systems and environments (involving home, peers, school, community). Second, interventions focus on the present and are action-orientated and target sequences of behaviour across multiple systems. Third, there is particular emphasis on empowering caregivers (parents, teachers) in order to promote their abilities as agents of change, in addition to the work done by the therapist. MST is essentially a home-based intervention in which therapists work intensely with families providing around-the-clock support. It is very labour intensive and consequently very expensive.

The effectiveness of MST has been assessed in a number of clinical trials and has been found to significantly reduce, for example, recidivism rates among adolescents who are persistent violent offenders (Henggeler *et al.* 1992). A small-scale trial with adolescent sexual offenders (Borduin *et al.* 1990) also showed promising results. A recent Cochrane systematic review of MST for 10- to 17-year-olds, however, suggested that the situation was not as straightforward as simply recommending MST for everything. The most rigorous tests of its use included in the review showed no significant differences between MST and other services. A slightly more inclusive look at the broader literature showed a small tendency for MST to show better outcomes, but the review concluded that it was not clear whether MST had clinically significant advantages over other services (Littell, Popa and Forsythe 2005). It is likely that the way in which MST is implemented is very important, and also that it will turn out to work better for some problems than for others. It may be that we need further research to untangle whether it is the intensity of the programme that is the key, rather than anything very specific about the method of delivery.

Multidimensional Treatment Foster Care

While MST focuses on working with young people living within their family homes, Multidimensional Treatment Foster Care (MTFC) is an approach based on working with young people who are living with foster carers. Community families are recruited, trained and closely supervised to provide MTFC to adolescents placed with them. The young people are given close supervision by foster carers in the home, in school, and in the community, with clear boundary setting and positive reinforcement for appropriate behaviour. In addition the young person's biological (or adoptive) family is taught to use the behaviour management system being carried out in the young person's foster placement with the ultimate aim of having the young person return home.

A US-based evaluation of this programme showed that young people who take part subsequently spent fewer days incarcerated, had fewer arrests, had significantly less hard drug use, and more quickly made the transition from secure/restrictive setting (e.g. hospital, detention) to community placements (Chamberlain and Mihalic 1998). A recent report of the use of treatment foster care in the UK by Farmer *et al.* (2003) suggests that the use of this specialised form of foster care needs to be further explored by research, as it has potentially more to offer than just being a 'step-down placement' from more restrictive settings (including group or residential homes). However, again, high levels of programme integrity and tailored use for particular problems are likely to be the key to longer-term success.

Residential / institutional treatments

Serious behaviour problems may result at some point in children receiving interventions in a range of out-of-home settings apart from foster care. These include children's homes both secure and open, residential boarding schools, young offender institutions of different kinds and sizes, and various residential mental health settings. The type and nature of these institutions and the services they deliver vary enormously by locality and by affiliation. Those within the criminal justice system have very different histories and philosophies, for example, to those arising from within the social welfare system or the health system, and there are big differences in types of provision between various states in the USA and countries in, for example, Scandinavia. As such it is impossible to provide any meaningful generalisations about their use. Quite apart from the different systems from which they arise, it is very difficult to untangle the elements of residential or institutional treatments that do or do not contribute to outcomes, as the intervention tends to cover so many elements of everyday life as well as specific targeted components.

There is some limited research on what happens in institutions that are part of the criminal justice system, used for children sentenced to custody in court. Overall, the conclusions from the literature tend to be that in order to have any impact, custody of one kind or another has to be carefully designed to include multimodal work of the type described above and post-treatment follow-up, and should include some cognitive-behavioural elements (Rutter *et al.* 1998). In a review of 83 studies of institutional treatment for serious juvenile offenders, Lipsey and Wilson (1997) concluded that the most effective treatment programmes could reduce reoffending by about a third. The characteristics indicating effectiveness included extensive use of individual sessions and interpersonal skills training, and inclusion of anger-management elements. Delivery was very varied, and included lots of room for practice, and lots of focus on aftercare and community supervision. As ever, the training and experience of staff, and their understanding of the underlying principles of the intervention together with an adherence to the procedures, is as crucial as the actual components of the regime. The evidence for any effectiveness from short sharp shock regimes (or 'boot camps') clearly points to a lack of added value from the harsher elements of delivery (Mackenzie and Souryal 1994).

However, as we have already seen in other chapters in this volume, these children are vulnerable and damaged themselves as well as being a risk to others, and there is a developing literature on the negative effects of any prison-type setting during the adolescent period (e.g. Goldson 2002). The UN Convention on the Rights of the Child clearly states that custody for children should only be used as a last resort, and at the moment both the UK and USA have relatively high rates of child custody per head of population. The research literature would seem to suggest that if children do have to be restrained to protect others and themselves, this is best done in an environment where staff are trained in child and adolescent development, and in child and adolescent mental health, and where meeting the child's many needs is part of the broader picture.

There is also a rather separate literature on interventions delivered in children's homes as they arise within the child social care field, as distinct from institutions used to deliver youth justice disposals. In the UK much of this work has been led by a few specific research units (e.g. Brown et al. 1998; Bullock, Little and Millham 1993; Gibbs and Sinclair 1999). The work has not, until recently, tended to be very international or comparative, and it has been difficult to develop robust studies using methodologies that truly allow us to separate out cause from effect and to compare different types of provision. In one rare example of a study that did compare regimes in young offenders institutions with secure forms of children's homes in the UK, the evidence seemed to suggest that outcomes were better from the more child-centred institutions (Ditchfield and Catan 1992), but this research is now rather dated given the enormous changes in the structure of service delivery in the UK in recent years. We return to questions of accommodation below in consideration of day-to-day care, as well as with respect to interventions.

Day-to-day management of placement

The previous section has shown that we know something of what works with serious antisocial behaviour, and that it is likely to be intensive, time consuming and expensive. We know there are also serious limits to the extent to which we can expect to make a difference, and expectations have to be realistic when dealing with problems that are as deeply entrenched as those of this very extreme set of children. However, we have some tools at our disposal. Yet key questions remain about the care of these children on a day-to-day basis while they may or may not receive specific interventions. They not only have to be treated, they have to be housed and looked after. In fact, despite the layout of this chapter, the latter has to come first. However good the intervention or specific programme that is delivered, it will not work on a child living in an unstable or chaotic environment – be that environment one that is provided by the family or by the state. This is where these children pose the most serious challenges for their families and social care staff. What we have available in the way of evidence on good practice in this regard is limited, and there is only a small and difficult literature to summarise. The quality of the research work that has been undertaken in this area is very variable, much of the writing being reliant on views and opinions and very small samples. However, the questions raised are crucial.

First, it is important to point out again that children and young people who commit serious acts of violence or sexual offences represent a very heterogeneous group. There will be no 'one-size-fits-all' solution to their day-to-day care. This heterogeneity is also evident in terms of the various 'career paths' that these young people experience (Little and Bullock 2004). These career paths vary depending not only on the characteristics of the young people, their families, their personal history or characteristics of their offences, but also as a function of the legal and administrative systems that they find themselves processed by over time. In England and Wales a shift towards the dovetailing of service approaches has begun in recent years, but has a long way to go, and in the meantime children can be unhelpfully catapulted between the systems, potentially adding to chaos and uncertainty.

Accommodation

Across all countries, even if the proportions vary, some children and adolescents who have sexually abused or committed violent acts remain within the family, and are offered support through community-based programmes that aim to rehabilitate. Others are assessed as needing to be accommodated away from family or the community because of the potential risk they pose to themselves and others. As we have seen above, this may involve placement in foster care, secure or non-secure residential settings, provided by health or social services, in addition to youth offending institutions.

Although there are risks associated with accommodating potentially dangerous children alongside other children in need, there are very few reliable figures about the level of abuse or harm that prevails in such situations. In a rare piece of work on peer abuse in residential care settings, Barter et al. (2004) reported high levels of peer violence and verbal attacks between young people in 11 of 14 homes in which they undertook interviews with young people and staff. Children in residential care were reportedly more at risk of physical and sexual assault from their peers than from staff. Earlier surveys on related topics also give some indication of the likely scale of the problem, with results from two non-representative studies showing that figures for risk of sexual abuse are quite high. An NSPCC report of children who had been abused (mostly sexually) while living in a residential care or educational setting showed that in half of cases the abuser was another child (Westcott and Clement 1992). In a study of sexually abused children in foster care, Macaskill (1991) found that in just over half of placements the abused children initiated sexual activity with another child within the foster or adoptive family. Utting's (1991) report *Children in the Public Care* advocated separation of children who have abused from children who have been the victims of abuse, but in practice finding appropriate accommodation for these cases is clearly a major challenge.

The detrimental effect that detention in secure accommodation conditions can have on the rehabilitation process was highlighted by Epps (1994). As well as the risk of abuse and of abusing others, many young people are accommodated some distance from family and friends, and the opportunities to establish healthy patterns of attachment and intimacy may well suffer. Nichol *et al.*'s (2000) survey of the views of 'troubling young people' also shows that most young people themselves express a preference for 'welfare' rather than 'penal' placements, which may have important implications for gaining their cooperation in dealing effectively with their difficulties. Hunter *et al.* (2004) noted an increasing trend in the US towards the use of court-ordered residential placements of young people who commit 'person offences', alongside a downturn in the use of community-based programmes for young people who sexually offend. The authors argue for a reversal of this trend on both economic and clinical grounds. However, it has been suggested that specialist secure facilities may be required to contain the relatively small number of young people who drop out of other forms of placement and remain at high risk to others (Whittle and Kurtz 2004) as non-completion of programmes seriously undermines their efficacy (Edwards *et al.* 2005).

A major dilemma for child welfare practitioners, therefore, is the difficulty of safely accommodating both victims and perpetrators given limited resources, and in these circumstances there is continuing debate over best practice models. It is not as if practitioners are not aware of this; the problem tends to be the difficulties of providing high-cost, flexible and intensive facilities for this small and varied group. A survey of practitioners' views revealed their own reservations about placing young sexual abusers in the same residential accommodation as child victims in light of the vulnerability of looked after children (Masson 1997–8). The survey raised many issues about the management of the sexually abused and abusing children including: inadequacies in placement planning; inadequacies in preparation, training, supervision and support of carers; differential responses to the sexualised behaviour of girls and boys both within and outside placements; inadequate use of existing child protection procedures to deal with continuing instances of abusing behaviour; inadequacies in meeting the mental health needs of the young people; and inadequacies in recognising the high levels of stress experienced by staff

(Masson 1997/8). A more recent summary of evidence suggests that this picture is largely unchanged (Green and Masson 2002).

The Report of the Committee of Enquiry into Children and Young People Who Sexually Abuse Other Children (National Children's Home 1992) recommended that children and young people who have abused need to have their behaviour addressed, managed or worked with if they are to be placed in residential settings with other children, and that provision of secure therapeutic specialist residential settings is needed for those young abusers requiring the highest level of security. Additionally, the report proposes that in the case of foster care placements provision should be made for specialist, intensive support for both the child and the carers.

The combination of a low baseline of incidence of these types of children, the high risk they pose to others, the tension between providing baseline stability and also flexibility, and the very high cost of providing for them, create real difficulties in their accommodation and day-to-day care. A louder and more joined up debate is necessary in order to get to grips with these issues. Specialist care and training are a priority. The next section looks at some of the implications these issues raised for development of services.

Implications for services

Training needs

The challenges for people coping with this small group of troubled children are enormous. The experience of foster carers, for example, raises questions about what constitutes the appropriate amount of training they receive and information they are given. Evidence suggests that a significant proportion of foster carers are not satisfied with the level of information that they are given about the backgrounds of sexually abused young people whom they care for (Farmer and Pollock 1998; Macaskill 1991). It has been suggested that greater training may, for example, enhance the ability of carers to respond to opportunities for the children to talk about their abuse (Macaskill 1991), a practice that has been linked to better outcomes for such children (Farmer and Pollock 1998). Foster carers may also need training to help children learn non-sexualised ways to offer and receive affection (Devine and Tate 1991).

Farmer and Pollock's (1998) study of sexually abused and abusing children in substitute care in two UK local authorities found that although the majority of the abusing young people were placed in foster care with experienced carers, foster carers were thought to be ill-prepared for reducing the risks of the child repeating their abusive behaviour. This was in part due to the lack of information that they were given about the young person's abusing behaviour (which was not passed on in over half of cases). Most worryingly, there was also very little therapeutic intervention aimed at addressing the children's abusive behaviour, and the authors suggest greater involvement of adolescent psychiatric services with specialist knowledge in this area. The main message to emerge from Farmer and Pollock's study is that when planning placements, greater thought needs to be given to the match between the needs of the child to be placed and others already in the setting, and the risks which each will pose to the other. They make a number of specific recommendations concerning the placement of sexually abused and abusing children, all of which are pertinent to children who sexually abuse or commit violent acts when it is borne in mind that they too are frequently the victims of such acts:

1. Caregivers should be given full information about children's backgrounds in order to make decisions about the suitability of a placement and plan to keep children safe.

2. Greater use of foster care placements where there are no other children or only much older children and use of single foster mothers or same-sex residential placements.

3. Greater assistance for foster carers in planning how to provide high levels of supervision.

4. Development of practice for residential care workers to provide higher levels of supervision of young people's activities when outside the home.

5. Provision of a method by which children in placements can communicate their concerns about being bullied or sexually harassed (such as a phone line to an independent agent).

These findings are generally supported by continuing work in the field of fostering in the UK (e.g. Sinclair and Wilson 2003; Sinclair, Gibbs and Wilson 2004; Sinclair, Wilson and Gibbs 2004), including a survey of over 1000 foster carers across seven local authority areas, which came to similar conclusions concerning ways of supporting carers and matching the child's needs to what the placement could provide.

In addition to the training needs of foster carers, research has also looked at the training needs of social care staff. A small-scale study of the attitudes of social workers to working with juvenile sex abusers showed they felt handicapped by their lack of specialist skills and knowledge in relation to this client group (Ladwa-Thomas and Sanders 1999). They particularly identified a lack of skills in being able to deal effectively with the denial of the abusers and their carers, and in conducting comprehensive assessments, including assessment of risk of reoffending. The study led its authors to suggest the following for improving practice in working with adolescent sexual offenders:

•   Increasing social workers' access to the latest knowledge and research in this area.

- Making abuse by juveniles a focus for local child protection committee dialogue.

- Greater training of social work staff in dealing with denial by abusers and carers, in being able to distinguish experimentation from abuse, and in conducting assessments of sexually offending young people.

- Earlier assessment and intervention of young abusers, in conjunction with greater provision of intervention services.

- Policies regarding service provision that are specifically based on knowledge of sexual abuse by young people rather than generic offending per se, in order to determine the most appropriate form of provision.

- Enabling practitioners to feel confident about facing new challenges to child protection through, for example, sharing practice via conferences, journals, professional forums and support groups.

Integrated services

The evidence that we have looked at so far suggests that what is needed is comprehensive assessment that acknowledges strengths as well as risks, married to timely provision of flexible and tailored services to meet the complex needs of the individual. This should be against the context of an expectation that what is required is long-term provision, including several years of fluctuating levels of support. Perhaps this small group of children more than any other highlight the need for joined up services to bridge the gap between the competing objectives of care and control. Therefore well-integrated youth justice and child welfare responses are required to meet their needs (Littlechild and Masson 2002). Similar conclusions are echoed by Tiffin and Kaplan (2004), who call for more integrated working of youth offending teams and Child and Adolescent Mental Health Services as well as better educational support to assist re-engagement with society.

Examples of close inter-agency working in the US in relation to young people who sexually offend are provided by Hunter et al. (2004). They include the Wraparound Milwaukee service, a care management organisation for young people thought to be at risk for residential treatment due to their complex emotional and/or behavioural needs. A care coordinator, who is not a treatment provider but a 'knowledgeable broker service', facilitates the provision of services appropriate to the individual needs of the young person and family. Early results from the programme show that sexual recidivism rates are 2 per cent, and 23 per cent for non-sexual offending.

Another service described by Hunter and colleagues in the US is the Norfolk Juvenile Sex Offender Program, which is particularly notable for its model of cross-agency working. The key underlying principle of the Norfolk programme is the belief that quality community-based sex offender treatment depends on successful legal and treatment service cooperation. The service involves very closely coordinated and strategically implemented legal management and clinical intervention services to adolescent boys between ages 12 and 20 years who have committed a sexual offence. Probation and parole officers are involved in assessment, planning and implementation of clinical interventions alongside treatment providers, and this integrated judicial and clinical team jointly makes key case management decisions. There is close collaboration of all agencies involved through, for example, shared assessment and treatment planning and shared training. In addition, juvenile court judges and related agency professionals are trained to understand the assessment approach and intervention methods, involving multisystemic and sex offender specific components. There is little information available at the moment about the effectiveness of this approach, though initial results with 25 young people who participated in its first year show that there have been no new sexual offences committed in the follow-up period, ranging from one to eight months (Hunter et al. 2004).

Yet in England and Wales at least, Little and Bullock (2004) paint a worrying picture of service provision for this group as piecemeal and haphazard. It seems that the level of joined up working by multiple agencies (including education, psychiatric, health, social services and youth justice services) is highly variable across the country, and in many cases falls short of what is required to meet the complex needs with which this group of young people presents (Masson 1995). For example, in a survey of 'severely troubled and troubling young people' located within both penal and welfare services in one local authority area, Nichol et al. (2000) identified significant shortcomings in assessment and provision of interventions for meeting mental health needs. Green and Masson (2002) also comment that while other areas of childcare provision have come on in leaps and bounds in terms of adopting a systematic approach to the identification, assessment and provision of services for children in need, the area of children who are regarded as dangerous is curiously lagging behind.

Recommendations for better inter-agency working in the field of high-risk children include: establishing who is carrying main responsibility for a case; agreeing a structure for responses when the needs cannot be met from the agencies' own resources; setting up both high level and ground level working groups that allow formal commitment and support throughout the agencies involved; agreeing of common work practices in relation to legislation, referral and assessment, agreed definitions and thresholds for intervention; flexible funding arrangements; a suitable location for the delivery of services by a range of agencies; and frameworks for collating data and information across agencies (e.g. Harker *et al.* 2004; Roaf and Lloyd 1995; Tomlinson 2003).

Conclusions

The struggle to strike a balance between the twin objectives of care and control of children and young people who have committed serious acts of violence or sexual offences is still evident at many levels, and across different countries. This is the case not only in relation to provision of services for this group, but is also reflected in the approach taken by evaluations of services. For example, what is striking about many evaluations of interventions for young people who have committed serious violent acts or sexually offended is the degree of focus on sexual and non-sexual recidivism rates as the sole outcome of interest. While this is undoubtedly an important measure of service effectiveness that needs to be considered, results focusing on other psychosocial outcomes for the young people are often missing. We are rarely given a sense, for example, of how personal and broader social elements of their lives may have changed post-intervention, such as their self-esteem, friendships and intimate relation-ships, family functioning, education, training or employment prospects. It is their ability to get along with other people, day to day, in their immediate social environment that is crucial.

It is true that results from specialist interventions with both seriously violent young people and those who are at risk of sexually abusing others show that many are amenable to change. Although we still lack detail on the aspects of particular intervention facilities that work best, there is a growing consensus that we know quite a lot about the components of effective interventions; the general principles are essentially agreed. However, more research is needed to help us understand how to diminish risks and enhance strengths, and build opportunities for growth and resilience, within the broader context of the everyday lives of these challenged and challenging young people. This needs specialist skills and a clear understanding of mental health needs, as well as an understanding of adolescence in general. Where we feel the particular gaps lie are in combining thinking on day-to-day care with thinking about interven-tion delivery. Stabilising children, providing appropriate care and attention, and keeping them and others safe has to be the starting point and the ongoing context for intervention. Looking at one side or the other of this equation on its own is to address only half of the picture.

References

Barter, C., Renold, E., Berridge, D. and Cawson, P. (2004) *Peer Violence in Children's Residential Care.* Buckingham: Palgrave.

Borduin, C.M., Henggeler, S.W., Blaske, D.M. and Stein, R.J. (1990) 'Multisystemic treatment of adolescent sex offenders.' *International Journal of Offender Rehabilitation 34,* 105–113.

Brewer, D., Hawkins, J.D., Catalano, R.F. and Neckerman, H.J. (1995) 'Preventing serious, violent and chronic juvenile offending: A review of evaluations of selected strategies in childhood, adolescence and the community.' In J.C. Howell, B. Krisberg, J.D. Hawkins and J.J. Wilson (eds) *Serious, Violent and Chronic Juvenile Offenders: A Sourcebook.* Thousand Oaks, CA: Sage.

Brown, E., Bullock, R., Hobson, C. and Little, M. (1998) *Making Residential Care Work: Structure and Culture in Children's Homes.* Aldershot: Ashgate.

Bullock, R., Little, M. and Millham, S. (1993) *Residential Care for Children: A Review of the Research.* London: HMSO.

Chamberlain, P. and Mihalic, S.F. (1998) *Blueprints for Violence Prevention, Book Eight: Multidimensional Treatment Foster Care.* Boulder, CO: Center for the Study and Prevention of Violence.

Devine, C. and Tate, I. (1991) 'An introductory training course for foster carers.' In D. Batty (ed) *Sexually Abused Children: Making Their Placements Work.* London: British Agencies for Adoption and Fostering.

Ditchfield, J. and Catan, L. (1992) 'Juveniles sentenced to serious offences: A comparison of regimes in young offender institutions and local authority community homes.' London: Home Office.

Edwards, R., Beech, A., Bishop, D., Erikson, M., Friendship, C. and Charlesworth, L. (2005) 'Predicting dropout from a residential programme for adolescent sexual abusers using pre-treatment variables and implications for recidivism.' *Journal of Sexual Aggression 11,* 2, 139–155.

Epps, K. (1994) 'Managing sexually abusive adolescents in residential settings: A strategy for risk assessment.' In N.K. Clark and G.M. Stephenson (eds) *Rights and Risks: The Application of Forensic Psychology.* Leicester: British Psychological Society.

Erooga, M. and Masson, H. (1999) *Children and Young People who Sexually Abuse Others – Challenge and Responses.* London: Routledge.

Farmer, E. and Pollock, S. (1998) *Substitute Care for Sexually Abused and Abusing Children.* Chichester: Wiley.

Farmer, E., Wagner, H., Burns, B. and Richards, J. (2003) 'Treatment foster care in a system of care: Sequences and correlates of residential placements.' *Journal of Family Studies 12,* 11–25.

Farrington, D.J. and Coid, J. (2003) *Early Prevention of Adult Antisocial behaviour.* Cambridge: Cambridge University Press.

Farrington, D.J. and Welsh, B. (2001) 'What works in preventing crime: Systematic reviews of experimental and quasi-experimental research.' *Annals of the American Academy of Politics and Social Science 578,* special edition.

Gibbs, I. and Sinclair, I. (1999) 'Treatment and treatment outcomes in children's homes.' *Child and Family Social Work 4,* 1, 1–8.

Goldson, B. (2002) *Vulnerable Inside: Children in Secure and Penal Settings.* London: Children's Society.

Green, L. and Masson, H. (2002) 'Peer sexual abuse in residential care: Issues of risk and vulnerability.' *British Journal of Social Work 32*, 2, 149–168.

Hagell, A. (2003) *Quality Protects Research Briefing: Understanding and Challenging Youth Offending*. London: Department of Health, Research in Practice and Making Research Count.

Harker, R.M., Dobel-Ober, D., Berridge, D. and Sinclair, R. (2004) 'More than the sum of its parts? Inter-professional working in the education of looked after children.' *Children and Society 18*, 3, 179–193.

Harrington, R. and Bailey, S. (2003) *The Scope for Preventing Antisocial Personality Disorder by Intervening in Adolescence*. Liverpool: National Research and Development Programme on Forensic Mental Health.

Hawkins, J.D., Catalano, R.F., Kosterman, R., Abbott, R. and Hill, K.G. (1999) 'Preventing adolescent health-risk behaviours by strengthening protection during childhood.' *Archives of Pediatrics and Adolescent Medicine 153*, 226–234.

Hedderman, C., Sugg, D. and Vennard, J. (1999) *Changing Offenders' Attitudes and Behaviours: What Works?* Home Office Research Study 171. London: Home Office.

Henggeler, S.W., Melton, G.B. and Smith, L.A. (1992) 'Family preservation using multisystemic therapy: An effective alternative to incarcerating serious juvenile offenders.' *Journal of Consulting and Clinical Psychology 60*, 953–961.

Henggeler, S.W., Schoenwold, S.K., Borduin, C.M., Rowland, M.D. and Cunningham, P.B. (1998) *Multisystemic Treatment of Antisocial Behaviour in Children and Adolescents*. New York: Guilford Press.

Howell, J.C., Krisberg, B., Hawkins, J.D. and Wilson, J.J. (eds) (1995) *Serious, Violent and Chronic Juvenile Offenders*. London: Sage.

Hunter, J.A., Gilbertson, S.A., Vedros, D. and Morton, M. (2004) 'Strengthening community-based programming for juvenile sexual offenders: Key constructs and paradigm shifts.' *Child Maltreatment 9*, 177–189.

Ladwa-Thomas, U. and Sanders, R. (1999) 'Juvenile sexual abusers: Perceptions of social work practitioners.' *Child Abuse Review 8*, 55–62.

Lipsey, M.W. (1995) 'What do we learn from 400 research studies on the effectiveness of treatment with juvenile delinquents?' In J. McGuire (ed) *What Works, Reducing Reoffending: Guidelines from Research and Practice*. Chichester: Wiley, pp.63–78.

Lipsey, M.W. and Wilson, D.B. (1997) *Effective Internevtion for Serious Juvenile Offenders: A Synthesis of Research*. Nashville, TN: Vanderbilt Institute for Public Policy Studies.

Lipsey, M.W. and Wilson, D.B. (1998) 'Effective interventions for serious juvenile offenders: A synthesis of research.' In R. Loeber and D.P. Farrington (eds) *Serious and Violent Juvenile Offenders*. Thousand Oaks, CA: Sage.

Littell, J.H., Popa, M. and Forsythe, B. (2005) *Multisystemic Therapy for Social, Emotional and Behavioural Problems in Youth aged 10–17*. Chichester: Wiley.

Little, M. and Bullock, R. (2004) 'Administrative frameworks and services for very difficult adolescents in England.' In S. Bailey and M. Dolan (eds) *Forensic Adolescent Psychiatry*. London: Arnold, pp.336–344.

Littlechild, B. and Masson, H. (2002) 'Children and young people who have sexually abused: Law and provision.' *Childright*, July/August, 16–18.

Loeber, R. and Farrington, D.P. (1998) *Serious and Violent Juvenile Offenders: Risk Factors and Successful Interventions*. Thousand Oaks, CA: Sage.

Lösel, F. and Beelman, A. (2003) 'Effects of child skills training in preventing antisocial behaviour: A systematic review of randomised evaluations.' *Annals of the American Academy of Political and Social Science 587*, 84–109.

Macaskill, C. (1991) *Adopting or Fostering a Sexually Abused Child.* London: Batesford.

MacKenzie, D.L. and Souryal, C. (1994) *Multisite Evaluation of Shock Incarceration. National Institute of Justice Research Report.* College Park, MD: University of Maryland Press.

McGuire, J. (1995) *What Works: Reducing Offending.* Chichester: Wiley.

Martinson, R. (1974) 'What works? Questions and answers about prison reform.' *Public Interest 35,* 22–54.

Masson, H. (1995) 'Children and adolescents who sexually abuse other children: Responses to an emerging problem.' *Journal of Social Welfare and Family Law 17,* 3, 325–336.

Masson, H. (1997/1998) 'Issues in relation to children and young people who sexually abuse other children: a survey of practitioners' views.' *Journal of Sexual Aggression 3,* 2, 101–118.

National Children's Home (1992) *The Report of the Committee of Enquiry into Children and Young People who Sexually Abuse other Children.* London: NCH.

Nichol, R., Stretch, D., Whitney, I., Jones, K., Garfield, P., Turner, K. and Stanion, B. (2000) 'Mental health needs and services for severely troubled and troubling young offenders in an NHS region.' *Journal of Adolescence 23,* 243–261.

Palmer, T. (1994) *A Profile of Correctional Effectiveness and New Directions for Research.* Albany, NY: State University of New York.

Roaf, C. and Lloyd, C. (1995) *Multi-agency Work with Young People in Difficulty.* Oxford: Oxford Brooks University.

Rutter, M., Giller, H. and Hagell, A. (1998) *Antisocial Behaviour by Young People.* Cambridge: Cambridge University Press.

Sinclair, I. and Wilson, K. (2003) 'Matches and mismatches: The contribution of carers and children to the success of foster placements.' *British Journal of Social Work 33,* 871–884.

Sinclair, I., Gibbs, I. and Wilson, K. (2004) *Foster Carers: Why They Stay and Why They Leave.* London: Jessica Kingsley Publishers.

Sinclair, I., Wilson, K. and Gibbs, I. (2004) *Foster Placements: Why They Succeed and Why They Fail.* London: Jessica Kingsley Publishers.

Tiffin, P. and Kaplan, C. (2004) 'Dangerous children: Assessment and management of risk.' *Child and Adolescent Mental Health 9,* 56–64.

Tomlinson, K. (2003) 'Effective interagency working: A review of the literature and examples from practice.' LGA Research Report 40. Slough: NFER.

Utting, W. (1991) *Children in the Public Care: A Review of Residential Child Care.* London: HMSO.

Utting, W. (1997) *People Like Us: The Report of the Review of the Safeguards for Children Living Away from Home.* London: The Stationery Office.

Webster-Stratton, C. and Hammond, M. (1997) 'Treating children with early-onset conduct problems: A comparison of child and parent training interventions.' *Journal of Consulting and Clinical Psychology 65,* 1, 93–109.

Westcott, H. and Clement, M. (1992) *NSPCC Experience of Child Abuse in Residential Care and Educational Placements: Results of a Survey.* London: NSPCC.

Whittle, N. and Kurtz, Z. (2004) 'The needs of young people who display sexually harmful behaviour and the effectiveness of interventions and service approaches to meet these needs and to prevent sexually abusive and criminal behaviour.' Unpublished report.

Worling, J.R. and Curwen, T. (2000) 'Adolescent sex offender recidivism: Success of specialised treatment and implications for risk prediction.' *Child Abuse and Neglect 24,* 965–982.

7

Implications of different residential treatments for young people who commit serious crimes

Gwyneth Boswell

Introduction

This chapter examines the residential regimes and careers of 10- to 17-year-old children in England and Wales who commit serious crimes, looking particularly at the extent to which those regimes meet their rehabilitative needs, and what happens to them as they reach adulthood. It draws briefly on research conducted by the author in the 1990s and more substantially on three pieces of research carried out in the period 2001–3.

These studies differ in their timing, scale and method, but they all focus upon those who have committed acts of serious violence (including murder and sexual violence) as children, and they all draw upon a combination of quantitative and qualitative material, including reconviction and other follow-up data. The findings will be used to describe briefly the regimes concerned and to outline their effects upon their young inmates as or after they reach adulthood.

Although these children's offending has frequently been at the extreme end of the seriousness spectrum, it is likely that all will return to their local communities at some point, and will continue to have a variety of needs that still require multidisciplinary participation in service delivery. In that respect, knowing more about their periods in custody is an important part of a bigger picture. There are also lessons to be learned from the impact of different types of residential regime on the outcomes for these children, which may be useful even in different settings within the community.

Custody for serious young offenders in England and Wales

In England and Wales, the automatic life sentence provisions for children who murder remain similar to those originally set out in the Children and Young Persons' Act 1933. However, a tariff date system now informs these children at the time of sentence of the earliest date at which they will be considered for release. The Criminal Justice Act 2003 has set the minimum 'starting point' for this tariff at 12 years, a notable increase on the previous average of eight years. Provisions for the sentencing of those who have committed other 'grave' crimes have, on the other hand, broadened considerably over time and have, arguably, been hostage to prevailing penological and political climates. As the National Association for the Care and Resettlement of Offenders' (NACRO) most recent review of this issue notes:

> Long-term detention, once regarded as a provision reserved for a small number of extremely serious offences, has come to occupy an increasingly broad space within the sentencing landscape for children and young people. (NACRO 2002, p.13)

This development over more than seven decades has served to highlight the welfare/justice dichotomy for young offenders, possibly more than in any other area of criminal justice. This dichotomy manifests itself not just in the criminal and legal processes, but also in the frequently lengthy custodial career paths followed by these young people.

Under the provisions of the Crime and Disorder Act 1998, the new Youth Justice Board for England and Wales (YJB) took over from the Home Office the responsibility for commissioning and purchasing places for all children and young people under 18 years of age detained within a reorganised juvenile secure estate. Essentially there are three different types of places where children might serve their custodial sentence: local authority secure children's homes (LASCHs); privately managed secure training centres (STCs); and 13 juvenile young offender institutions (YOIs). Prior to 1998, Home Office policy was to place all children under 16 years in Department of Health secure facilities. The YJB now places children aged 15 upwards in YOIs unless they are deemed to be particularly vulnerable. In LASCHs, where children's backgrounds, needs and vulnerability levels are often indistinguishable from those who have arrived there via the 'welfare' constituency of the Family Proceedings Court under the provisions of the Children Act 1989, they will experience high staff–child ratios and good access to education, employment and social skills training facilities (Boswell 1996; Goldson 2002). For those who reach adult prison at the age of 21 years, these facilities will be only sporadically available and they will be serving the 'punishment and retribution' element of their sentence (Boswell 1991, 1996). Thus, what happens to them when they enter a juvenile secure setting, at a stage of development (adolescence) where they are still maturing

IMPLICATIONS OF DIFFERENT RESIDENTIAL TREATMENTS / 131

and open to change, may be crucial to their eventual chances of successful rehabilitation. The role of professional staff they encounter in such settings is likely to play a vital part in this process.

The backgrounds of young people who commit the most serious offences have been the subject of much research over the years. There is now a considerable body of information on the risk factors for serious offending (summarised in Chapter 3 of this volume, for example), and a number of comprehensive reviews exist. While it is difficult to predict specifically to certain types of antisocial behaviour, there is broad consensus over the main factors that are important, including those that are individual, family based, school based, neighbourhood driven, and so on. The picture is, inevitably, very complicated, but essentially most research concludes that children who kill, in particular, tend to come from disturbed, often abusive backgrounds, having experienced serious psychosocial adversity (Rutter, Giller and Hagell 1998).

Research by Boswell (1996), specifically with the children who had murdered or committed grave crimes, found that of a sample of 200 (over one-quarter of that population at the time), 72 per cent had experienced one or more forms of emotional, physical, sexual or organised abuse and 57 per cent had experienced significant loss of family or others close to them. Of the sample, 35 per cent had experienced both these phenomena and, given that this was a population at the most serious end of the violent offending spectrum, this figure lent support to the suggestion that exposure to multiple types of maltreatment may be linked with offence severity (Smith and Thornberry 1995). Over half of juveniles in custody have a history of being in care or other involvement with Social Services (HMIP 1997). Other common characteristics of the incarcerated juvenile population in general include coming from a black or minority ethnic background, and physical, behavioural and mental health problems, including depression, self-harming and suicidal behaviour (Social Exclusion Unit 2002).

Against this catalogue of characteristics which, arguably, would contribute an unpromising prognosis for any young person, there is a need for criminal justice policy decisions which meet both society's requirement for punishment and the individual young offender's need for a regime containing a programme of facilities and activities in which staff are able to address the 'deficits' listed above, and help to steer the young person towards rehabilitation.

Regimes for children who murder or commit other grave crimes

Despite the fact that the various custodial facilities for young offenders can be quite different, studies of young offender regimes in this country are thin on the ground. An exception is Ditchfield and Catan's (1992) study, which compared YOI and local authority secure units (LASU) regimes, as the present LASCHs then were, for children who had committed grave crimes. They found that the level of services (notably education and training) and quality of life (i.e. privacy, autonomy and staff–inmate relationships) in LASUs was manifestly superior to that in YOIs. They considered that the lower reconviction rates for those from LASUs could be attributed directly to their care/treatment ethos, as opposed to the security/control ethos in YOIs.

Similar conclusions were reached by Boswell (1991, 1996) in an exploration of the needs and experiences of these types of serious offenders during the early 1990s. The research involved a representative study of 200 offenders in custody aged 14 to 59 years, sentenced to be detained during Her Majesty's Pleasure (some for life) under section 53 of the Children and Young Persons Act 1933, now subsumed under sections 90 and 91 of the Powers of the Criminal Courts Act 2000 (Boswell 1995, 1996). At this time two Department of Health youth treatment centres (subsequently closed down) also provided a high level of services and quality of life to these types of offenders. At that time also (with the exception of one YOI, which ran dedicated units), section 90/91 offenders placed in the YOI system were merely assimilated into the regime for the rest of the population. As a consequence, staff at one YOI studied 'considered that they did not treat section 53 offenders any differently to other inmates, though they were acutely aware of the particular problems they presented, and of the fact that they had often been sentenced at a young age' (Boswell 1996, p.78).

Although YJB policy has moved to the placing of most 15-year-olds in YOIs, in recognition of the fact that many of these young people can be located at some point along a continuum of vulnerability, and of the YJB's new main aim of 'preventing offending', the Prison Service issued Prison Service Order 4950 (HM Prison Service 2000). The Order stated that regimes for prisoners under the age of 18 years should do all they can positively to motivate young people via individually tailored programmes, and to honour the principles of the Children Act 1989. This included the principle that safeguarding a child's welfare is of paramount importance, but with provisos relating to the safety of other inmates, staff and visitors.

A key feature of the Prison Service's response to this Order was the setting up of three 'Enhanced Units' specifically to house the most vulnerable section 90/91 young prisoners. These units were developed to deliver a particularly high level of regime activities and individual support to this group of young people. The intention was that they should provide a model of intervention in secure facilities and that, as stated in the policy document 'What should a Section 53 Unit Provide?', this model should consequently be monitored and evaluated 'to a greater extent than elsewhere in the Prison Service Under 18 estate' (YJB 2001, p.2).

The main differences between an Enhanced Unit and a standard regime for section 90/91 offenders are that the former is a purpose-built unit (in the case of one unit for no more than 30 trainees) with a high staff–trainee ratio, a wide range of education/training options in small classes, easy access to appropriate groupwork programmes, one-to-one work with personal (prison) officers, prison probation officers and proactive support in maintaining family contact. A standard regime tends to have a much larger intake (240 trainees in the case of one YOI, of whom 45 are serving section 90/91 sentences) with proportionately less access to the above range of facilities and without a special focus on the needs of section 90/91 trainees. In recommending placement or transfer to an Enhanced Unit, the managing body, the section 53/91 Placement Unit in Prison Service HQ, is advised as follows by Prison Service Order 4960 'Detention Under Section 92 of the Powers of Criminal Courts (Sentencing) Act 2000':

> The Enhanced Units will be particularly appropriate for 15 year olds or for the more vulnerable or challenging 16 and 17 year olds who may need a regime that is more akin to that found in the LASCHs. (HM Prison Service 2001)

Thus, it seemed important that the experience emerging from Enhanced Unit innovation should be reviewed, gaps and weaknesses identified and addressed, and good practice highlighted, developed and disseminated.

Studies of contrasting regimes for different kinds of young offenders

Building on our earlier work in the 1990s, three further pieces of research on regimes were thus undertaken in the early 2000s (all institutions' names are pseudonyms):

1. The first was a whole population study of an 'Enhanced Regime', known as the Warwick Unit, housing 26 section 90 and 91 offenders (24 of whom agreed to participate in the research) within a juvenile YOI (Boswell and Wedge 2003).

2. The second was a study of a representative sample of 24 out of 45 section 90 and 91 offenders, housed within a standard regime for juvenile prisoners, in Blenheim YOI (Boswell and Wedge 2003). Where they could be traced, those young men who had completed their sentences at Warwick Unit and Blenheim YOI were followed up between nine months and two years after release, by which time they had become adults.

3. We also undertook a third study, a pilot evaluation of McGregor Hall, a therapeutic facility for adolescent male sexual abusers, which followed up as many ex-residents as could be found (15) between

two and five years after they left the facility and set their reconviction rates alongside those of a comparison group (Boswell and Wedge 2002, 2003).

The main findings from these first two studies are presented in this section; the findings from the third are given in the next section. Although the results from these first two studies are contained in a single report, it is important to note, as the report does, that since the Blenheim YOI study began a year later than the Warwick Unit study, was based on a pragmatic choice of establishment, and with a number of other variables, it is not possible to refer to its respondent sample as a control group. It is, however, possible to draw on the findings from each group to make some comparisons. Thus, for convenience, the methodology and findings are summarised here in a form that enables the similarities and differences in regimes to be easily discerned. A more detailed account of the entire research process can be found in Boswell and Wedge (2003).

Methodology

This section provides a summary of the research tools utilised and the samples to which they were applied in the Warwick Unit and Blenheim YOI studies (Table 7.1).

Table 7.1 Trainee samples and their progress through the study

	Warwick Unit	Blenheim YOI	Totals
Whole section 90/91 population	26	45	71
Refusals	2	N/A	2
Purposive selection	N/A	24	24
First stage samples	24	24	48
Refusals/transfers at first stage	–	4	4
First stage interviews/psych. tests	24	20	44
Refusals/untraceable at second stage	3	5	8
Second stage samples	21	15	36
Second stage interviews/psych. tests			
In custody	11*	14**	25
In community			
in person	6	–	6
by telephone	4	1	5

* figure includes one trainee reconvicted and serving a Detention and Training Order (DTO) sentence
** figure includes two trainees reconvicted and serving DTO sentences

INTERVIEW SCHEDULES

The interview schedules containing problem checklists were administered to trainees (in some cases after release) in the early and late stages of their sentences, in order to establish their responses to their respective YOI regimes and the extent to which their self-reported problems had reduced/increased/ stayed the same over time.

PSYCHOLOGICAL TESTS

The seven psychological tests were likewise administered in the early and late/post-release stages of their sentences. They sought to establish the extent of change in their beliefs, attitudes and behaviour in relation to: social responsibility; self-esteem; aggression, depression; and positive outlook. One test also sought to establish the presence or absence of post-traumatic stress disorder (PTSD) at each stage.

ADJUDICATION DATA

Adjudication data were obtained in respect of Warwick Unit trainees (over an average stay of 13 months) and of Blenheim YOI trainees (over an average stay of 10 months) for the purposes of assessing the level of disciplinary offences in each regime.

OFFENDER RECONVICTION DATA

Data were obtained for the purposes of assessing the levels of reoffending in respect of each regime. However, because the Blenheim YOI study had begun 18 months after the Warwick Unit study, fewer Blenheim trainees had been released at the time of follow-up. As a result, the figure of 11 released Warwick Unit trainees had to be matched by a combination of six released Blenheim trainees from the substantive study and a further group of five released Blenheim trainees who had not been part of that study.

TRAINEE CASE RECORDS

Trainee case records were searched to confirm and supplement information they had provided about their personal and offence-related characteristics.

OFFENDING BEHAVIOUR GROUPS

Offending behaviour groups were observed on two occasions to establish and confirm content and process as outlined by staff and trainees.

STAFF INTERVIEWS

Staff from Warwick Unit (14) and Blenheim YOI (17) were interviewed on one occasion each about their experiences and views of the regime in which they operated. Due to (their) shortage of time, six staff members took the schedule away, completed it as a questionnaire and then returned it to the researchers. This process contributed to the triangulation of evidence surrounding the nature and effectiveness of regimes for section 90/91 offenders.

Sample characteristics

The majority of respondents from both samples had arrived in their respective YOIs at the age of 16 years. About a sixth in each had arived at age 15 and a sixth at 17. The Blenheim Unit sample contained two-thirds of respondents of black and ethnic minority origin as opposed to one-quarter in the Warwick Unit sample, which was already disproportionately high. This may, to an extent, reflect the different ethnic make-up of the catchment areas of each establishment, but of course is a major cause for concern in the criminal justice system generally.

Although 'vulnerability' is not really defined in any of the relevant policy documents, comparative characteristics of the two samples suggested that while a majority in each had damaged and disturbed backgrounds, this appeared to be more the case with the Warwick Unit trainees, indicating that accurate assessments were being made to allocate them to Warwick as an Enhanced Unit.

Trainee problem areas

The problem areas in all these trainees' lives prior to their section 90/91 sentences were many and wide ranging. They included problems relating to family, finance, education, employment, accommodation, offending, abuse, loss, addiction and mental health. Although the extent of damage in the backgrounds of Blenheim trainees may have been slightly less, this is merely relative to that of the Warwick trainees. However, the 'before and after' problem checklists showed a clear pattern of problem areas reducing whilst trainees were at Warwick Unit; more Blenheim trainees began and ended their sentences with reported problems than did those at Warwick.

Psychological test findings

The 'before and after' psychological tests confirmed the above trend, demonstrating that the Warwick Unit sample's scores for self-esteem improved and their reported levels of aggressive behaviour, and beliefs supporting aggression, reduced significantly over time. The Blenheim sample's depression levels increased significantly over time.

A small proportion of Warwick Unit trainees (four) scored positive for current (PTSD) at first interview, but this had halved by second interview. A further three scored positive for lifetime PTSD (i.e. at some previous point in their lives). This compared with only one Blenheim trainee scoring positive for current PTSD at both interviews, but four others coming close to scoring positive for lifetime PTSD. The diagnostic criteria for PTSD are generally agreed to be over-rigid. Between a quarter and a third of each sample were either in or close to the PTSD category, and a number of traumatic experiences were recounted to researchers, including abuse, loss, witnessing war atrocities and so on. Despite a mandatory healthcare requirement in Prison Service Order 4950 for a multidisciplinary team skilled and experienced in adolescent mental health, this facility did not appear to be present in either regime.

Support from external services

Following on from the above observations, trainee and staff responses in interview suggested that the quantity and quality of external services for these young men tended to be on the disappointing side both during and after sentence. Staff turnover for agencies providing services for drug abuse and for mental health problems, for example, was very high, and there was a shortage of trained personnel. This meant that trainees assessed with these needs received services on rather a hit-and-miss basis. While there was a reasonable level of satisfaction with YOT worker and probation contact, a significant minority felt very let down by the lack of support (as opposed to licence 'enforcement') after release. However well they are prepared for returning to the outside community, they need sustained post-release support, for this is when their risk of reoffending is at its highest.

Trainees' ratings of their regime

Trainees were invited to rate the main constituents of their regime on a scale of 1 to 5, where 1 was 'helpful' and 5 was 'unhelpful'. This consisted of the following checklist: association/mealtimes; staff; one-to-one sessions; groups; work experiences; education; sport; friends on the unit; family contact; probation/YOI worker visits; unit rules; bedroom/cell; food; décor; indoor activities; outdoor activities; outings/town visits. The specialised regime at the Warwick Enhanced Unit was rated highly in most respects by trainees and staff alike. In contrast, while some aspects of the Blenheim regime (education, sports, outdoor activities and family contact) were highly rated by trainees, most other aspects were not.

Staff interviews

Staff interviews at both establishments revealed high levels of commitment to the work against a backcloth of grave dissatisfaction with the low effectiveness of non-dedicated section 90/91 units. Longer serving staff were also able to compare this with very positive experiences of working on two dedicated section 90/91 wings during the 1990s.

However, despite the emphasis placed by Prison Service Order 4950 on rigorous selection, training, management and support of staff, there was little evidence that this is taken sufficiently seriously in either establishment. Warwick Unit prison staff were all experienced with young offenders, but made only written applications for their posts, where interviews were supposed to be the norm. They had only minimal training in the early days of the unit and had had none since. They did not feel supported and valued by the wider prison, region or YJB, but rather that they, the trainees and the unit were 'paraded' only when important visitors were being shown round. The Blenheim staff's comments showed that they felt seriously demoralised by the same set of deficiencies.

Adjudications and reoffending

The Offenders' Index results, placed alongside other information, effectively showed that one-third of each released sample had reoffended. In the case of the Warwick Unit sample, only one trainee had been convicted of a crime serious enough to warrant a further YOI sentence (and this had been committed before the original sentence). Two trainees from the Blenheim YOI sample had received further YOI sentences for robbery. The only real differential, therefore, lay in the levels of crime seriousness, which were somewhat lower for the Warwick Unit sample. Adjudication records showed that offence rates and types were also very similar during sentence.

In summary

A wide range of problems, as outlined above, was identified by both these samples. In as far as these contribute to offending (and there is much research which suggests they do), the public is being protected from violent offences while these young men are in custody, whether at Warwick Unit or at Blenheim YOI. However, in as far as juvenile regimes have a duty of welfare to these youngsters and in as far as the statutory main aim of the YJB is to prevent reoffending, then it is difficult to discern a longer term purpose to custody if these problems are not addressed within it. Although Blenheim YOI trainees felt that they had been helped with problems of offending and emotional abuse to and from others, primarily through offending behaviour groups, the difficulty here, and with education about which they also felt positive, was the likelihood of their being moved on before they had completed groups and courses. In other aspects most of them did not feel helped.

At Warwick Unit, trainees found that most of their problems were addressed by a range of groups, one-to-one and educational experiences as well as by continual positive engagement with staff who had time for them. The Warwick Unit study chronicles a regime in which antisocial characteristics were replaced by prosocial characteristics, where educational and constructive leisure pursuits were opened up, and broken family relationships were healed. Staff were clear about their aims, and this was reflected in the fact that almost all aspects of the regime were rated positively by the trainee sample, and individual comments suggested that it was the holistic '24/7' nature of this supportive and respectful regime that equipped trainees for ultimate rehabilitation. Despite some frustrations, job satisfaction levels amongst this group of staff were mostly very high, and trainees realised that this was 'the best chance they'd ever get'. Warwick Unit continued to be used as a support system by trainees after they had left the unit.

This is not to suppose, however, that Blenheim trainees should not also have access to Enhanced Units, nor that less vulnerable trainees should not be provided with regimes based on Warwick Unit's 'enhanced' model. If anything is clear from this study (and most other studies and inspections which precede it), it is that this group of long-term young offenders has a catalogue of problems and needs which detention in an 'ordinary' custodial regime does little to address.

A study of a residential therapeutic regime for adolescent male sexual abusers

McGregor Hall is a voluntary children's home registered with the Department of Health. As such it is a very different type of establishment from a young offender institution. At any one time it houses around 15 particularly damaged male adolescent sexual abusers, most of whom have been criminalised and are on a condition of residence attached to either a supervision order or a community rehabilitation order. A decreasing minority have not been criminalised and have reached the residential community via the childcare referral system. Apart from their residents' histories of inappropriate sexual behaviour, the community's description of the typical presenting problems of these young men could apply to many section 90/91 YOI trainees: challenging behaviours; denial/minimisation of offending; poor relationship skills; childhood history of abuse/trauma/neglect; limited ability with words; educational disadvantage; moderate learning difficulties; history of multiple care placements.

Following a staged individual resident assessment process, the therapeutic programme at McGregor Hall moves through a range of settings and activities to provide a consistent therapeutic approach 24 hours a day, 7 days a week.

Based on restorative justice principles, the programme operates on the premise that self-esteem and confidence develop through mutual respect and valuing rather than through punishment. It comprises individual counselling, groupwork, on- and off-site work experience, education, creative arts, leisure activities and a specialist relapse prevention programme for addressing the perpetration of sexual abuse. Community meetings, held at the beginning, middle and end of each day, where behaviour is reviewed and decisions made, are the cornerstone of the therapeutic programme in that they encapsulate the ongoing 'milieu' of relationships amongst residents and staff. Within them, young people's behaviour is both nurtured and challenged so that they learn to conduct themselves in ways which will be socially acceptable when transferring to other day-to-day settings. Also encouraged, where appropriate is family contact; the healing of damaged relationships; a gradual move towards independence culminating in a period living in a bungalow in the grounds with minimal staff support; and an after-care support facility. High levels of supervision and ongoing risk assessment are integrated into what is essentially a psychodynamic approach to understanding why these young men have sexually abused, and to helping them progress through adolescence to a point where they can take personal responsibility for their actions.

As outlined in the introduction, this research constituted a pilot study. The research population in question had not been studied previously and there was no comparable study on which to draw. The survey of the 15- to 19-year-old residents was retrospective; that is, ascertaining information from them and a range of other sources about their lives both before and after McGregor Hall. It aimed to establish a basis for a longitudinal survey. The first question which had to be answered, therefore, was whether it was feasible to conduct this kind of study with this type of population. The study did, in fact, prove feasible and the longitudinal study is now into its fourth year. As recounted above in the YOI study, the trainee interview schedule and problem checklist had been piloted previously, and the most recent versions were in fact tested within this McGregor Hall study (Boswell and Wedge 2002).

Although the study was a pilot in respect of its methods, it was in itself a whole population study. The two criteria for the respondents' selection were that they should have left the therapeutic community between two and five years prior to interview and should either have completed the two-year therapeutic programme or left in a 'planned' way; that is, with the agreement of all concerned that they had completed the work necessary to bring them to an optimum point for return to the outside community. The 15 who formed the research sample were the only ex-residents on the register for that period who satisfactorily met both these criteria. Similarly, a comparison group was formed from the only 14 youngsters with a similar range of problems, who had been referred to McGregor Hall in the same period but, for a range of reasons, had not become residents. In the event, only ten of each group could be traced.

The methodology for this study was identical in most respects to that outlined in some detail in respect of the YOI study and need not be repeated here. The only substantial difference was that psychological tests were not deployed since a population of adolescent sex offenders tends, on the whole, already to have received the attentions of psychologists or psychiatrists. The interview schedules and problem checklists posed a small number of extra questions which related specifically to sexual offending but otherwise were the same.

In brief, referral to McGregor Hall over the period being studied appeared to have resulted in placements for those convicted of/otherwise known to have engaged in sexual abuse but not normally in other kinds of offending. For this client group, sexual conviction post-departure had reduced dramatically. Those who did not become resident at McGregor Hall (i.e. the comparison group) were much more active criminals, mainly in respect of non-sexual offending both before and after referral; five of them also offended sexually post-referral as compared with only two ex-residents.

Compared with their lives before McGregor Hall, the majority of ex-residents reported significantly fewer problems two or more years down the line. Additionally, none of them was in denial about their previous sexually abusing behaviour. When asked what they saw as the best things about McGregor Hall, five ex-residents commented as follows:

> The staff and residents; feeling safe; boundaries; the friendliness of staff.

> Their whole attitude. They know you're there for sex offending but they give you a chance and don't treat you like that.

> Forming attachments with staff – these are still important after two years, and gave me confidence in who I am.

> I couldn't give a best thing – it was just everything. When I was there, fair enough, I hated it, but towards the end I could understand and looking back I can see it was necessary.

> Support from staff and residents. It's the sort of place where you get institutionalised slightly because it's one happy family. I broke down in tears the day I left.

Their remaining problems were not, however, insignificant but most of them, often despite lacking family support, appeared to have acquired from McGregor Hall the necessary techniques for coping without precipitating crises. Two to five years after leaving, the impact of McGregor Hall remained firmly imprinted upon them, encapsulated in the advice offered by one ex-resident, who had left three years previously, to current residents: 'It's hard work, but you'll be grateful after.'

Summary and pointers for the future

This chapter began by highlighting the serious dilemma posed for society when children between the ages of 10 and 17 years commit acts of violence, thus constituting a risk to the general public. Previous research has demonstrated with some consistency that those convicted of violent crimes have invariably experienced childhoods featuring, singly or in combination, conflict, broken families, loss, abuse, neglect and their associated variables. The results of three studies have been reported here in order to provide a perspective on the characteristics, backgrounds and outcomes for groups of these children respectively placed in statutory sector standard and enhanced custodial regimes and a voluntary sector therapeutic regime. Although the latter two regimes cater for children assessed as particularly vulnerable, it was clear that such children also populated the standard custodial regime.

Outcomes in terms of reoffending were slightly better for the enhanced than for the standard regime and considerably better for the therapeutically treated group as against a non-treated comparison group. Psychological testing for the two custodial groups showed significant improvements over time for the enhanced regime group in respect of self-esteem levels and reduction in aggressive beliefs and behaviour; they showed significant increase in depression levels for the standard regime group. Both the enhanced regime group and the therapeutic regime group reported significantly fewer problems respectively at the end of, and two to five years after, their placements. The standard regime group reported an increase in problems towards the end of or after their placements.

It should be reiterated that the above findings are based on comparisons of children from a similar age range who have committed acts of serious violence, rather than on closely matched control groups. It can nevertheless be broadly deduced that the two regimes providing a high staff–inmate ratio for relatively small groups of children, with a range of closely supervised education/training/treatment facilities led to better outcomes in terms of reoffending, problem reduction, self-esteem and coping levels, than did the non-dedicated standard regime for large numbers of juveniles, of whom the section 90/91 trainees formed only just over 25 per cent of the population.

In thinking about the implications of these findings for the future disposal and management of these young people, it is necessary to consider all the stages and stakeholders in the penal process: crime prevention; criminal justice policy; custodial career management; the enhancement of public understanding; and further research developments:

1. In respect of crime prevention, education and publicity are needed at community level to encourage both children and adults to recognise and report incidents of abuse and trauma. Parent support and parenting classes (many, interestingly, now being run in YOIs) can

help present and future parents avoid the pitfalls of abusive or damaging parenthood.

2. Criminal justice policy might afford some attention to the rest of Europe, where 14 years is the average age for criminal responsibility. In respect of those from whom society needs to be protected until their risk levels can be minimised, these findings suggest a need for smaller establishments with dedicated staff who can ensure that individual treatment and education needs are not only identified but implemented and sustained.

3. Staff working in these regimes need to be fully furnished with knowledge about relevant research findings, and with professional assessment skills, with investigation routinely made into abuse, loss and other prevalent background factors. Such assessments should aim to offer a root cause explanation of the offending behaviour, a realistic estimate of the security level required for the protection of society, and an appropriate programme of action which will specifically seek to ensure that the young person does not repeat their violent behaviour. In cases where unresolved childhood trauma is found, post-traumatic stress counselling should form a specific part of that programme.

4. Criminal justice professionals are well placed to interact with the public to provide serious rather than salacious information about young people who commit acts of serious violence and to emphasise the importance for community safety of replacing condemnation with understanding. Through a range of local and national networks, they can involve the public in discussing the action each sector can appropriately take to minimise the risk of this happening in their communities.

5. The Beijing Rules on the administration of juvenile justice (UN 1986) have established standards for the integration of research programmes into the process of policy formulation and application, with mutual feedback and learning across international networks. It behoves all researchers to adhere to these standards.

In the above ways, it should be possible to respond to child violence by pinpointing preventative measures, assessment and intervention techniques relevant to the complexities of contemporary culture, and applicable within and across coherent flexible systems of child welfare and youth justice.

References

Boswell, G.R. (1991) *Waiting for Change: An Exploration of the Experiences and Needs of Section 53 Offenders.* London: The Prince's Trust.

Boswell, G.R. (1995) *Violent Victims.* London: The Prince's Trust.

Boswell, G.R. (1996) *Young and Dangerous: The Backgrounds and Careers of Section 53 Offenders.* Aldershot: Avebury.

Boswell, G.R. and Wedge, P. (2002) *Sexually Abusive Adolescent Males: An Evaluation of a Residential Therapeutic Facility.* Community and Criminal Justice Monograph 3. Leicester: De Montfort University.

Boswell, G.R. and Wedge, P. (2003) 'An evaluation of the regimes for Section 90/91 offenders at HM young offender institutions, Blenheim YOI and Warwick Unit.' Unpublished report to the Youth Justice Board of England and Wales.

Ditchfield, J. and Catan, L. (1992) 'Juveniles Sentenced for Serious Offences: A Comparison of Regimes in Young Offender Institutions and Local Authority Community Homes. Research and Planning Unit Paper 66. London: Home Office.

Goldson, B. (2002) *Vulnerable Inside: Children in Secure and Penal Settings.* London: The Children's Society.

HMIP (Her Majesty's Inspectorate of Prisons) (1997) *Young Prisoners: A Thematic Review.* London: Home Office.

HM Prison Service (2000) *Prison Service Order No. 4950: Regimes for Prisoners Under 18 Years Old.* London: HM Prison Service.

HM Prison Service (2001) *Prison Service Order No. 4960: Detention Under Section 92 of the Powers of Criminal Courts (Sentencing) Act 2000.* London: HM Prison Service.

NACRO (2002) *Children Who Commit Grave Crimes.* London: NACRO.

Rutter, M., Giller, H. and Hagell, A. (1998) *Anti-social Behaviour by Young People.* Cambridge: Cambridge University Press.

Smith, C. and Thornberry, T.P. (1995) 'The relationship between childhood maltreatment and adolescent involvement in delinquency.' *Criminology 33,* 451–477.

Social Exclusion Unit (2002) *Reducing Re-offending by Ex-Prisoners.* London: Office of the Deputy Prime Minister.

United Nations (1986) *Beijing Rules: United Nations Standard Minimum Rules for the Administration of Juvenile Justice.* New York: Department of Public Information.

Youth Justice Board (2001) 'What should a Section 53 unit provide?' Unpublished policy document.

8

'Hard to place' children and young people

A commentary on past, present and future approaches to care and treatment

Kevin J. Epps

Introduction

This chapter provides a brief commentary, from a personal perspective, on some of the changes and developments that have taken place in Britain in approaches to working with 'hard to place' children and young people. Over the past few years I have attended various conferences and seminars concerned with this group of young people and have been struck by the fact that virtually no attention has been given to historical approaches. I qualified as a clinical psychologist in 1986, just 20 years ago, yet find myself harking back to researchers, practitioners and theoretical models which seem to have been lost in the mists of time, but have much to contribute to current debates. The existence of 'hard to place' young people is not new, and yet many practitioners seem to approach this issue as if it is a novel problem. It is difficult to trace the events that have contributed to this state of affairs, but the content of training courses is surely one factor. Conversations with mental health professionals working with children and adolescents who qualified in recent years suggests relevant knowledge and skills are often absent from training courses, no doubt due to the pressure for courses to keep up with more recent developments. For example, there is no guarantee that newly qualified clinical psychologists have any training or experience of applied behavioural analysis, behavioural modification or behavioural family work, all of which are extremely relevant when working with severely conduct disordered children.

Defining and describing 'hard to place' children and young people

One of the difficulties from a research perspective, particularly since the advent of computerised search engines and databases relying on key words, is that terminology has changed over the years. 'Hard to place' young people defy simple categorisation or labelling. No mental health diagnosis, psychometric label or defined cluster of personal, family or demographic variables sufficiently captures their essence. What, exactly, makes this group of young people so hard to place? How are they different to other 'difficult' young people? Each generation of researchers and clinical practitioners seems to invent their own brand of terminology, often reflecting current social, legal and theoretical trends. Inevitably, literature searches fail to capture huge swathes of relevant historical information. Terms such as 'delinquent', 'seriously maladjusted', 'emotional and behaviourally disturbed (EBD)', 'seriously emotional damaged', 'troubled and troublesome', 'difficult and dangerous', 'seriously antisocial', 'mentally disordered young offenders', 'severe problems of adjustment' and 'seriously conduct disordered' all compete with one another, and yet none of these alone captures the essence of why some young people are 'hard to place'. However, most local authority looked after children service managers, particularly directors of social services, will easily identify at least one or two young people in their care who are hard to place and who account for hugely disproportionate amounts of money, time, resources and stress, the latter often reflected in staff anxiety, sickness and absenteeism.

Characteristics of 'hard to place' children and young people

So, who are these 'hard to place' children and young people, and how have they been dealt with in years gone by? In response to the first question, following on from the earlier discussion, the answer is that we still do not know how best to capture the essence of this group of young people. The international research work led by NCH – The Bridge Child Care Development Service under the auspices of the Oak Foundation will hopefully shed further light on how best to identify and describe these young people, building on the profiles identified in the chapters in Part 1 of this volume. Many of these young people will undoubtedly present with serious emotional, behavioural and learning problems of a kind and nature that makes caring for them extremely difficult.

These problems often include a combination of the following: persistent aggression and violence to adults (often to carers) and to peers, often of a severe, impulsive and unpredictable nature (and sometimes exacerbated by large physical build); lack of self-care, often accompanied by self-injurious or reckless, risky behaviour, including persistent absconding and substance misuse; inappropriate sexualised behaviour, sometimes aggressive and coercive in nature; high levels of over-aroused, irritable, overactive, restless behaviour; high levels of personal distress resulting from an array of diffuse, poorly defined, emotional states (including anxiety, self-loathing, worthlessness, anger, depression and low self-esteem); poor peer relationships, often associated with being unpopular and victimisation through bullying; poor relationships with adults, frequently associated with significant attachment difficulties; and resistance to help from adults, characterised by persistent non-compliance and refusal to engage in therapeutic work. A common thread running through the lives of many of these young people is that they find it hard to 'connect' with other people around them, both peers and adults. They do not form relationships easily, with peers or with adults, and do not fit easily into schools, children's homes, or even into prison settings, causing professionals to want them removed to a more 'appropriate' setting, which unfortunately often does not exist.

As the research reviewed in Chapter 3 shows, the origins of these emotional, behavioural and learning difficulties can often be traced back to infancy, when patterns of dysfunctional emotional and behavioural responding have been established and reinforced through damaging life experiences, including repeated and persistent serious trauma (severe physical and/or sexual abuse, exposure to violence, significant emotional loss through bereavement, abandonment or separation); early neglect and deprivation; grossly inadequate parenting; educational failure; substance abuse; and exposure to deviant peers. By the age of six or seven years some of these children will already be suffering from the effects of significant social marginalisation. Ironically, behaviour that is deemed 'maladaptive' in older years may well have served an adaptive (survival) function in infancy and toddlerhood. For example, habitual patterns of aggressive behaviour that proved useful in a family context where aggression is the main problem-solving and survival strategy become undesirable and maladaptive in the nursery or infant school setting. If the child's behaviour does not adapt to the new context he or she is perceived as challenging and difficult and the behaviour is likely to become even more deeply ingrained and resistant to change in subsequent settings.

This pattern may well continue through to adolescence, where physical size, past reputation and increased skill in using aggression all add to the problem of providing adequate care. These young people exist at the periphery of their age group, destined for a life of unpopularity, stigmatisation, vulnerability to abuse and exploitation, eventually finding their way into statutory care, incarceration and unable to settle anywhere for long. A significant proportion also find themselves referred to mental health professionals, who struggle to find a form of words to neatly describe the presenting problems or to identify a treatable condition, where treatment more often than not refers to psychiatric treatment using medication, which does little to change entrenched patterns of behaviour, emotion and thinking. Even where a diagnosable, treatable, condition is identified, treatment often takes place against a backdrop of chaos and amid numerous other social, educational and family problems, which ameliorate the success of treatment.

Past and present responses to 'hard to place' children and young people

Historically, many different approaches have been used in an effort to deal with these 'hard to place' children and young people, some more successful than others. The term 'success' needs to be clarified when used in this context. Practitioners working with these young people soon learn to adjust their expectations of what is deemed a successful outcome. If a child aged 12 years has not been in mainstream school due to behavioural problems since the age of seven years, it is probably best not to consider full-time integration into the local high school as a realistic short-term goal. In some instances, success can be very small, but still highly significant, changes. A reduction in self-cutting from an average of nine times each day to twice each day, for example, is a step in the right direction and to be encouraged, even when all other challenging behaviours remain unchanged. Most practitioners make this type of adjustment to their thinking and expectations when they work long term with this group of young people.

The concept of 'hard to place' children and young people is in many ways a relatively recent concept, mirroring the development of state-funded children's services. By definition 'hard to place' children are identifiable only because they fall outside of mainstream provision, which has not always existed. It is perhaps worth remembering that the hanging of young children used to be 'by no means unusual' in England during the eighteenth and nineteenth centuries (Cristoph 1962). It is likely that many 'hard to place' children shared this fate in days gone by. Others would have been placed in orphanages, although the most difficult and challenging children would inevitably have been refused entry or rejected, and lived on the streets. Others languished with adults in prisons, lunatic asylums and, more recently, in the back wards of large psychiatric hospitals. For example, Parkhurst Prison on the Isle of Wight received boys from 10 to 18 years of age for 25 years following the 1838 Parkhurst Act.

Even today it is not unusual to find some of the most difficult young people aged 16 or 17 placed with adults in psychiatric units because of an inability to find a placement designed for young people. This, in essence, is the problem: accommodation designed for 'specific types' of young people with defined characteristics will exclude those who do not fit the admission criteria. 'Hard to place' children are difficult to define, do not fit into established groupings, and therefore find themselves being moved between various forms of unsuitable accommodation, like an unwanted package that cannot find a home. This is perhaps truer today than ever. In clinical practice it is not unusual to find 'hard to place' young people who have experienced 30 or 40 placements since birth, and in exceptional cases more than 100. One girl seen by the author in secure accommodation at the age of 12 years had been in 92 placements. She was subsequently readmitted to the same secure unit on five separate occasions over the following two years due to placement breakdown in the community and an escalation in her violent and challenging behaviour. At the time of writing she continues to be held in secure accommodation, and to date she has had 107 placements. Needless to say, her future looks uncertain and she has significant attachment and relationship difficulties.

Local authority secure accommodation

The England and Wales Children Act 1989 was designed to meet the needs of most children most of the time. However, it was not designed to meet the needs of children who present with exceptionally difficult and challenging behaviour, who fall outside the scope of mainstream provision and for whom traditional approaches have been wholly unsuccessful. Consider, for example, the use in England and Wales of local authority secure accommodation. Under section 25 of the Children Act 1989, a child must meet the threshold criteria for secure accommodation before a court will grant a Secure Order that extends beyond 72 hours in any 28-day period. Many children undoubtedly benefit from a brief stay in secure accommodation, allowing time for a period of safe care and education, and time for professionals and family to focus their attention on resolving difficulties that have previously hindered placement in an open community placement. However, outcomes for 'hard to place' young people placed temporarily in secure accommodation are often less positive. Local authority secure units are designed to provide care, containment and education over the short to medium term (i.e. three to six months) (see Epps 1997; Harris and Timms 1993). These units do not have a remit to provide long-term intervention programmes designed to systemically change behaviour. Further, the current legislation does not support this type of approach. Secure Orders under the 1989 Children Act are short-term measures to be used as a last resort, with the onus on moving the young person to an alternative non-secure community placement in a planned way as soon as possible. As such, they are not conducive to addressing deeply entrenched behavioural and psychological difficulties through the use of long-term interventions in a specific, stable, secure placement. 'Hard to place' young people sometimes find themselves subject to several short-to-medium periods of secure accommodation, often in different secure units across the country, with no long-term progress in their presenting difficulties. Indeed, their problems often become more numerous and more entrenched until a point is reached, usually around the age of 16 or 17, where children's services begin to withdraw and look to other agencies to deal with the young person. In some instances the case file is closed, leaving the young person with no statutory service involvement.

During this period these young people may thus pass through a whole range of short-term, often inappropriate, placements, spending periods of time in custody, private sector crisis intervention units, or even in bed and breakfast accommodation. It would no doubt come as a shock to members of the public to discover that some of the countries' most difficult and risky young people are living in bed and breakfast accommodation because they are too difficult to manage in any form of childcare unit, including secure accommodation. This does not protect either the child or the public and clearly does not offer any intervention or treatment that might help to ameliorate the problem.

The reality in Britain today is that there are no residential treatment facilities for young people presenting with the most serious forms of antisocial behaviour and conduct problems. The term 'treatment' used in this context does not refer solely to the use of medical or psychiatric treatment, but the use of long-term, planned, systematic, theory-driven programmes of intervention designed to promote behavioural and psychological change. Consequently, these young people bounce back and forwards between various agencies and forms of accommodation, with no realistic long-term care plan and no real hope for the future, at enormous cost to the responsible funding agencies. The weekly cost of providing a sufficiently containing community placement, often with two or three staff dedicated to constantly supervising the young person, can be as much as £8000. Many of these placements are unable to provide any meaningful education or therapeutic work simply because the context is not conducive to the young person engaging in this type of work. The focus is on containment, risk management and providing acceptable levels of basic care that meet statutory requirements. Tasks or demands that provoke the young person to escalate aggression and disruption (e.g. insistence on attending education, or talking about their thoughts and feelings in therapy sessions) simply add to the day-to-day management difficulties and may even jeopardise the viability of the placement. It is not unknown for funding agencies to complain about the lack of education and therapy, and to move the young person to a placement that claims to be able to offer these activities, only to discover that the situation actually worsens following the move due to the disruption and discontinuity in care and the inadequacy of the new placement.

Youth treatment centres

In the past, however, there have been significant attempts to deal with these exceptionally difficult, 'hard to place' young people. The most notable of these was the creation by the Department of Health (DOH) of the youth treatment centres (YTCs) by constitution of Parliament in the 1970s, prompted in part by the case of Mary Bell who, in 1968 when aged 11, was found guilty of having at the age of ten killed two small boys, aged three and four (see Sereny 1974, 1995). At this time there was no appropriate accommodation for girls in which she could serve her custodial sentence. The YTCs, both now closed, were therefore set up to provide long-term care, education and residential treatment to Britain's most difficult and troublesome young people. The first YTC to open, in 1971, was St Charles in Essex, which adopted a psychodynamic approach to residential care that was prevalent during the 1960s and 1970s. The second YTC, Glenthorne, opened in Birmingham in 1978. This centre was a purpose-built unit that adopted a social-learning approach (Bandura 1971, 1973), strongly influenced by the Achievement Place model in Kansas (Phillips *et al.* 1972). The treatment model was based on behavioural parenting and the use of structured behavioural approaches to analyse and modify behaviour within a family living type environment. A third YTC was planned but never opened. At this time several other local authority resources, including Aycliffe Children's Centre in Durham and Orchard Lodge in South London, offered specialist programmes in extensive secure and open accommodation to very difficult young people. Orchard Lodge, for example, provided a behavioural programme (Unit One), also intended to replicate the Achievement Place model (Brown 1987). These facilities, along with several others, began to establish a countrywide network of services dealing with very challenging young people. The YTCs were subject to considerable research and follow-up, most notably by the Dartington Social Research Unit, resulting in a large number of publications between 1989 and 1998 (see Bullock, Little and Millham 1998). Interested readers will find in these publications a wealth of information about the lives, backgrounds, and care careers of some of Britain's most challenging young people.

Glenthorne Youth Treatment Centre

Numerous other publications originated from both St Charles and Glenthorne, particularly the latter, which from the beginning had close links with the School of Psychology at the University of Birmingham. The model of care and intervention adopted at Glenthorne was unique in that from the beginning it was designed specifically for working in secure and open residential conditions with young people with the most serious forms of antisocial and conduct problems, many of whom were convicted of grave crimes such as murder, rape and arson. Most young people remained at the centre for at least one year, although those serving a long custodial sentence remained considerably longer before being released into the community or moved to adult provision. One young person, convicted of murder at the age of 11, remained for more than six years. The centre therefore adopted a long-term approach to care and treatment, developing plans to suit each young person and setting outcome goals that were achievable and realistic according to the length of stay. Several years after opening one of the secure units was converted into an open unit, allowing for the graded rehabilitation of young people into the community.

Glenthorne's philosophy and practice was heavily influenced by the scientist-practitioner approach to care and intervention, particularly Philip Feldman's seminal work at Birmingham on psychological approaches to understanding criminal behaviour (Feldman 1977). During its 22-year history the centre developed particular expertise in providing residential care and treatment to exceptionally behaviourally challenging young people from across Britain, many of whom would meet the psychiatric diagnostic criteria for conduct disorder using ICD-10 or DSM-IV. Glenthorne, however, was not a psychiatric facility, and did not adopt a diagnostic approach to problem formulation. Rather, it used a contextual functional-analytical approach, construing challenging behaviour as learned responses to inappropriate social environments, usually beginning in the home in early childhood under the influence of parents and subsequently persisting in other environments (e.g. nursery, school, community). The primary intervention task within the centre, therefore, was to understand the factors that served to maintain and perpetuate inappropriate patterns of behaviour and to arrange the social and physical environment in such a way to promote and encourage new patterns of appropriate behaviour in each young person.

The process of planning and implementing interventions depended heavily on all members of the staff team working together in a consistent manner with each young person in an effort to have a powerful positive influence on behaviour (see Gentry and Ostapiuk 1989). For example, in any one case specific behaviours would be targeted for reinforcement, whilst other behaviours would be ignored (i.e. removal of adult attention, which is a form of punishment). This residential team approach would be complemented by other intervention approaches that were consistent with a social learning model, including individual and group skill training (e.g. social competence and self-management), individual cognitive behavioural therapy (CBT) and, where possible, family therapy (usually behavioural or systemic in orientation). Good basic childcare and physical and mental healthcare were seen as essential and would underpin the intervention programme. Where necessary, medication was prescribed by visiting GPs or psychiatrists and used only with the young person's consent to treat identified medical conditions (including mental health symptoms, such as anxiety or depression), not to control or manage behavioural problems.

The writings of Martin Herbert, particularly his seminal book on conduct disorders (Herbert 1978), had a tremendous impact on the theoretical and operational approaches adopted at Glenhorne YTC. Those responsible for the early development of the centre also had the wisdom to realise that, to sustain a consistent social learning approach to working with residents, all staff members required extensive training in social learning theory and practice.

Consequently, a diploma course was set up, originally under the auspices of Herbert at the University of Leicester, later moving with Clive Hollin to the University of Birmingham. For many years this course provided a steady stream of residential workers (with backgrounds in residential social work, teaching and psychiatric nursing) who worked in teams to provide 24-hour care and intervention, with input from clinical and forensic psychologists, social workers and visiting psychiatrists. Although not without its problems, this total organisational commitment to social learning theory was tremendously successful in dealing with extremely damaged and challenging young people, most of whom had been excluded from all other forms of accommodation and could without exception be considered 'hard to place' (see Bullock, Little and Millham 1994).

Current provision for 'hard to place' children and young people

There can be no doubt that the closure of the YTCs by the DOH in 2000 left a large gap in provision for 'hard to place' young people. Young people who would have been referred and admitted to the YTCs now move between various placements and institutions with no consistent long-term care or education. Most of these risky young people at one time or another are now referred to the Forensic Child and Adolescent Mental Health Services (CAMHS), community outpatient teams that are being developed in various parts of the country (Lengua et al. 1997; Williams 2004). In an evaluation of 40 community assessment reports prepared by the multidisciplinary West Midlands Forensic CAMHS, Epps (2005) found that conduct disorder was the most frequent Axis 1 diagnosis (35%) in the 37 reports that provided an ICD-10 classification. Attention deficit disorder (ADD), autistic spectrum disorder (ASD) and attachment disorder were also common. Psychotic symptoms were identified in only 13.5 per cent of the 37 cases, and were stated as a reason for referral in only 2.5 per cent. Seventy-six per cent received more than one Axis 1 diagnosis, typically a combination of the above in association with complex post-traumatic stress disorder (PTSD). Eighty-four per cent also received an Axis 5 diagnosis (Associated Abnormal Psychosocial Situations), indicating significant family and social difficulties.

In essence, therefore, most of the young people seen by this particular Forensic CAMHS team were presenting with significant risk to others in association with complex behavioural, developmental and psychosocial problems. It is perhaps not surprising, therefore, that the majority of referrers requested advice about behavioural management (70%) and risk management (40%). Advice about placement was provided in 70 per cent of the cases. Placement recommendations frequently included reference to the need for a safe, structured, highly supervised placement with experienced residential care workers and access to specialist services (e.g. for sexually inappropriate behaviour, sexual abuse, psychiatric oversight). It is noteworthy that mental illness (e.g. psychosis, schizophrenia, bipolar disorder) is relatively rare in this population, although many can be considered as having mental health difficulties in the broadest sense. The term 'mental health problem' is often mistaken to mean mental illness (another source of confusion) but is actually a more inclusive term referring to a whole host of psychological, emotional and behavioural problems, including suicide risk, self-injury, substance abuse, attention and learning difficulties, and emotional and behavioural problems arising from abuse (Bailey, Thornton and Weaver 1994; Huckle and Williams 1996; Nicol *et al.* 2000). In their survey of the perceptions of relevant service providers of the mental health needs of young people considered for secure placement, Kurtz, Thornes and Bailey (1998) comment that 'young people with difficult and dangerous behaviour tend to be categorized as criminal or mentally ill.' The misunderstanding and confusion surrounding the terms 'mental health' and 'mental illness' when used with young people cannot be underestimated. There is frequently an implicit assumption that a young person who commits a serious antisocial act such as rape must have a diagnosable psychiatric disorder that can somehow explain away their behaviour; further, that this disorder can be successfully treated, thereby returning the young person to a state of 'normality' and eliminating risk. The difficulty is that deeply entrenched, inappropriate patterns of behaviour, thinking and feeling do not fit an illness model: they are not transient departures from normal functioning and cannot be remedied through medical treatment.

The absence of a range of appropriate secure and open community treatment facilities for 'hard to place' conduct disordered young people has also been raised as a concern by academics and practitioners interested in the prevention and treatment of adult antisocial personality disorder at a recent National Programme on Forensic Mental Health Research and Development Seminar (2003). Although research in this area is lacking, there is growing evidence that serious conduct problems in childhood are a significant predictor of later personality problems (Bernstein *et al.* 1996). A significant proportion of adults diagnosed as having antisocial personality disorder had a childhood history of conduct disorder (Myers *et al.* 1998). Whilst most practitioners accept that a significant proportion of seriously conduct disordered adolescents will resist treatment approaches, it is nevertheless a matter of concern that many of these young people are held in care and custodial settings, often at considerable cost to the taxpayer, with no opportunity to engage in systematic intervention work to address their difficulties.

It seems sensible to suggest that some of this money would be better spent if it were directed towards properly designed and evaluated intervention programmes, linked to existing programmes that deal with persistent young offenders, such as the Intensive Supervision and Surveillance Programmes (ISSP) operated by the Youth Justice Board (YJB). Part of the difficulty, however, is the absence of a legal mandate to treat this group of young people. As noted earlier, the Children Act 1989 Secure Accommodation legislation is not designed for treatment purposes, but for welfare and safety. In contrast, the 1983 Mental Health Act is treatment oriented, but is designed primarily with adults in mind. Further, under current arrangements, the psychiatric profession bears the burden of responsibility for use of mental health legislation. Many psychiatrists do not consider the treatment of serious conduct problems in adolescence as falling within their bounds of training or expertise. They are even more wary of using the Mental Health Act to detain this group of individuals, and are also cautious about the medicalisation of behavioural and social problems. Consequently, there are no NHS inpatient adolescent psychiatric units devoted to the treatment of conduct disorder, and it is rare to find a young person detained under the category of psychopathic disorder, although this does occasionally happen in forensic adolescent inpatient settings.

An integrated range of specialist provision is required for this group of 'hard to place' children and young people, including small community group homes, specialist family fostering schemes (employing highly trained foster carers), secure residential treatment facilities, forensic inpatient CAMHS, and individually tailored community placements offering placements to one or two young people requiring care away from other children and young people. Successful intervention with these young people will ultimately depend on matching young people to appropriate environments and interventions ('ecological matching'). Whilst a tremendous amount of clinical literature has been devoted to the assessment of young people, there is a dearth of literature on describing and quantifying social environments.

Conclusions and future directions

In summary, there remains a small but highly significant group of children and young people who present with extraordinarily complex behavioural and psychological difficulties that make them 'hard to place' in childcare facilities. These young people defy simple categorisation, are often impossible to engage in formal therapeutic work, and prove unmanageable in most forms of accommodation, even that designed for difficult and troubled young people. Current national service provision for these young people is inadequate, poorly organised and fragmented. It is also hugely expensive, relying on short-term, crisis-focused placements, with an emphasis on behavioural containment and risk management with no long-term care plan or systematic approach to intervention. However, in looking to the future with a view to developing better services, it is important not to forget the past. Examples of past good practice and 'outdated' theoretical approaches are often overlooked in the search for new solutions. The youth treatment centres, for example, amassed considerable knowledge and skills in the care, management and treatment of exceptionally difficult young people, yet much of this experience was lost when the YTCs were closed. Whilst there will never be a single or simple solution to providing care and treatment to these young people, it is important to learn from past experiences, so that past mistakes are not repeated. With respect to the future, it is possible to identify a number of priorities for improving services for these children and young people. These are outlined below:

1. The development of research programmes to identify and describe 'hard to place' children and young people. Who are they? Why are they hard to place? Where are they now? How much money is currently being spent on this group? What happens to them?

2. Related to the above, research aimed at specifying the diverse needs of these young people, using a broad multimodal needs analysis tool.

3. Drawing from the above research, an analysis of gaps in service provision. Some gaps may be small and simply require integration of existing services. Other gaps may be larger (e.g. appropriate residential care and treatment) and require considerable expenditure and service planning and development.

4. The development of research aimed at measuring and quantifying care environments so that young people can be better matched to their placement and care programme. Current practice relies on a random hit-and-miss approach, with practitioners searching for placements, often with little idea of what is most appropriate and whether the service provider will actually deliver what they promise. Assessments are sometimes of little use because they do not address the critical issues and there is little attempt to match the young person to the placement.

5. Attention also needs to be given to developing theoretical frameworks for understanding this group of young people. No single framework is likely to suffice, but some frameworks probably have more to offer than others in response to specific problems. The evidence base for 'what works' is growing. Whilst this evidence is mainly applicable to the less complex and more common problems encountered in clinical practice, it is sometimes possible to extrapolate to more complex difficulties, such as conduct disorder (see Scott 2004).

6. Finally, there needs to be debate between services about the best way to deal with 'hard to place' children and young people, particularly those identified as having a serious conduct disorder and those with a mild to moderate learning disability, who often fall between existing services. Agreement needs to be reached on the roles and

responsibilities of each service for these young people. It seems, for example, that there is agreement that conduct disorder in older children and adolescents is primarily a social rather than a mental health problem, although a significant number of these young people do have associated mental health difficulties, such as ADHD, depression and substance misuse (Dubicka and Harrington 2004; Hill 2002). However, the treatment of non-health problems, such as antisocial behaviour, particularly conduct disordered adolescents who are beyond parental control and resistant to traditional clinic-based outpatient treatment, falls outside the remit of child and adolescent mental health services. These services do not have a legal mandate or the necessary resources or treatment infrastructure to deal with these young people. However, the same can also be said of local authority social services departments, who often refer these young people to local CAMHS on the grounds that they have a psychiatric disorder. Thus in clinical practice a stalemate situation is often reached, with no single agency accepting responsibility for the young person. Practitioners with statutory case responsibility, such as social workers and youth offending team workers, are often left puzzled and confused about how to access appropriate services and issues about placement funding are difficult to resolve. Hopefully, the merging of health and social care under current government initiatives, and the revision of mental health legislation, may begin to pave the way for the resolution of these difficulties.

References

Bailey, S., Thornton, L. and Weaver, A. (1994) 'The first 100 admissions to an adolescent secure unit.' *Journal of Adolescence 17*, 207–220.

Bandura, A. (1971) *Social Learning Theory.* Morristown, NJ: General Learning Press.

Bandura, A. (1973) *Aggression: A Social Learning Analysis.* Englewood Cliffs, NJ: Prentice-Hall.

Bernstein, D.P., Cohen, P., Skodol, A., Bezirganian, S. and Brook, J.S. (1996) 'Childhood antecedents of adolescent personality disorders.' *American Journal of Psychiatry 153*, 907–913.

Brown, B. (1987) 'Behavioural approaches to working with adolescents in trouble.' In J.C. Coleman (ed) *Working with Troubled Adolescents: A Handbook.* London: Academic Press.

Bullock, R., Little, M. and Millham, S. (1994) *The Experience of YTC Look-Alikes Sheltered in Other Settings.* Dartington: Dartington Social Research Unit.

Bullock, R., Little, M. and Millham, S. (1998) *Secure Treatment Outcomes: The Care Careers of Very Difficult Adolescents.* Aldershot: Ashgate.

Cristoph, J.B. (1962) *Capital Punishment and British Politics.* London: Allen and Unwin.

Dubicka, B. and Harrington, R. (2004) 'Affective conduct disorder.' In S. Bailey and M. Dolan (eds) *Adolescent Forensic Psychiatry.* London: Arnold, pp.124–143.

Epps, K.J. (1997) 'Looking after children and young people in secure settings: Recent themes.' In A. Peake (ed) *Children Away from Home. Educational and Child Psychology 15*, 42–52.

Epps, K. (2005) 'A retrospective analysis of community referral assessment reports prepared by a regional forensic child and adolescent mental health service.' Paper presented at Ardenleigh Forensic CAMHS case conference, Birmingham, January.

Feldman, P. (1977) *Criminal Behaviour: A Psychological Analysis*. Chichester: Wiley.

Gentry, M.R. and Ostapiuk, E.B. (1989) 'Violence in institutions for young offenders and disturbed adolescents.' In K. Howells and C. Hollin (eds) *Clinical Approaches to Violence*. Chichester: Wiley.

Harris, R. and Timms, N. (1993) *Secure Accommodation in Child Care: Between Hospital and Prison or Thereabouts?* London: Routledge.

Herbert, M. (1978) *Conduct Disorders of Childhood and Adolescence: A Behavioural Approach to Assessment and Treatment*. Chichester: Wiley.

Hill, J. (2002) 'Biological, psychological and social processes in the conduct disorders.' *Journal of Child Psychiatry and Psychology 43*, 133–164.

Huckle, P. and Williams, T. (1996) 'Adolescent offenders referred to a forensic psychiatric service.' *Psychiatric Bulletin 20*, 258–260.

Kurtz, Z., Thornes, R. and Bailey, S. (1998) 'Children in the criminal justice and secure care systems: How their mental health needs are met.' *Journal of Adolescence 21*, 543–553.

Lengua, C., Bhatti, V., Vostanis, P., Rothery, D. and Cope, R. (1997) 'Psychiatrists' views on the need for the development of an adolescent forensic service.' *Journal of Forensic Psychiatry 8*, 635–643.

Myers, M.G., Stewart, D.G. and Brown, S.A. (1998) 'Progression from conduct disorder to antisocial personality disorder following treatment for adolescent substance abuse.' *American Journal of Psychiatry 155*, 479–485.

National Programme on Forensic Mental Health Research and Development Seminar (2003) Expert seminar held on 12 March 2003, Manchester, England.

Nicol, R., Stretch, D., Whitney, I. *et al.* (2000) 'Mental health needs and services for severely troubled and troubling young people including young offenders in an NHS region.' *Journal of Adolescence 23*, 243–261.

Phillips, E.L., Phillips, E.A., Fixsen, D.L. and Wolf, M.M. (1972) *The Teaching-Family Handbook: Group Living Environments Administered by Professional Teaching-Parents for Youths in Trouble*. Lawrence: University of Kansas.

Scott, S. (2004) 'Childhood antecedents of juvenile delinquency.' In S. Bailey and M. Dolan (eds) *Adolescent Forensic Psychiatry*. London: Arnold, pp.97–111.

Sereny, G. (1974) *The Case of Mary Bell*. London: Arrow.

Sereny, G. (1995) *The Case of Mary Bell: A Portrait of a Child who Murdered*. London: Pimlico.

Williams, R. (2004) 'A strategic approach to commissioning and delivering forensic child and adolescent mental health services.' In S. Bailey and M. Dolan (eds) *Adolescent Forensic Psychiatry*. London: Arnold, pp.315–335.

9

Challenges to meeting the needs of these children effectively

An overview of an international research study in Germany, Greece, England and Wales

Ann Hagell

Introduction

Anecdotal evidence from social care agencies suggests that most of them are responsible for a small group of children who may have committed or may be at risk of committing serious interpersonal violence. They may have overlapping mental health problems and be very difficult to place in company with other children, as they clearly pose a threat of either physical or sexual abuse to others. This threat will nearly always be because of behaviour they have already exhibited, although they may or may not have been subject to criminal justice proceedings as a result of that behaviour. Generally it is those who have already posed some kind of threat, but who have not been prosecuted, who are the most difficult to care for. There may also be some who have not yet acted inappropriately but who threaten to do so. There is evidence that treatment facilities for these children are limited and unregulated and that they pose particular challenges for agencies who do not know what to do with them. As a result, there is a tension between meeting the children's needs and protecting society, which may result in compromises of care that contribute further to the risk that they will continue to pose a threat to other children.

Two things make placement of these children especially difficult. The first is that this group of children, with their extensive emotional and behavioural difficulties, are particularly difficult to deal with because they are often challenging and stressful to be around. Second, given the current structure and resourcing of children's services, it is very hard to allocate sufficient budget and energy on provision for a very small minority. Two case studies graphically illustrate the types of children who provoked our interest in this group. They are presented in Boxes 9.1 and 9.2.

Box 9.1 Child A: Greg

Greg is 15 years old and has been in the care of the local authority since he was ten. He has always been large for his age and could easily be mistaken for a 20-year-old. He first came to the attention of the local authority because his mother was unable to manage his violent behaviour. The trigger incident was when he threatened her with a knife during an argument.

Greg has had a number of placements in different care homes and on two occasions there have been allegations from other younger boys that Greg sexually abused them, but neither case was substantiated. Greg was recently moved from his most stable placement to date (15 months) because he had developed an obsessive relationship with a girl there, whom he followed everywhere and constantly sent letters to. When challenged he had resisted staff violently and the placement ended. Greg is currently living at home with his mother, but the assessment is that the arrangement will not last – he is not supervised and believed to be a danger to local children. He is not attending school and has been back to his previous placement three times since leaving two weeks ago, each time in pursuit of his ex-girlfriend. On each occasion the police had to be called and a secure escort arranged to bring him back.

The option of a secure placement has been recently discussed at a planning meeting, where there were differing views about both his dangerousness and the best placement for him. The outcome was that he should undergo an assessment from an expert organisation dealing with young abusers. However, such projects are often reluctant to undertake assessments of young people who do not admit they have been involved in abusive behaviour, as in Greg's case.

All attempts to provide an alternative placement have been unsuccessful. When they hear of Greg's history, unit managers say they could not guarantee the safety of other children in their units. He remains at home with a view that he will stay there with support, or be placed in a secure unit. There is concern that this arrangement will continue until a crisis precipitates an emergency application to a secure unit. However, Greg's advocate continues to argue that there are not currently grounds for a secure placement and that she would support legal action against the authority if he were placed in such a setting.

Box 9.2 Child B: Paul

Paul was the eldest son of Bernadette, a teenage mother. When Paul was about a year old, his mother met Michael, 15 years her senior, a heavy drinker who appeared kind and affectionate. They married after three months and Bernadette quickly became pregnant again. The relationship between Paul and his stepfather was difficult from the start. Paul was unused to male figures and cried at Michael's approaches and clung to his mother.

At the time of the birth of the second child, Paul was looked after by a cousin of Michael's who also had three older sons. On one occasion the boys locked Paul into the dark cupboard under the stairs for a number of hours. Paul was terrified and traumatised by this experience. When returned to his mother, Paul appeared to be regressed in his speech and toilet training. He was even more clingy and very jealous of his little brother, S, prodding or pinching him behind his parents' backs, for which he was physically disciplined. Domestic violence resulted in a number of parental separations, although another baby was born when Paul was four years old.

Paul's behaviour at school was problematic. He was aggressive to other children, hyperactive and disruptive in lessons. His mother attended meetings with staff but couldn't understand his difficult behaviour. Aged seven he stole a bicycle and ran away for two days. Three months after, he was picked up by police for playing on an electrified railway with a group of much older boys. Paul appeared to have no concept of other people's feelings. Aged 10 he 'kneed' old people out of his way on buses and broke his brother's arm by twisting it. The neighbour's dog, which he had taken for a walk, was found strangled in a muddy pool on the marshes.

Eventually his mother requested that the local authority (LA) accommodate him. He ran away from experienced foster carers and it was felt unwise to place him in the borough's only community home which already had disruptive teenagers. He was therefore placed in a small unit for four people with one-to-one supervision. Here he jumped out of a first-floor window, stole a bottle of vodka from a local shop and was eventually found unconscious and admitted to hospital.

Following two further similar incidents, the LA applied to the Secretary of State for him to be held in secure accommodation, when Paul was 11. Here he provoked fights with boys twice his size. His mother visited occasionally but was adamant that she would not be able to cope with him back home. After six months Paul had made progress both in controlling his behaviour and educationally, and was therefore moved to a small unit of ten children with its own school. He settled reasonably well and by age 14 it was decided by both his mother and the LA that returning home was a viable option and an intensive rehabilitation plan was put into operation. By age 15, however, it was apparent that Paul could not cope with an unstructured setting. He was drinking heavily, stole kitchen knives as weapons and slashed a younger child across the cheek. He also sexually abused the family's pet cat and a neighbour's seven-year-old daughter.

In discussion with both the local education authority (LEA) and NHS, the LA agreed to make an application to a unit in the North of England, where he would once again be held securely whilst a psychiatric assessment was made.

It seems likely that the situation with regard to this small group of difficult to place children will be the same within most European countries. However, although the children may be quite similar, the ways in which they are dealt with may be rather different. It may be possible to learn from these differences. This chapter will describe an exploratory piece of comparative fieldwork, comprising a survey of social care staff in three areas – England and Wales, Germany and Greece – to assess how many children raise these types of challenges to care provision, and to look in more detail at how these countries meet these challenges. Our research questions thus included:

- In the average child social care agency of these three areas, how many children are there who are very difficult to place, and do they share key characteristics?

- What makes these children difficult to place – to what extent are the challenges posed by the system and to what extent by the children and the families themselves?

- Where do most of these children end up in the current systems available?

- What do we know about what would be the best forms of care and treatment for these difficult to place children?

Shared methods

Each of the three surveys undertaken as part of this research project was based on a shared methodology, which included:

1. *A set of core definitions*, particularly on the terms 'children', 'serious crime' and 'provision'. Children were defined using the UN definition as people up to and including 18 years of age. However, in the UK for example, this is different from our local legislation, which excludes 18-year-olds, and attention is drawn where different age ranges have been used in the report of the English study. Serious crime was defined as murder, manslaughter and attempts to do both

of these, acts of interpersonal violence, threatening behaviour if it is serious and/or includes use of weapons and sexual offences. Provision was defined as any sort of attempt to house the children, or support them while they stay with their families, or interventions to treat the underlying antisocial behaviour problems.

2. *A common sampling strategy.* It was specified that all social services departments or similar agencies with responsibility for child services and protection in each country would be asked to take part in the survey. Alternatively, a sample could be selected if it was not manageable to send the questionnaire out to all departments (Germany is much larger than England in terms of potential agencies, for example). The sample was also to include voluntary provision if appropriate.

3. *A shared survey questionnaire.* A postal questionnaire was designed for the study and translated into Greek and German. The questionnaire presented two brief case studies to clearly identify the types of children in whom we were interested, and asked the respondent agency representative some straightforward questions about the numbers of children like these who were the responsibility of their agency. More detail was then collected on a subset of up to four of these children, and the most information was collected on a further subset of two of the children. Questions included: 'Where has the child been living?' 'What risk factors are present in their background?' 'What have been the main problems in placing the child?'

4. *A shared procedure.* The approach included gathering some initial information on who was the most appropriate person in each agency to approach, and then posting of questionnaires to these people (or distribution of email versions). If there was no response within approximately four weeks, a follow-up telephone call was to be made. After six weeks it was suggested that non-respondents be sent a second copy of the questionnaire, and a final telephone call was anticipated at around eight weeks, after which efforts to extract data from that particular agency would cease. In practice, all three countries followed slightly different (locally appropriate) forms of this protocol.

Presentation of survey findings

It was a challenge to know how best to present the results of three related but separate studies. The rather different setting in each country meant that each country had to evolve a slightly different version of the project, suitable for their own systems. There were also differences in our approaches to the treatment of the quantitative data, reflecting in part the rather different sample sizes and response rates achieved in the three related studies, with Germany achieving the largest sample. We have thus chosen here to present each of these fieldwork studies separately in the next three brief chapters, but in the next section here we have included overarching conclusions that arise from a reading of all three together. What emerges, despite the differences, is remarkable consensus about the characteristics of these children, the problems they face and the best case scenarios we would like to achieve for them.

Conclusions from the three research areas
Common themes, interesting differences and messages for good practice

In this study we have attempted to make some initial stabs at establishing the prevalence of difficult to place children and the range of problems they present. However, the participating countries all struggled with response rates and we cannot assume that the information we have collected is representative of the target population in any statistical sense. The real value of this project has been in tackling questions about the range of difficulties posed by these children and the various ways in which different societies are addressing them. What is remarkable is that, given differences between the countries with regard to the history of child social care and the cultural differences, and the heterogeneity of the groups of children being described, there is so much similarity in the stories between Greece, Germany and England. The things we have particularly noted include the following:

- *Similarities in the characteristics of the children.* We had specified that we were interested in certain types of children and this of course meant that there were similarities in the children described back to us in all three countries. However, it was notable that the gender distributions were very similar, with more boys than girls in all three countries, and the average age of the group, at around 14 to 15 years, was also fairly constant. In all three countries the proportions of ethnic minorities in the sample was very low, just a small handful of children. In all three countries gender differences were consistent, with the girls presenting more problems of self-harm and inappropriate sexual behaviour in the form of promiscuity, while the boys presented more problems through their violence and abuse of others.

- *Similarities in the ordering of the risk factors* that social workers think exist in the backgrounds of these children's lives. Generally, in all three countries, a wide range of risk factors was indicated for all the children, as would have been anticipated given the severity of the problems the group had to show in order to be of interest for this study. In all three countries, the emphasis was on parenting difficulties. In all three countries, there was less emphasis on hyperactivity and neurological factors. As we discussed in the English section, this may in part reflect disciplinary preferences for certain explanations for behaviour, and a lack of assessment expertise in these issues.

- *Similarities in the reasons why the child is so difficult to manage or place.* At the individual level these were commonly attachment problems, violent behaviour, physical and mental health issues: at the family level, violence and neglect and a lack of cooperation; at the institutional level, lack of appropriate services, problems getting ownership for the child. System difficulties were recounted to be as challenging, if not more challenging, than the children themselves.

- *Similarities in the numbers of various options that had already been tried with these children.* In all three countries a wide range of options had been tried, widest in Germany and England/Wales. Use of psychiatric hospitals for placements was highest in Germany and very low in England/Wales and Greece. The factor analysis undertaken in Germany revealed two distinct groups of placement histories among their sample: a group with multiple placements in all sorts of locations outside the family, and a second group with a relatively stable family placement but temporary psychiatric hospitalisation. This second group does not seem to feature as strongly in the reports of the other countries although the data did not stretch to replicatory factor analysis on this occasion. However, interesting avenues for further research are suggested by these results.

- *Similarities in what would be the best options for these children.* Specialist input, often therapeutic, and specialist residential care were the most oft cited preferred options in all countries.

The pictures from the three pieces of fieldwork were not, however, identical. The differences relate mostly to the current circumstances of the children. It was particularly noticeable that in Greece these children had been retained within their families or with relatives (70%) to a greater extent than in England (less than 10%) or Germany (28%). Foster care was particularly rare in Greece, more common in Germany, and most common in England. Use of residential care was most common in Germany and England. The main difference with respect to the current placement of children was between Greece versus both England and Germany.

All three studies indicate the great difficulties and challenges facing staff trying to manage the care and treatment of these potentially violent children. The German report described the process as one of 'a strategy of trial and error'. A considerable issue raised was the instability of placements. As the respondent quoted at the end of the English/Welsh study stated, one main component of her wish list for her client was a placement that could respond to his needs for as long as necessary.

The consistency of these three fieldwork reports leads us to conclude that we know about these children. We know what their characteristics will be and we know what the challenges will be, and these are very similar across different cultural contexts and in the face of different resources. But the reports were also very consistent in reporting real problems in meeting the needs of this group, despite this knowledge. This is where the effort needs to be directed. We know what they are like, we know what they need. Now we have to invest in what will be, of necessity, very expensive, intensive, long-term, individually tailored specialist care if we are to untangle the knot of multiple risk factors in order to change the trajectory of the children's lives. We also need to anticipate that these efforts may not be welcomed by these challenging and uncooperative families. More research is needed on successful delivery of services in these circumstances.

10

Working with violent children in German youth services

Results of a survey

Doris Bender and Friedrich Lösel

Introduction to the German context

As in other countries, Germany has a differentiated system of services and measures for seriously aggressive children and their families. Before the age of 14 years, youngsters are not held responsible for criminal offences in Germany. This means that they are not referred to the criminal justice system but treated by the youth and family services. Even above the age of 14 years, German criminal law for young offenders is based on the principle of education rather than punishment (Streng 2002). Youth services cooperate intensively with the justice system, for example, in carrying out assessments for the juvenile penal court or delivering alternative treatment measures (Dünkel, Geng and Kirstein 1998).

At younger ages, there are various options for managing risks for particularly aggressive children. As long as the family seems to be basically intact, social workers, family counselling or therapy can offer ambulatory measures. When the child needs to be removed from the family, a first option is placement in a family-like group linked to a residential home, limited to six weeks ('acute measure'). Various options are available for longer-term care. One is placement with foster parents who are paid for each child in their care. Although the foster family must fulfil some basic criteria, parents do not need to undergo special training or possess special qualifications. A similar solution on a professional basis is placement in families in which at least one parent is a social worker by profession. This service is more expensive than regular foster care, and this measure is reserved primarily for younger and particularly difficult children.

Such children can also be placed temporarily in psychiatric hospitals or, for longer periods, in residential care institutions such as halfway houses or more or less closed homes, available in most German states. For adolescents who do not need residential care but supervision and help, there are three forms of residential groups (with eight to ten youngsters). These differ in terms of the intensity of care by social workers. Supervision and care can range from five to eight hours a week to permanent residence with the group, staffed by several social workers. In another type of programme, a couple lives with one to three difficult adolescents in a fixed location outside Germany (e.g. in a village in Greece) for about one year ('project abroad'). The other programme is special 'intensive individual socio-educational care' in which one social worker lives with one child in a remote location such as an alpine pasture for up to six months.

Method of the field study

We contacted the main youth welfare departments in Germany (610 institutions in 16 states) and sent them a translated version of the questionnaire with an accompanying letter providing information on the European project, which explained the relevance of the study for current German practice. Institutions from 12 states participated in the survey. Four states did not take part because of existing statewide regulations prohibiting such assessments. The mean response rate of institutions across participating states was 23 per cent.

Results of the field study

Description of children

Professionals mentioned 459 children with difficulties comparable to those described in the two case studies with whom they were currently working. Individual numbers ranged from 1 to 20 children, with an average of 4.4 (SD = 3.62) per questionnaire. Professionals were asked to select a maximum of four children and describe why each individual child was difficult to place. Eighty per cent of the questionnaires contained information on two children, 50.8 per cent on three and 40.8 per cent on four children.

A detailed description was provided for 352 children. Their mean age was 14.6 years (SD = 2.34; range = 6–20 years). The relation of boys to girls was approximately 3:1 (73% boys vs. 27% girls). The majority (84.3%) were of German nationality, 4.3% came from other countries of the European Union and 2.4% from South-Eastern Europe. The sample also contained single children from Africa, North and South America, Vietnam and Turkey. No information on nationality was given for 7.1 per cent of the children.

Difficulties in placing the child

When analysing the answers to the question why these children were difficult to place, we found 64 qualitatively different reasons. The most frequent single category (30.4%) was the child's high level of aggression. Answers could be classified into problems referring to deficits in the child (75%), in the parents or the family (17.2%) or in the institutions involved (7.8%). Figure 10.1 presents the main results on child-related features. To some extent, categories with similar content have been aggregated in this figure.

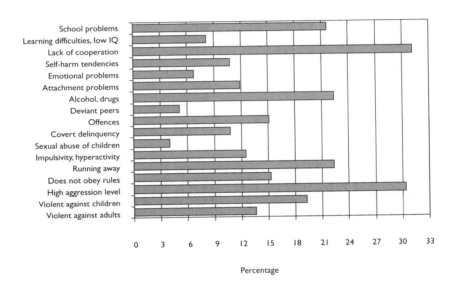

Figure 10.1 Reasons for difficulties in placing the child: characteristics of the child

Difficulties in placing the child were attributed most frequently to the child's behaviour. Taking related categories together, violence against others and a general high level of aggression were the main problem in nearly half of all cases (48.3%). Other important reasons were the child's lack of cooperation with social services and professionals (31.2%), consumption of alcohol and/or drugs (22.4%) and serious problems at school (21.6%). These included truancy, refusal to go to school and suspension. Running away from institutions (22.4%), not obeying rules and limits (15.3%) and having committed official offences (15.1%) were further frequent reasons for difficulty in placing the child.

Table 10.1 shows the main results in family and institution related difficulties. Parents' lack of cooperation and failure to support social services measures were the most frequently mentioned reason for failure. This was followed in second place by parental problems. These included psychological disorders, alcohol problems or excessive stress. In total, parental problems and deficits played a role in 42 per cent of the children's problems. Social workers also

Table 10.1 Difficulties in placing the child: family and institution problems

Problem	%
Child maltreatment	8.0
Child neglect	10.5
Child sexual abuse	6.3
Parental problems (e.g. alcohol)	13.9
Parental relationship problems	4.0
Parent–child problems	5.7
Parents' lack of cooperation	19.0
Refusal of institutions to take the child	8.2
Lack of places/institutions	6.0

named domestic violence/child maltreatment, child neglect or sexual abuse quite frequently. Summing up these items, 20.2 per cent of the children were victims of abuse within their immediate living environment.

Problems linked to institutions were also mentioned as reasons for difficulties in placing children. These categories contained answers like 'institutions refuse to take the child' or 'there is a lack of adequate services or not enough places'.

GENDER DIFFERENCES

Comparisons between boys and girls revealed that girls caused more frequent problems through promiscuity ($r = 0.24$, $p < 0.001$), deviant peer groups ($r = 0.13$, $p < 0.05$) and running away ($r = 0.14$, $p < 0.01$). They more frequently became victims of sexual abuse ($r = 0.13$, $p < 0.05$) and were more difficult to place because of self-harm and suicidal tendencies. In contrast, boys caused more problems through violent behaviour and the sexual abuse of other children ($r = 0.13$, $p < 0.05$). They also more frequently committed official offences ($r = 0.20$, $p < 0.001$). Overall, boys showed significantly more externalising and less internalising problems than girls.

Characteristics of individual cases: current living situation

We obtained detailed descriptions of up to two children per agency, resulting in descriptions of 232 children. Data on the current living situation are presented in Figure 10.2. Nearly a third of the sample (27.6%) was currently living either with both parents, one parent or another family member. A substantial number of children (22.8%) were in residential care. As Figure 10.2 shows, very few children were living with foster parents, were in closed units or in prison, in a

children's psychiatric hospital or participating in intensive care projects outside
Germany.

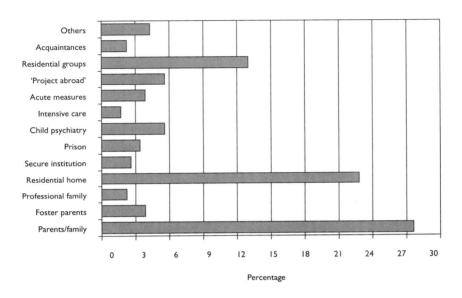

Figure 10.2 Children's current living situation

Prior placements

A similar picture emerged when we looked at the children's prior placements.
On average, they named 3.1 (SD = 1.77) placements per child (range = 0 to 8).
Frequencies of individual nominations are shown in Table 10.2.

At some time in their past, the majority of children had lived with their
family of origin. However, more than half the sample had already been in residential care as well, and half of them had stayed in a children's psychiatric
hospital. A substantial number of children had experienced the above-mentioned 'acute measures'. More than a quarter had lived in residential groups,
slightly fewer in foster families and ten per cent in a closed unit. Approximately
seven per cent had lived with a family in which one parent was a social worker
('professional families').

Relations between different prior placements

Factor analysis of prior placements (using placement categories with frequency
greater than 5%) revealed two factors. The first factor (24% of variance) clearly
indicated a trend towards multiple different placements outside the family. The

Table 10.2 Children's prior placements

Placement	%
Parents/family member	83.6
Foster parents	19.9
'Professional' families	7.3
Residential home	59.1
Secure institution	10.3
Prison	0.4
Child psychiatry	50.0
Intensive individual care	0.9
Acute measures lasting maximum six weeks	38.4
Project abroad	4.3
Residential groups	26.7
Acquaintances/partner	1.7
Others	8.2

second factor (15% of variance) pointed to children who lived in relatively stable family conditions but required temporary psychiatric hospitalisation. (Details of the factor analysis are available from author on request.)

Problems in the child's background

Professionals were asked to give one of four ratings to problems in the child's background: definitely present, might be present, clearly not present, or no available information. Results are shown in Figure 10.3.

According to the social workers in our study, almost the entire sample had problems at school such as truancy or suspension (92.3%). The majority of children had learning difficulties (69.9%), behaviour problems since early childhood (76.8%) and experience of family conflict and violence (85.3%). Approximately half of the sample misused substances (47.3%), had delinquent peers (46.1%), were high-risk personalities (46.7%), and were probably victims of neglect or abuse (51.4%). The other factors were present for a third of our children.

Services to which children had been referred

In terms of referrals to other services, on average 4.1 different services were reported per child (SD = 1.82; range = 0 to 9). Services provided are shown in Figure 10.4. As could be expected, the allocated social worker was named in nearly 100 per cent of cases. The majority of children (78.0%) had been

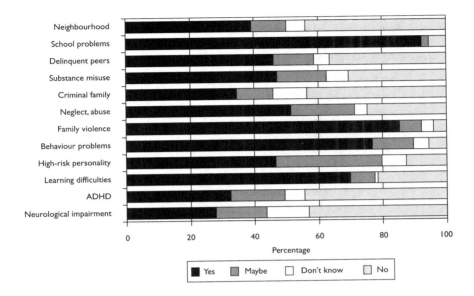

Figure 10.3 Child's background factors

referred to a child psychiatrist and more than half (53.4%) to a counselling centre. More than a third (37.9%) had attended a school psychologist, and a third (33.2%) a paediatrician. Approximately a fifth (20.3%) had been referred to a paediatric clinic and 15.6 per cent received any kind of therapy. Approximately 10 per cent had received services for their substance misuse, and a similar proportion had been supervised by probation services. Special programmes such as intensive individual care or staying abroad were each applied in less than 5 per cent of cases.

Analysis of referrals to services that the children had not received (although recommended by professionals) showed that nearly a quarter of the children should have been referred in each case to a child psychiatrist (23.3%), a counselling centre (22.8%), a family therapist or an individual therapist (22%). Substance misuse services were also recommended for a substantial number of children (16.4%).

Reasons for non-availability of services

The social workers listed various reasons why children had not yet been referred to the services they had recommended. One reason was lack of availability (Figure 10.5). Among non-available services, the most frequently named service was intensive individual care in which one social worker looks after one

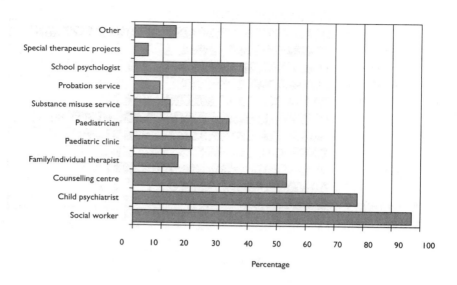

Figure 10.4 Services to which children had been referred

child (12%). Any kind of therapy (10.1%), a secure unit (7.4%), and special socio-educational measures (5.6%) were also mentioned in more than 5 per cent of cases. However, non-availability was not the main reason for 20.3 per cent of answers.

In general, other reasons for non-uptake by services fell into three categories: reasons concerning parents, children and institutions. About half of the answers (48.3%) applied to the family (parents and children) that originally should have benefited from the service. Already more than a third of the answers referred to the described child. In particular, serious problem behaviour (13.1%) or lack of motivation and cooperation in the child (15.9%) were named as reasons why services could not be offered or ended with early dropout. In nearly a fifth of cases (19.3%) the reason was a lack of parental cooperation with individual services or professionals. A similar proportion of reasons was attributed to the institutions themselves (22.1%). Typical answers were a lack of places, a long waiting period, considerable distance from the child's place of residence or high expenses.

Best option for the child

Professionals were asked to recommend a best option for the child independently of whether the service was available or not. Results are presented in Figure

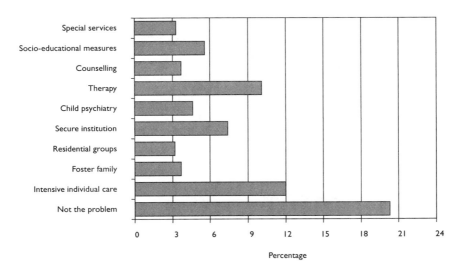

Figure 10.5 Unavailable services

10.6. On the one hand, answers contained services already described above. On the other, more psychosocial interventions were recommended. For example, the child should be taken out of a negative environment (12.7%), placed in a well-structured context (10.9%) and given a stable and caring reference person (10.9%). The most frequently mentioned specific services were individual therapy for the child (23.5%) followed by intensive individual care (17.4%) and educational training measures (15.7%). The professionals also recommended more parenting support for the family (11.2%). In 7.8 per cent of cases respectively, they suggested placing the child in either a foster family, in a residential home or in a secure unit. Only a tenth (9.1%) thought that the current service was the best option for the child described. Finally, they considered that it was too late for a further option in less than 5 per cent of cases.

Discussion and conclusions: German fieldwork study

Although we cannot claim that our findings are representative for all youth services throughout Germany, we do have a relatively broad database. It contains information from 121 social workers on 352 children, with 232 of these children being described in more detail. The response rate of 23 per cent in the participating German states lies within the normal range, particularly as we can assume that a proportion of services did not participate because they were currently not working with any cases from our target population.

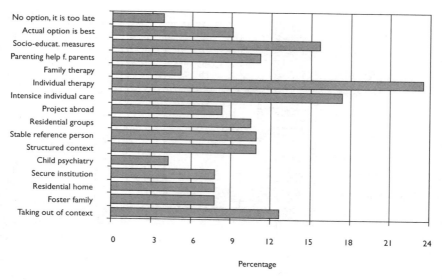

Figure 10.6 Best option for the child

On average, social workers name just over four children with a mean age of 14 years who fit the case descriptions of serious and persistent aggression. This confirms that our group represents only a small proportion of the prevalence of 7 per cent of youngsters exhibiting conduct problems in Germany (Ihle and Esser 2002). However, the problems of the children described in our survey are particularly serious and persistent. Whereas most children with some antisocial behaviour stay in their families and receive only temporary ambulatory treatment or even no treatment at all, the majority of our group have already been referred to a number of different placements and services. Hence, only about a third of the children are living with their family of origin at the time of the survey. Such findings indicate the great difficulties youth services have with these children. Despite their attempts to find a good and stable solution in each case, they sometimes end up applying a strategy of trial and error.

Overall, however, the need for multiple placements and measures is plausible because of their multiple problems and deprivations, which confirm the knowledge gathered from prospective studies on risk factors for serious and violent young offenders (Loeber and Farrington 1998; see also Lösel and Bender, Chapter 3 this volume). As expected, there are far more boys than girls in our group. They also reveal more violence and externalising behaviour, whereas the girls show a stronger tendency toward self-harm and internalising problems.

Ninety per cent of the answers describing difficulties in placing the child refer to child and family related deficits. Accordingly, the children and their families often find it hard to cooperate with youth services, and they refuse measures. Taken together, these prove to be more frequent reasons for not receiving a service than lack of availability. We do not know how valid these attributions are. However, treatment of antisocial behaviour always bears the risk of interpreting motivational problems more as a client characteristic and less as an interactive issue (McMurran 2002). It is important to note that in a fifth of the cases social workers also named practical obstacles related to their services. In addition, for many respondents the best options are not those currently or previously given to the child. In particular, they emphasise the need for more intensive, individualised and therapeutic measures along with a stable, structured context containing a caring reference person.

This issue of best options brings our findings to bear on the current state of research and practice in the field of seriously antisocial children in Germany. Although numerous services and measures are available, there is a clear lack of controlled evaluations of their outcomes (Lösel 2004; Lösel and Beelmann 2003). More systematic research on risk assessment, prevention and treatment is needed to help high-risk children and their families at the earliest stage in development and as effectively as possible.

References

Dünkel, F., Geng, B. and Kirstein, W. (1998) *Soziale Trainingskurse und andere ambulante Maßnahmen nach dem JGG in Deutschland [Social Trainings and Other Ambulatory Measures Specified in the German Juvenile Court Act]*. Bonn: Forum Verlag.

Ihle, W. and Esser, G. (2002) 'Epidemiologie psychischer Störungen im Kindes- und Jugendalter: Prävalenz, Verlauf, Komorbidität und Geschlechtsunterschiede' [Epidemiology of psychological disorders in childhood and adolescence: Prevalence, course, comorbidity and gender differences]. *Psychologische Rundschau 53*, 159–169.

Loeber, R. and Farrington, D.P. (eds) (1998) *Serious and Violent Juvenile Offenders: Risk Factors and Successful Interventions*. Thousand Oaks, CA: Sage.

Lösel, F. (2004) 'Multimodale Gewaltprävention bei Kindern und Jugendlichen: Familie, Kindergarten, Schule' [Multi-modal prevention of violence in children and adolescents: Family, kindergarden, school]. In W. Melzer and H.-D. Schwind (eds) *Gewaltprävention in der Schule: Grundlagen – Praxismodelle – Perspektiven*. Baden-Baden: Nomos, pp.326–348.

Lösel, F. and Beelmann, A. (2003) 'Effects of child skills training in preventing antisocial behavior: A systematic review of randomized evaluations.' *Annals of the American Academy of Political and Social Science 587*, 84–109.

McMurran, M. (2002) 'Motivation to change: Selection criterion or treatment need.' In M. McMurran (ed) *Motivating Offenders to Change*. Chichester: Wiley, pp.3–13.

Streng, F. (2002) *Strafrechtliche Sanktionen: Die Strafzumessung und ihre Grundlagen [Penal Law Sanctions: Sentencing and its Principles]*. Stuttgart: Kohlhammer.

11

Children who commit serious acts of interpersonal violence

A field study in Greece

Helen Agathonos, Vivi Tsibouka and Angeliki Skoubourdi

Introduction to the Greek context

Greece, a European Union country with a population of 11 million, of which 2.7 million are under the age of 18 years, is undergoing a substantial evolution that is linked with political, economic and social changes at national level as well as in relation to its strategic geographical position. A traditionally homo-geneous country in terms of ethnicity and religion of the population, Greece is becoming the host country to large numbers of economic and migrant workers and political refugees, transit, temporary or permanent. These phenomena have had positive consequences on the one hand (i.e. increasing the workforce), while on the other, negative findings suggest a rising trend of juvenile criminality.

A small number of studies in Greece have been addressing the issue of juvenile offending. The association between maltreatment in childhood and juvenile offending has been the subject of studies in the last decade (Hadzichristou and Papadatos 1993; Kourakis and Milioni 1995). A follow-up study of physically abused and neglected children during he first five years of life disclosed a significant association with offending behaviour in early adolescence. At mean age 11.5 years, 44 per cent of children victims had already been involved in at least one act of serious interpersonal violence (Agathonos-Georgopoulou 2004). A high association between exploitation in childhood and juvenile offending was found in a recent study in Thessaloniki: 41 per cent of juveniles were victims of physical or sexual abuse and 65 per cent were neglected and exploited by their families (Papanastoulis 2003). Two studies of children in secure accommodation focused on issues of discrimination as to the right to equity and access to education among youths (Panteliadou 1993; Petropoulos et al. 2000). Lastly, the question of imprisonment or social support and reintegration has been the subject of an open debate among professionals in Greece (Atsalakis 1996).

Until recently, juvenile justice in Greece has been functioning on the basis of a 1950 Penal Code and Code of Penal Procedures and their various amendments. Nevertheless, new phenomena made necessary modifications to meet emerging needs. In 2003, under the influence of international conventions and recommendations introduced primarily by the United Nations and the Council of Europe, the Greek Parliament adopted Act 3189/2003 on the 'reform of the legislation concerning minors', while amendments and additions were made to the Code of Penal Procedure. The protection of juvenile victims was also strengthened with Act 064/2002. Both were incorporated in the Greek Penal Code. A Bill establishing 'Units for the Care of Youngsters' (delinquents and victims at risk) is at present in preparation (Spinellis and Tsitsoura 2004).

The new legislative framework, which is quite progressive, requires the creation of infrastructure in conjunction with a new ideology towards children, from being 'dangerous' to others to being 'in danger'. The results of the field study in Greece confirm the need for policy measures that would prioritise primary and secondary prevention while orienting tertiary prevention within the special provisions of the UN Convention on the Rights of the Child 1989.

Methodology

The field study in Greece was carried out over a five-month period from January to May 2004. The questionnaire was translated into Greek and adapted to comply with the local situation as to classifications of employment and other minor differences. Questionnaires were sent to 202 services, the total service network pertaining to the various sectors dealing with at risk children, with an accompanying letter describing the aims and the implications of the study results at national level. The agencies contacted belonged to the following sectors: Welfare (74), Justice (68), Mental Health (50), NGO/other (10).

Results

Characteristics of services

From the 202 agencies contacted 89 (44%) responded, an attrition rate of 56 per cent. Among those having responded, 64 (79%) answered that they do not have such cases while 25 (21%) replied positively. As a result, the field study comprised 25 services distributed as follows: Welfare, 10 (40%), Justice, 11 (44%), Mental Health, 3 (12%) and NGO, 1 (4%).

Characteristics of children

Professionals were asked how many children in their current caseload present with difficulties similar to those in the two case studies included in the questionnaire. An average of three children was known in each service, with a range from one to eight cases.

Among the 25 services, a total of 60 children were identified as meeting the requirements of the study. Of these, 47 (78%) were boys and 13 (22%) were girls. Their age ranged from 10 to 17.5 years (mean age 14.8 years). All children were of Greek ethnicity. Information on present and past place of domicile of the children was obtained in 43 cases (Table 11.1).

Table 11.1 Child's present and past place of domicile (n = 43)

Place	Present		Past*	
	Number	%	Number	%
At home with parents/relatives	22	52	29	67
Relatives only	7	16	3	7
Institution	12	28	11	25
Hospital's special unit	1	2	3	7
Secure unit	–	–	1	2
Other	1	2	3	7

*More than one placement

Of the children, one in two were found to live at home, while over one in four lived in institutions at the time of the study, followed by a small number living with relatives, while one child was undergoing treatment at a special psychiatric unit of a children's hospital. It is obvious from Table 11.1 that in the past some children had more than one placement.

Professionals were asked to identify factors pertaining to the history of each child. Answers ranged from 'yes' to 'no' as follows: (a) Yes – definitely true; (b) Unsure – might be the case; (c) No – clearly not a factor; (d) Don't know – not enough information. Table 11.2 depicts the risk factors in the child's history reported as 'Definitely true', by order of frequency.

School problems characterise the background of almost all children, followed by experiences of poor parenting and possible abuse. A large number of children grew up in violent families, while one in four children had delinquent siblings and/or other adult family members with criminal behaviour. One in two children participated in a gang or in a delinquent peer group while more than one in three children lived in a problematic neighbourhood. School problems seem to be associated with learning difficulties, behaviour problems,

Table 11.2 Risk factors in child's history reported as 'definitely true'

Risk factors	%
School problems	88
Poor parenting – possible abuse	74
Family conflict and violence	67
Learning difficulties	64
Behaviour problems since childhood	59.5
Delinquent peers or gang participation	48
Neighbouring problems	38
High-risk personality	36
Hyperactivity	36
Criminality of family members/delinquent siblings	26
Substance misuse by child	14
Neurological impairment	12

hyperactivity, neurological impairment, a personality described as 'high risk', and in a few cases substance misuse.

In their efforts to manage the child, services had referred children to other more specialised settings while a considerable number had asked for consultation. In total there were 101 referrals or 2.4 per child, while 53 consultations were asked or 1.3 per child. Most referrals were to mental health services or private services (56%), followed by an allocated social worker (18), special education (7), paediatrician (6) and substance misuse service (4), while ten referrals were to 'other' settings. A similar distribution was found for consultations asked.

Professionals were asked to state the reasons why children were difficult to manage or to place. Their responses disclosed a population of children with multiple problems and a heavy load of adverse life circumstances. These were grouped into four categories (Table 11.3).

In their efforts to help children or to find a 'good enough' placement for them, professionals are challenged with a variety of problems, as depicted in Table 11.4. Problems related to the system outnumber others, followed by difficulties related to family factors and last, those associated with the child. It is worth noting that in only one case had professionals not been challenged by any difficulties so far.

When help was sought for the children, system related problems were the most frequent obstacles. Difficulties in access, high costs and insufficient intra-service collaboration were described in 30 cases, while family and child related factors were found in seven and four cases respectively. In two cases only were services described as sufficient.

Table 11.3 Reasons why child is difficult to manage/place
(more than one reason reported for many children)

Reasons related to the child	34	Attachment problems, violent/challenging behaviour, refusal to cooperate, school problems or dropping out, sexually abusing other children, health problems linked with violent behaviour.
Reasons related to the family	37	Poor parenting, family problems/violence, attachment problems, rejection/neglect of child, parental death
Reasons related to the system	32	Lack of therapeutic services, insufficient/bad intra-service collaboration, services cannot meet child's needs, child 'unwanted' by system
Family refuses to cooperate	10	

Table 11.4 General problems and challenges
in helping/placing child

Child related reasons	13	Refused to cooperate, dropped out of care
Family related reasons	22	Multi-problem family, poor parenting, rejection of child, uncooperative
System related reasons	24	No services available or difficult access because of distance and costs, insufficient/inappropriate services for children's needs, 'unwanted' case, placement breakdown
No difficulties encountered so far	1	

Professionals were asked for their opinion on the best option for each child. Individual therapeutic treatment (19, or 36%) and therapeutic residential care (18, or 35%) were their primary options, followed by individual treatment of parents or family therapy (9, or 17%). In four cases (8%), the child staying on or returning to his or her own family but with support was considered as the best option, followed by placement in a foster family in two cases (4%).

Discussion: Greek fieldwork study

The results of the field study confirm the knowledge already existing on the links between the prevalence of severe and multiple risk factors in early childhood and the early onset of aggressive, disruptive and antisocial behaviour (English, Widom and Brandford 2002; Falshaw and Browne 1999; Widom 1989). In spite of the difficulties characterising these children in conjunction with their adverse family situations, one in two lives at home, with one or both natural parents or in a reconstituted family, while one in three lives in an institution. These findings seem to be different from those of other EU countries in which most of these children live in residential or in foster care. Within the Greek reality, in which children in care comprise 0.1 per cent of the child population aged between 0 and 18 years, a 28 per cent rate depicts a population with special characteristics, causing severe problems to their families. It seems as though these families cannot draw resources from their relatives and neighbourhoods, being themselves disrupted, socially isolated and 'unwanted' by their communities, just as their children are 'unwanted' by them. Under these circumstances, the child's life with its family can be regarded as either a risk or as a protective factor. A Greek follow-up study of physically abused and neglected children disclosed that those who stayed at home with professional support presented with fewer behaviour problems in comparison with those placed in residential care (Agathonos-Georgopoulou, Browne and Sarafidou 2004).

The high preponderance of boys over girls is not surprising; nevertheless, the early onset of delinquency in this population is quite alarming. Considering the seriousness of the problems these children are presenting with, interventions in their families must commence very early in their lifecycle so that intergenerational continuities in deprivation and family psychopathology are prevented.

The accumulation of problems in children and their seriousness are expected to cause learning difficulties and school problems such as bullying (as victims or victimisers), absenteeism and dropping out. These are accentuated by the fact that in Greece special education is addressed to children who have learning disabilities or suffer from mental handicap, in the absence of serious behaviour disorders. Meanwhile, there are no therapeutic settings offering schooling for children presenting with such difficulties. This situation leads to their social exclusion and to the perpetuation of a cycle of deprivation and violence. It is obvious that professionals in Greece find themselves in extremely difficult situations as they have no tools they can work with. Most of the problems that professionals are challenged with are system related. There is a total lack of specialised services while those existing are mostly inappropriate, inefficient, understaffed and characterised by a high professional burn-out.

The situation in the welfare sector is no different. Placing these children in residential care is very problematic as settings require a social worker's and a mental health worker's report on the child's 'health and mental capacity'. This requirement excludes children with a history of severe behaviour problems whereas those who may be admitted are not usually kept for long or drop out. The failure of the welfare system to help these children acts as an open door to the juvenile justice system in which most of them are found when they leave the care system at age 18 years.

The field study in Greece depicts a relatively small population of children who are not only unwanted by their families but also by the system. Unfortunately, decision makers responsible for the prioritisation of problems and for the allocation of resources tend to prefer the political correctness of funding programmes that cure ill health rather than intervene in families' 'asylum' after they fail to parent their children. In Greece, a country in which the traditional extended family is no longer the norm and where the support of the community is gradually replaced by the social isolation of urban environments, there is a need for the development of preventive programmes at community level. In the late 1990s, the law for decentralisation allocated responsibilities to prefectures and municipalities, without necessarily allocating the funds involved in many programmes addressed to children and their families. This gap has to be filled, together with the introduction of innovative therapeutic services for children who 'do not fit' into the existing system, while professional training and staffing of services within a multidisciplinary approach are essential. There is a need for evidence-based, cost effective programmes that, while taking into consideration the complexity of the phenomenon, are scientifically robust and politically convincing.

References

Agathonos-Georgopoulou, H. (2004) 'Child abuse and neglect and juvenile delinquency: Communicating chambers?' *Psychology 11*, 2, 141–161 [in Greek].

Agathonos-Georgopoulou, H., Browne, K.D. and Sarafidou, J. (2004) 'An evaluation of abused children's behavior following intervention: A follow-up study in Greece.' In H. G. Eriksson and T. Tjelflaat (eds) *Residential Care: Horizons for the New Century*. Aldershot: Ashgate.

Atsalakis, M. (1996) 'Imprisonment of juvenile delinquents or social support and rehabilitation? Suppression or prevention?' *Mandragoras 10–11*, 22 [in Greek].

English, D.J., Widom, C.S. and Brandford, C. (2002) *Childhood Victimization and Delinquency, Adult Criminality and Violent Criminal Behavior. A Replication and Extension.* Final report presented to the National Institute of Justice, Grant No 97-IJ-CX-bo17.

Falshaw, L. and Browne, K.D. (1999) 'A young man referred to specialist secure accommodation.' *Child Abuse Review 8*, 419–432.

Hadzichristou, Ch. and Papadatos, Y. (1993) 'Juvenile delinquents' perception of childhood parental rearing patterns.' *Child Abuse and Neglect 17*, 487–494.

Kourakis, N. and Milioni, F. (1995) *A Survey in Greek Prisons. A: The Special Detention Centres of Korydallos and Kassavetia.* Athens-Komotini: A.N. Sakkoulas [in Greek].

Panteliadou, S. (1993) 'Fifth Panhellenic Conference of Psychological Research.' *Adolescence 77*, 90–92 [in Greek].

Papanastoulis, B. (2003) 'The children of abuse: Juvenile delinquents have a history as victims.' *Eleftherotypia*, 4 April [in Greek].

Petropoulos, N., Laganas, N., Makridis, G. and Papaioannou, M. (2000) 'The educational needs and the interests of juveniles in educational and secure accommodation institutions.' In E. Daskalakis, P. Papadopoulou, D. Tsambarli, I. Tsinganou and E. Fronimou (eds) *Criminals and Victims at the Step of the 21st Century.* Daskalakis, Athens: National Centre for Social Research [in Greek].

Spinellis, C.D. and Tsitsoura, A. (2004) *Juvenile Justice in Greece* (in press).

United Nations Convention on the Rights of the Child (1989) UN Doc. A/Res./ 44 /25. Geneva: UN.

Widom, C.S. (1989) 'The cycle of violence.' *Science 244,* 160–166.

12

Dealing with the children who are hardest to place

Results of a survey of childcare agencies in England and Wales

Ann Hagell and Emily Hill

Introduction to the English/Welsh context

The organisation of English and Welsh social care for children is a system in some flux at the time of writing. A new Children Act is introducing major changes to the organisation of children's services, with a new director of children's services covering education, health and children's social care in each local authority area, delivering both prevention and intervention to children in need in a coordinated and systematic way. At the time of the research these changes had not come into effect (such as the establishment of new 'Children's Trusts'). However, the aims of social work with children will remain essentially the same – to safeguard children and young people and to promote their welfare. Provision comes from the statutory authorities, as directed by government and as delivered by the 150+ local authorities covering England and Wales, but also from the voluntary sector and the private sector.

The majority of children falling into the 'very difficult to manage' category will be children who are 'looked after' – some of these are looked after by the local authority with parental agreement and can return home at any time, while others are in care under a compulsory order. Some are looked after by other members of their family or by friends; others are placed in foster homes, others in residential homes, which can be open or secure. They nearly all have backgrounds of neglect, abuse, or other family problems. Fostering is an option and there are also some independent and private fostering options. The children live in a home, but are not legally adopted by their foster parents. It is expected that the placement will not be permanent (unlike adoption). There is much concern about the national shortage of foster parents and the instability of all types of care placement, as well as the consistently demonstrated poor outcomes for children in state care.

For the most difficult children within the child social care world, there are the secure local authority children's homes. There are 28 of these types of unit across the country placed within local communities, accommodating around eight or so children at any one time. Children who have been prosecuted for violent offences, as opposed to those who seem likely to be violent but are being maintained within the social care network, are processed through the Youth Justice System. While a very small proportion end up in local authority units, the remainder of those sentenced to custody will go either to secure training centres or to prison service accommodation – young offenders institutions (YOIs). Secure training centres are part of the prison estate and house around 40 children in a 'junior' version of YOIs. They do not bear much resemblance to local authority secure units, which are more like homes. The children are there as part of a criminal sentence, not for care purposes. The sentences are either time limited or indefinite in cases of children who murder or commit the most serious violent offences.

However, for the children who are difficult to place with other children, either within or outwith the prison service, there are few options. This is particularly the case for those not on a custodial sentence – but even those locked up in prison service accommodation return to their local communities at some point. We now describe the English/Welsh portion of the comparative fieldwork assessing how many children raise these types of challenges to care provision, how they are dealt with, and whether examples of good practice can be identified.

Sampling and methods

Sample

After receiving full approval from the Association of Directors of Social Services (ADSS), all 168 social services departments in England and Wales with responsibility for child protection services were asked to take part in the survey. Out of the 168 agencies, 31 responses were received (18%), despite a concerted effort to contact the relevant key personnel. The low response rate is very common among postal and telephone surveys of social care staff, particularly at a time of reorganisation.

Survey questionnaire

An English version of the questionnaire was administered via the post during February 2004. A series of follow-up phone calls and contacts were made over a nine-month period to increase the response rate.

Background data on the respondents to the survey

Responses were from agencies within England (n = 25) and Wales (n = 6). The majority of respondents were working for departments within Children and Families Services, ranging from looked after children and child protection teams to disability and residential childcare teams. Other agencies that completed the survey included a children's home and a secure unit.

On average, each social service had 6.7 children that met our description of a child that was potentially dangerous and difficult to treat. If we extrapolate from this to the country as a whole, assuming the same number of 'difficult to place' children in all local authorities, we can guess that there are over 1000 children classified by their social services department to be in this category.

Demographics of these difficult to place, potentially threatening children

Social services respondents were asked to identify four of their difficult children on whom to provide a little more data. There were 99 children in the resulting baseline sample of difficult to place children. Over half of the sample (64%) were boys. The average age of the children was 14 years, with the mode (most frequent) being 15 years (n = 27). Most (86%) were white, 6 per cent were black and the same proportion were of mixed ethnicity; 1 per cent were recorded as Asian.

Social care staff then provided more detailed information on any two of these four children. For those children in the 'individual cases' sample (n = 59), questions were also asked about the child's current and previous living situation. As Figure 12.1 shows, the majority of children (n = 29, 48%) were accommodated in residential care (e.g. a children's home). The next largest group were living in a regional or secure unit (n = 8, 13%) or in a form of accommodation other than what was listed. Amongst the 'other' living circumstances was an independent council flat, a specialist therapeutic placement (not local authority [LA]) and a bed and breakfast. Only a small number of children (n = 6, 10%) were accommodated in some form of foster care with a local authority carer, with a specialist or secure carer, or in an independent placement. Three children lived at home with a family member.

When looking at previous accommodation situations of these children, as well as having lived with a family member (n = 39, 65%) again the majority had also been in some form of residential placement (n = 39, 65%). While almost two-thirds (62%) of these children had previously lived in some form of foster placement, only 8 per cent (n = 3) were still living in foster care, suggesting potentially high levels of breakdown of foster care placements.

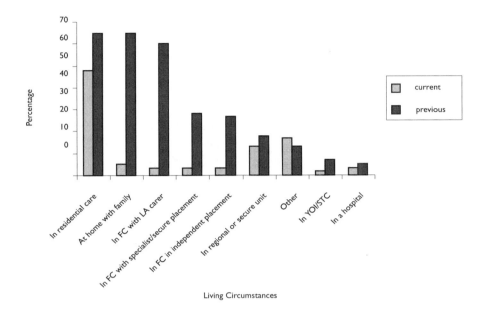

Figure 12.1 Current and previous living circumstances of the children for whom more detailed data were provided. Base = 59; 'FC' = foster care; YOI / STC = young offenders insitution or secure training centre

Characteristics of potentially dangerous children

Figure 12.2 highlights the 'risk factors' that respondents thought were 'definitely' associated with the child's current problems. Of the 59 children that this question was asked about, family conflict and violence was shown as being the factor most present in the child's background (88%). This was followed closely by poor parenting/possible abuse, and behavioural problems (present for 81% and 82% respectively). Neurological impairments were only definitely said to exist in 7 per cent of the children's backgrounds. However, a third of respondents (33%) were 'unsure' and thought that it might be the case for these children.

Essentially the patterning of risk factors is pretty much as one might expect from the research literature, except where it is likely that social care staff were not qualified or experienced enough to judge (for example, neurological problems of some kind are more likely than this patterning of risk factors suggests).

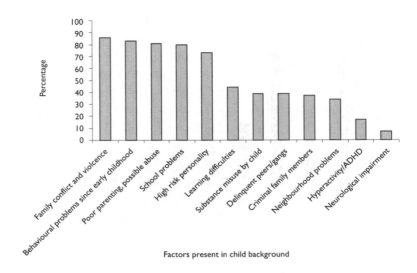

Figure 12.2 Risk factors reported to be 'definitely' present in the child's background. Base = 59

Services accessed by these children

Figure 12.3 highlights the services that such children have been referred to, either currently or in the past. As we would have expected, all children (bar two who were missing data) had an allocated social worker. Only two children did not appear to have been referred to a mental health professional (e.g. child psychologist, psychiatrist) at any point in their lives. Most of the services on the list are likely to have been fairly specialised and only used in extremes by social care staff, so the wide range indicates the multiple efforts that staff were making to draw in extra help for these particularly troubled young people.

Why are these children difficult to place?

Challenges posed to social care services

Respondents were asked to comment on the general problems and challenges that their department had faced in placing such children. First, as may be expected, difficulties transpired due to the characteristics of the child and these are listed in Table 12.1.

In addition, for many of the children, their own refusal to be treated or stay in a particular placement also proved to be a huge issue:

Her inability and unwillingness to engage in any therapeutic or stable relationships is a fundamental factor. Periods of absconding when her behaviour became extremely dangerous often meant identifying placements at the point of crisis.

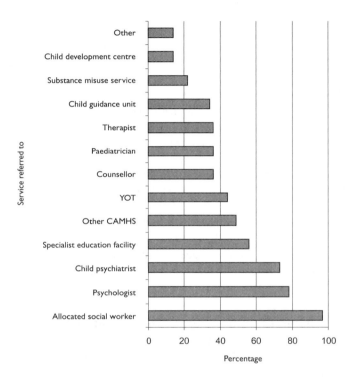

Figure 12.3 Range of statutory services that these children have been referred to. Base = 57 (2 missing data)

Thus, due to such extreme behavioural problems, the qualitative data reflected that numerous placements had broken down for these children, and so placement history has made other agencies reluctant to care for these young people.

The second group of difficulties were found in the characteristics of the family, as Table 12.2 shows. Such children often came from backgrounds with a history of family violence, poor parenting and abuse. In some cases, parents would be an influential factor as to why a child was not able to access the most appropriate treatment/placement. As one professional highlighted:

The parents wanted their child to remain in their care for as long as possible and would not consider specialist placements earlier in his life.

Table 12.1 Characteristics of the child that could affect placement

Characteristics	Includes
Behavioural difficulties	Disruptive placements; danger to animals; physically/verbally abusive; impulsive/hyperactive; offending; soliciting; physically domineering; negative attitude to women; lack of respect for authority figures; sexualised behaviour
Mental health problems	Attachment disorder, ADHD, conduct disorder, bipolar disorder, etc.; psychotic episodes; emotional problems
Special needs	Learning disabilities; special needs (e.g. deaf, special educational needs)
Child difficult to engage	Lack of remorse; not conforming; refusing treatment
'Needy' child	History of abuse (sexual, physical, emotional); exposure to domestic violence; vulnerable/placing themselves at risk
Multiple placements	Absconding from placements; requires individual placement as can't be placed with younger children
Self-harming/overdosing	Cutting; suicide attempts
Sexual abuse of children and others	High risk of sexual behaviour when with other children
Arson/damaging property	Fire-setting history; vandalism
Substance misusing	Drug/alcohol abuse
Disruptive education	Exclusions, little or no education

Table 12.2 Characteristics of the child's family that could affect placement

Characteristics	Includes
Family difficult to engage	Reluctance to engage with services for child
Violent/offending siblings	Siblings with history of violent behaviour; spent time in custody
Relationship problems	Attachment issues; difficult relationship with parents; unresolved family issues

Other reasons why family circumstances would hinder placements included reluctance to engage, poor parental involvement, parents undermining placements if they could see their child was settling and the influence of the child's siblings on their behaviour.

Third, and perhaps most revealingly, characteristics of the agency also came out of the qualitative analysis as a prominent factor in the difficulties surrounding placement of such children. As one social worker described their dilemma:

Lack of agreement between health, education and social services over the degree of learning disability this young person has and whether or not he has mental health issues…has led to resources not being available.

Table 12.3 outlines the types of systematic issues that social care professionals deemed a problem when trying to successfully place a 'difficult' child. For the types of children we were focusing on, it was evident that they required a whole range of specialist services. As one social worker described:

[The] placement required needed to be specialist, including therapeutic input for sex behaviour, speech therapy, education as well as social needs.

However, due to issues around agency cooperation, lack of specialist carers to manage such children and funding, specialist services were not that easy to obtain, particularly within the local area.

Table 12.3 Characteristics of the agency that could affect placement

Characteristics	Includes
Unclear assessment	Resistance from agencies to 'label' the child
Lack of agreement between agencies	Inconsistencies between agencies
Lack of specialist services	Lack of therapeutic input; child too high risk for service; need carers to cope with complex risks
Placement not adequate to meet child's needs	Placement breakdowns; reluctant agencies
Threshold criteria between services	Confused roles of agencies
Limited regional facilities	Limited resources for post-16
Funding issues	Excessive cost of placement; lack of appropriate funding

What would have been considered good practice?

In terms of the best option for the child, social care staff felt that they did not have enough access, at early enough ages, to specialist provision such as residential school placements, specialist foster care, specialist family placements, specialist therapeutic input, specialist assessment, specialist forensic advice, and so on. The themes emerging from responses, in addition to the need for any sort of specialist (trained) input, included:

- very small units of only one to three children that were family-like in ethos

- individually tailored care packages that addressed the child's unique needs, and these children were very different from each other in this respect

- highly trained foster parents, able to anticipate and cope with the problems likely to be exhibited by the children

- earlier intervention, earlier removal from families

- more therapeutic input.

In just a handful of cases (out of the 59 individual stories that the social workers relayed), the social care staff felt that in fact the child was in the most appropriate placement. These were local authorities who were lucky enough to have some placement that looked like the wish list above. However, these facilities were few and far between.

Conclusions: English/Welsh fieldwork study

A number of things make placement of these children peculiarly difficult. By our own definition, they had to be considered a threat to the safety of themselves and other children or adults. However, what the research showed was the enormous variety that was encompassed within this broad definition, and it is the heterogeneity of the group, together with the low baseline of just six or seven per local authority, that makes provision so difficult. What these children need is enormous investment of time, energy and resources, in the form of personally tailored multi-agency specialist care, and it is very difficult to provide this type of care for such small numbers of children. Only 4 per cent of the sample were living with a specialist carer in a secure environment. The difficulties are compounded by the depressed state of the social care profession, with very high turnover of staff and lots of vacant posts (40% unfilled jobs not being unusual). In addition, the social care departments were struggling with the need to provide both early prevention and intervention, and also later specialist treatment, and some of the responses to the research suggested considerable conflict in achieving both these aims with the children who were in their care.

On the basis of the responses to open-ended questions it was clear that the children were both very varied, but that some also fell into some distinct groups. More research with larger and more representative samples could investigate our hypotheses, but in the first instance our impression was that there were children who (a) had early symptoms of emerging personality disorder; (b) were learning disabled or had other developmental disabilities; (c) were persistent young offenders with whom all systems were struggling including the criminal justice system; and (d) had been extremely badly treated but were otherwise unclassifiable.

Overall, several things stood out. The physical as well as behavioural characteristics of the children presented a challenge – size and weight being mentioned as challenging along with the unpredictability of behaviour, attachment problems and anger. As we might have expected, self-harm was a particular problem among the girls, and a negative attitude to people in authority was a problem with both groups, but poor attitudes to women staff particularly a problem among some of the boys. Altogether the reluctance to accept help both on the part of the children and their families posed a real challenge to care and intervention. Yet these difficulties were compounded by problems posed by the agencies themselves including lack of agreement between services, differing priorities, resistance to labelling, lack of suitable options for placement, and a general lack of trained, experienced, specialist staff.

A range of different factors were pointing to considerable instability in the lives of these young people, generated both by their own destructive behaviour but also by the agency context. The children described in this survey were not those for whom we are unsure of whether poor outcomes are indicated. All of the warning lights had already been lit and were blazing red. The question for the staff was one of placement suitability and availability. One wrote to us to describe what she wanted for her client:

> A therapeutic environment where he could have been controlled with loving care, his behaviour managed and redirected whilst offering firm boundaries within a nurturing environment. A placement that would give a clear commitment to him on a long-term basis, irrespective of his challenges, and work with him until the damaged and sad little boy inside could be reached. A placement whose cost was reasonable enough to ensure it could be funded for whatever period was necessary. It is doubtful that such a placement exists.

13

Conclusions

Messages for good practice

Renuka Jeyarajah-Dent and Ann Hagell

Children who have committed grave crimes, or even those who threaten to do so, cause society to be frightened and angry. Every parent will identify with the sense of unease experienced when a troublesome child enters the neighbour-hood. The overwhelming instinct is to protect your children by separating them from the other child, even if your conscience tells you otherwise. Yet it is this sense of being separate from others that appears to be one of the most important factors in fuelling a child towards violence. For many of these children the very essence of being human – a warm responsive relationship with particular adults – is missing from the beginning of their lives.

As Lösel and Bender show in Chapter 3 of this volume, there is evidence that biological factors do predispose children to difficult behaviour, but there is also evidence cited in this book that appropriate care at an early age is import-ant in setting children off on a pathway that leads to resilience. In fact, Bowlby's early research in 1944 was based on the lives of 44 thieves who he discovered had been separated from mothers for significant periods at an early age. In order to form a secure attachment to their child, a parent will need to be available, dependable and benevolent. Indeed, an ongoing lack of these elements in the early years can in itself threaten brain development and growth (Glasser 2000). At one level, the reasons for violence seem very simple and the solutions easy to define (if a child has been abused or neglected then make up for this). They also seem frightening in that the absence of something that is so taken for granted – good parental care – can lead to such poor outcomes. However, the pathways to violence are indeed more complex.

Children are born with their own inherent characteristics into particular families living in certain contexts and communities. They set off on a particular pathway but various factors can change or interact with other factors to become more or less influential. There are many influences on parenting including material factors, support from friends and family, the degree of reliance on drugs and alcohol, mental illness or learning difficulty. All these factors make parenting more or less difficult, but parenting is not simply the provision of a series of tasks like feeding, clothing and keeping warm. It also includes the capacity to put oneself in a child's shoes and know what it feels like for them. It means giving a child a sense that someone, somewhere, is always thinking about them, and that they thus exist, in some fundamental way. This capacity in a parent is often linked to warm responsive parenting and for some children the lack of it makes them susceptible to other risk factors and propels them down a pathway leading to violence. In its simplest sense, a lack of being valued makes it more difficult to value others.

So in some cases things go very wrong. The result is a group of children who cannot be placed in the company of others because of the danger they pose. It is not necessarily anyone's fault, but picking up the pieces and changing the trajectory is clearly a terrific challenge. The important thing is that while pathways matter, people can be diverted from them often enough to make it worth the effort of trying. However, these children are generally adolescents before their behaviour is serious enough to force a professional response. Often by this time and as illustrated in the field study (Chapters 9–12) professionals have a limited choice of placement and the onus tends to be on protecting others by separating the individual from them and, if the law is involved, punishment. Yet what this book repeatedly reminds us is that an equally important element of the response has to be an intervention that attempts to address some of the root causes for the behaviour. This is difficult, especially when the adolescent is unwilling to engage and often positively hostile.

What did we learn from the work represented in this book? The messages that emerged related to the description of the problem, the assessment and diagnosis of these children, the challenge of providing day-to-day services in ways that protect them and others around them, and to the task of actually addressing the problems and trying to change trajectories. We learned from other countries that the children who we were all most worried about were universal in the patterning of their needs and risks. It is the accumulation of risk factors rather than any single factor that characterises them.

We learned that there are problems in squeezing very complicated children into existing diagnostic schemes, and that assessing children and classifying disorders are useful but not an end in themselves. It is also clear that spotting the warning signs is the result of experienced practice and understanding of a wider literature. Children still slip through these nets, not spotted and not communicated about. By the time these adolescents have been labelled as a danger to others they have fallen out of the arena of health and education because their problems are now associated with a conduct/personality disorder and not a mental illness and they are difficult to contain in school. There are particular gaps for children who are considered untreatable, or so unsettled as to be unsuitable for treatment. As Derbyshire describes (Appendix 5), the social worker is often the one left to solve the problem as by this time the adolescent is probably also under the auspices of the statutory child protection services.

Whatever the location, we learned that services for these challenging children tend to remain disparate and reactive rather than matched to need. There are of course examples of good practice, but what stands out more is the wishes of the practitioners for the children in their care, and the universal problems they had in providing a care package that in any way met those wishes. The reasons for this are understandable. The actual number of children who pose a high risk to other children and who are in the care of local services is small. This combines with the wide variation in their needs and the enormous cost of doing it properly. What is needed is agreement that we will invest in this group, not just to keep them out of sight, but to try to intervene where possible. The specific ingredients of successful interventions have still to be reliably catalogued. What we know is that services have to be multi-agency and responsive to the needs of the 'whole' child. This means that services work together with the individual child, the family and the community contexts in which they live, for example, the school and the child's peers, and that attention to problems is immediate. In some cases interventions will not work. A significant proportion of these children will always have severe problems. There seemed to be issues in acknowledging that this would be the case, yet still finding ways to 'hold' these children and to meet their human rights, rights that are not forfeited because of the risks the children pose.

We would be the first to acknowledge that the countries we invited to take part, and the disciplines from which the professionals came who wrote these chapters for us, have affected the content of this book in ways that we might not have anticipated at the outset at the original conference. We are aware now, as we draw this book to a close, that this collection of chapters represents a certain perspective, and that some aspects of thinking about these issues are missing. We have no representatives from Sweden or Norway; given the advanced state of social care in those countries, they might have provided a new way of looking at some of these problems. We have no sociologists on the contributors list and no lawyers or criminal justice practitioners. However, we were surprised more by the similarities between the messages in these chapters than the differences. We thought at the outset that we had a rather disparate set of pieces to pull together, but throughout each one virtually the same themes began to emerge: the mixed nature of the group; the difficulties of professionalising aspects of parenting that had gone so wrong for so many of them; the issues of providing a hierarchy of care that first stabilised and made the child secure, and then delivered an intervention.

There are some messages in this book that are internationally relevant in setting up services for children with dangerous behaviour. These are as follows:

1. Intervene early. Abusive, neglectful families harm children. Identify quickly those families who lack the capacity to relate to the child with warmth, to such a degree that the child feels constantly denigrated. This is tied with poor outcomes in children and if the situation cannot change then action is required.

2. Make sure every child is in receipt of a good enough education which promotes learning through teaching and through nurturing. This is also important at the secondary level and not just for young children, so design your school so that even the average teacher can have time to attend to a vulnerable child. Schools can provide a place for relationships that help make up for those missed at home.

3. Involve other agencies if problems cannot be sorted or if you think there will be repercussions for the child later on in life.

4. Remind health agencies, education and social services that even if there is no diagnosis problem solving with other agencies is crucial.

5. Obtain relevant advice in order to put together a treatment package based on a shared assessment.

6. If the child is thought to be too dangerous to allow to wander freely then the following considerations become pertinent:

   - The child is likely to want to feel secure. This is in relation to a long-term plan and also to physical boundaries in relation to adults being in control and sometimes even physical barriers to absconding or contact with inappropriate friends.

   - The child should continue to receive an education as this is a statutory right and an ongoing vehicle to future resilience. Good healthcare should also continue in relation to physical health. The environment should look and feel nice.

   - Qualified staff should oversee a treatment programme. Various chapters identified treatment techniques that have been shown to work, particularly Multi Systemic Therapy (MST). This is expensive but reflects the needs of the child as by this stage they are probably suffering from a multiplicity and complexity of needs.

   - Provide for frequent team discussion with a person who is outside of the case as there is a danger that those involved become embroiled in the dynamics.

- Have clear rules for the establishment that mean that children are treated as children first and not objectified as can easily happen when similar children are placed together. Rules should also inhibit staff from identifying too much with the children.

- Have inspection regimes that recognise the difficulty of the task but also demand transparency in treatment approaches and outcomes. There will be problems but careful review rather than a mechanistic response is required.

- Basics like a stable workforce and funding for the placement over time are important. These children will have experienced instability and being somewhere long enough to begin to feel safe and become understood will be very important.

- Talk frequently to the child through treatment interventions but also provide for others to do so in other settings.

- Have a range of provision. It may be necessary for some adolescents to be kept in secure accommodation but others may benefit from specialist foster care.

- Remember that these adolescents, even when incarcerated in prison, will also have the needs of others of a similar age for nurturing and care. In fact they are likely to need more of it because of their particular histories. Make sure their problems are being addressed through treatment. Research shows that many will have mental health needs that will need addressing.

- Even if there are no facilities that offer treatment, remember that these adolescents will need to be somewhere where they feel secure. They may be boys (as they often are) who are hard to control and presenting as bad, but often it is the element of sadness in their lives that is fuelling their behaviour. Remember what sad children need and attempt to provide it.

7. Respect and reward staff, wherever they are working. Working with these children needs patience and expertise and you need to keep your staff in post.

8. Learn from your experience. There is no better way.

References

Bowlby, J. (1944) 'Forty-four juvenile thieves: their characters and home life.' *International Journal of Psycho-Analysis 25*, 19–52, 107–127.
Glaser, D. (2000) 'Child abuse and neglect and the brain: A review.' *Journal of Child Psychology and Psychiatry 41*, 97–116.

Appendices
Brief commentaries

Overview

Ann Hagell and Renuka Jeyarajah-Dent

The international seminar on which this edited collection is based was an unusual event. NCH – The Bridge Child Care Development Service and the Oak Foundation were determined to convene an event that was truly international in composition, and by that we meant international in the sense of beyond the usual suspects, that is, to include more than simply other English-speaking countries. Our work doing consultancy in Eastern Europe had already led us to believe that while the stage of development of childcare services in many ways lagged behind that of the UK, in other ways there were many similarities and things to learn in both directions. To this end we specified that a proportion of the invited delegates to the seminar should come from other countries.

We were keen not only to have a clear and broad international perspective, but also to invite delegates from a real range of disciplines, so that we could get, for example, psychiatrists, anthropologists and speech therapists together to discuss the care and welfare of this extremely difficult group of children, rather than leaving the conversation in the domain of social care staff.

In practice, achieving our inclusive aims for the participants was much more difficult than we had perhaps anticipated, despite the Oak Foundation's generous funding of travel for delegates. Problems arose partly because most UK practitioners and researchers do not have wide networks within countries such as Bulgaria and Russia, so locating the right people to invite was one challenge.

However, we were delighted in the end that the majority of the delegates were either from outside our own disciplines and/or from other countries. We were keen not to lose this dimension in the book. While some of the delegates contributed full chapters, we also invited others to contribute brief commentaries for us from their own perspective, as additional pieces to complement the main body of the text. The word limit was set at around 2000 and the content of these short contributions was very much left to the authors to decide. The result is in no way intended to give comprehensive coverage of the issues or ways of dealing with them, nor does it necessarily reflect our own views, but what it does do is represent snippets from worlds not usually brought together, demonstrating both the universality of the problems faced by practitioners working with these children, and also the wide range of issues that bear on how we think about them, such as assessment, diagnosis, attachment, autism and Asperger's Syndrome.

The use of structured instruments in the assessment of violence risk

Paul A. Tiffin and Graeme Richardson

General considerations

The use of structured instruments can potentially enhance the task of assessing the risks posed to others by a young person presenting to professionals. They can guide interviews, helping ensure that relevant areas are inquired about and may summarise information in a way that is easily communicated to other agencies. In addition, such instruments can assist with identifying the current needs of young people, facilitating the planning of risk management and treatment strategies and interventions.

Before discussion of some of the possibilities, the limitations of such approaches must be acknowledged. Instruments are only as good as the information their ratings are based on. In addition, children and adolescents may be difficult to engage with for several reasons. Information should be obtained from a variety of sources (e.g. parents, carers, social workers, youth offending workers, police reports, etc.) in order to maximise validity. Risk is a dynamic phenomenon and the changing developmental background to any assessment must be borne in mind. In children, social environment plays an influential role in their behaviour and professionals should be prepared to reassess risk in the event of a change of home circumstances, parenting, care placements, educational placement, or peer relations and influences. Most instruments are designed to offer some predictions regarding the risk of violent offending over the short term (one to two years) but speculation based on findings regarding longer term outcomes should be avoided. Risk evaluations have a relatively short 'shelf life' (not valid much beyond 6 to 12 months) and need to be reviewed and revised, especially in response to changing life circumstances.

Special caution must be exercised when employing instruments in a medico-legal setting, as one must be prepared to defend one's expertise in using the instrument. The practitioner ought to undertake formal training in the use of the particular assessment instrument if and when this is available. Additionally, it may prove difficult to communicate the limitations of the instrument to the Court, where simple answers are often sought. Formal training often addresses this very issue.

Wherever possible, professional clinical experience, up-to-date knowledge and skills should be employed to obtain the information required for the instrument. With use, evidence accumulates for the validity of the particular instrument as well as its limitations. The main instruments in use at the time of writing are briefly outlined in this chapter, which complements the information in Chapter 3 by Lösel and Bender in this volume. These instruments are predominantly North American (USA and Canada) in origin and development. Equally, empirical support for the validity of these instruments is based on North American studies with North American populations. A significant limitation for them is the absence of validation studies with UK populations. For a more comprehensive review of this and related topics the authors would recommend some recent reviews and book chapters (Kroll 2004; Richardson, Cawthorne and Graham 2004; Sheldrick 2004; Tiffin and Kaplan 2004).

The assessment of psychopathic traits in youth

More recently, assessment of 'psychopathy' is used to aid risk assessments, rather than derive a clinical diagnosis. 'Psychopathy' is a term used to describe a subgroup of individuals who are callous, remorseless, devoid of empathy and apparently without conscience. Psychopathic, and in particular callous and unemotional traits in young people, may be the most useful predictor of violent reoffending (Frick and Ellis 1999).

In adults a diagnostic clinical rating instrument known as the Psychopathy Checklist (PCL-R) has been developed. A derivative of this instrument has been modified for the purpose of identifying emerging psychopathic traits in young people aged 12 to 17 years and is known as the PCL-YV (PCL-Youth Version) (Forth, Kossen and Hare 2003). The questionnaire covers 20 domains, including 'Pathological Lying' and 'Grandiose Sense of Self Worth' and is scored on the basis of all the information available to the assessor and a semi-structured interview with the young person. Unlike the adult PCL-R, the PCL-YV does not currently have a cut-off score, although a score of 30 or more is cited as 'high' in the current empirical literature. The PCL-YV requires training to administer and score. Depending on the available information and the interview time with the young person, completion of the PCL-YV is likely to take several hours. This instrument may be purchased from Mental Health Systems Inc (MHS).

A further derivative of the PCL-R, designed for use in children aged between 6 and 13 years, is the Antisocial Process Screening Device (APSD; Frick and Hare 2001). The authors advise more weight to be placed on informant information rather than direct interview. A teacher and/or parent/carer may rate it, and a combined score can be obtained. The instrument contains 20 items covering three domains of behaviour: Callousness, Narcissism and Impulsivity, taking around 10 minutes to administer. It is intended for use as a research instrument and as a screening device for emerging psychopathic traits in children. The young age of the subjects demands that interpretations of findings are made with extreme caution. This instrument may also be purchased from Mental Health Systems Inc (MHS).

Instruments for violence risk assessment

The Structured Assessment of Violence in Youth (SAVRY) is designed to guide violence risk assessment in both boys and girls aged 12 to 18 years (Borum, Bartel and Forth 2003). It contains 24 items making up three scales: Historical; Social/Contextual; Individual/Clinical. There is also a protective scale, which focuses on resilience factors. Once all the required information has been collected, coding and recording takes approximately one hour. Although numerical scores are not generated, each risk factor is assigned a rating of Low/Moderate/High risk based on coding guidelines. The SAVRY is suitable for professionals who are experienced in conducting risk assessments, although further training was recommended for the rating of item 21: 'psychopathic traits' (recently replaced with 'empathy/remorse'). Research is in the preliminary stages but early indicators are that there is a moderate to strong relationship between SAVRY summary scores and violent reoffending at one year follow-up (Catchpole and Gretton 2003). The adult version from which the SAVRY is derived is known as the HCR-20 (Webster *et al.* 1995) and is designed to predict institutionally based violence, informing the management of violent individuals in hospital and prison settings. The SAVRY may be purchased from the authors via a website (www.specializedtraining.com).

Of similar format to the SAVRY, but aimed at a younger age group (under 12 years), the Early Assessment Risk List for Boys (EARL-20B) was designed to assess risk for general antisocial behaviour in children (Augimeri *et al.* 2001). It consists of 21 items covering the family environment, the child, and the responsiveness of the child/family to interventions. A 21-item version for use with girls (EARL-21G) is also available in consultation form (Levene *et al.* 2001). As with the SAVRY each category is rated to indicate whether the risk is low, moderate or high. Once all the required information has been collected, coding and recording takes approximately one hour. Preliminary research indicates acceptable inter-rater reliability and some predictive validity for the EARL-20B (Augimeri and Walsh 2004). These instruments may be purchased from the Child Development Institute via their website (www.childdevelop.ca).

Sexual offending

The limited amount of research and the previous dearth of specialised services have contributed to the lack of validated instruments for assessing the risk of sexual violence in young people. However, several developments in this area are worthy of mention.

The Estimate of Risk of Adolescent Sexual Offense Recidivism (ERASOR, Worling and Curwen 2004) is a clinically derived tool, based on the adult SVR-20 (Boer *et al.* 1997) designed to assess the short-term risk of sexual reoffending in 12- to 18-year-olds. The ERASOR is composed of 25 items divided into five categories including sexual interests, attitudes and behaviours, family/environment functioning and historical sexual assaults. To date there is some tentative empirical support for the predictive validity of this instrument. As yet the ERASOR is not published although copies are available from the authors on request.

A separate clinically derived instrument, similar in format to the SAVRY, is currently being developed and due for publication in the very near future. The Sexually Harming Adolescent Risk Protocol (SHARP; Richardson in press) is designed to be a developmentally sensitive schedule for collating and summarising risk factors relating to sexual offending in young people. This includes items relating to the emotional, sexual, social and personality development and adjustment of the young person, to mental health difficulties, and to the nature, extent, and duration of their sexually abusive behaviour. Risk in each area is summarised as low, moderate or high. This instrument will be available from the Cognitive Centre Foundation (CCF) who may be contacted via their website (www.cognitivecentre.com).

There has been one attempt to develop a statistically driven ('actuarial') instrument that predicts recidivism in young sex offenders: The Juvenile Sex Offender Assessment Protocol-II (J-SOAP-II; Prentky and Righthand unpublished) is derived from literature reviews regarding the characteristics of both juvenile and adult sex offenders, and of particular risk factors associated with sexual recidivism. This has produced a 28-item instrument divided into four scales: Sexual Drive/Preoccupation; Impulsive/Antisocial; Intervention; Community Stability/Adjustment. This approach to developing a risk assessment instrument has been hampered by the relatively small number of sexual recidivists (Prentky *et al.* 2000). This instrument is available directly from the authors.

Needs orientated tools

Recently there has been an increasing emphasis on needs led assessment. This refers to the identification of a range of social, education, health, criminogenic, and case management/therapeutic needs.

The Youth Level of Service/Case Management Inventory (YLS/CMI; Andrews and Hoge 1999; Hoge and Andrews 2002) is a 42-item checklist that assesses a wide range of risk factors associated with the individual, their peer group, and within the family. It contains a section where specific goals are established and the means of achievement noted. This creates a case management plan, which aims to reduce risk factors and enhance protective elements in the individual or environment. An abbreviated 8-item version of the YLS/CMI is also available as a tool to screen for the need for further assessment. These instruments may be purchased from MHS.

The Salford Needs Assessment Schedule for Adolescents (SNASA; Kroll *et al.* 1999) is a more general assessment instrument but can be used in a forensic setting and includes questions regarding violence to others. The SNASA covers 21 areas of need divided into mental health, educational and social areas. Through interview, information is obtained on symptom severity, the level of cooperation shown by the young person and key worker stress. 'Cardinal problems' (i.e. significant problems requiring intervention) are divided into 'unmet need', 'suspended need' (ongoing intervention) and 'persistent needs' despite interventions (PDI). Research indicates acceptable inter-rater and test re-test reliability. The SNASA and manual are available online (www.ru-ok.com/downloads/SNASAclinical.doc).

Conclusions

The use of structured instruments is helpful in complementing a thorough clinical assessment. Care should be taken when selecting the most appropriate instrument for use with the particular young person. The findings from structured instruments must be placed in the context of a general clinical appraisal and treated cautiously, particularly in developmentally younger children. Be aware that this is not an exact or particularly well researched science. Thankfully, clinical and professional judgement has not yet been superseded by statistics!

Five points for practice

1. Formal instruments can be used to complement a clinical risk assessment; they are a useful guide to information gathering and highlight the appropriate list of risk factors to be assessed.

2. Such assessment instruments can summarise information about risk/protective factors, current needs and short-term predictions regarding outcomes in a way that is easily communicated to other professionals and agencies.

3. Always ensure that the instrument is appropriate to the situation and characteristics of the young person being assessed, and that training in administering the instrument has been received where necessary.

4. Be aware of the limitations of the instrument and that young people who are unusual 'outliers' may not necessarily be picked up as high risk. In addition, be particularly cautious regarding their use in legal proceedings.

5. Place any summarised scores or ratings in the overall context of everything that is known about the young person and their situation, bearing in mind that these may be constantly changing in developing young people. Consequently, ratings will only be valid for 6 to 12 months at most and reassessment will be required after this time or with changing circumstances.

References

Andrews, D.A. and Hoge, R.D. (eds) (1999) *Youth Level of Service/Case Management Inventor.* Dinas Powys: Cognitive Centre Foundation.

Augimeri, L. (2004) 'Antisocial young children: Gender issues in risk assessment and clinical risk management.' Paper presented at the American Psychology-Law Society Annual Conference, Scottsdale, AZ (www.fiu.edu/~apls2004).

Augimeri, L.K., Koegl, C.J., Webster, C.D. and Levene, K.S. (2001) *Early Assessment Risk List for Boys: Version 2.* Ontario: Earls Court Child and Family Centre.

Boer, D.P., Hart, S.D., Kropp, R. and Webster, C.D. (1997) Manual for the Sexual Violence Risk-20. Professional Guidelines for Assessing Risk of Sexual Violence. Vancouver: Simon Fraser University and Psychiatric Services Commission of British Columbia.

Borum, R., Bartel, P. and Forth, A. (2003) *Manual for the Structured Assessment of Violence Risk in Youth: Version 1.1 – Consultation Edition.* Tampa, FL: University of South Florida.

Catchpole, R.E.H. and Gretton, H.M. (2003) 'The predictive validity of risk assessment with violent offenders at one-year examination of criminal outcome.' *Criminal Justice and Behavior 30*, 688–708.

Forth, A., Kossen, D. and Hare, R.D. (2003) *The Hare Psychopathy Checklist – Youth Version (PCL:YV).* New York: Multi-Health Systems.

Frick, P.J. and Ellis, M.L. (1999) 'Callous-unemotional traits and subtypes of conduct disorder.' *Clinical Child and Family Psychology Review 2*, 149–168.

Frick, P. and Hare, R.D. (2001) *Antisocial Process Screening Device: Technical Manual.* New York: Multi-Health Systems.

Hare, R.D. (1980) 'A research scale for the assessment of psychopathology in criminal populations.' *Personality and Individual Differences 1*, 111–119.

Hare, R.D. (1991) *Manual for the Hare Psychopathy Checklist – Revised.* Toronto: Multi-Health Systems.

Hoge, R.D. and Andrews, D.A. (2002) *Youth Level of Service/Care Management Inventory: User's Manual.* Toronto: Multi-Health Services.

Kroll, L. (2004) 'Needs assessment in adolescent offenders.' In S. Bailey and M. Dolan (eds) *Adolescent Forensic Psychiatry.* London: Arnold.

Kroll, L., Woodham, A., Rothwell, J., Bailey, S., Tobias, C., Harrington, R. and Marshall, M. (1999) 'Reliability of the Salford Needs Assessment Schedule for Adolescents.' *Psychological Medicine 29*, 891–902.

Levene, K.S., Augimeir, L.K., Pepler, D.J., Walsh, M.M., Webster, C.D. and Koegl, C.J. (2001) *Early Assessment Risk List for Girls: Version 2.* Ontario: Earls Court Child and Family Centre.

Prentky, R. and Righthand, S. 'The Juvenile Sex Offender Assessment Protocol – II (J-SOAP-II).' Unpublished manuscript.

Prentky, R., Harris, B., Frizzell, K. and Righthand, S. (2000) 'An actuarial procedure for assessing risk with juvenile sex offenders.' *Sexual Abuse: A Journal f Research and Treatment 12*, 2, 71–93.

Richardson, G. (in press) *Sexually Harming Adolescent Risk Protocol.* Cardiff: Cognitive Centre Foundation.

Richardson, G., Cawthorne, U. and Graham, F. (2004) 'Risk practice and principles in a forensic mental health service for children and young people.' *Issues in Forensic Psychology 5*, 126–143.

Sheldrick, C. (2004) 'The assessment and management of risk.' In S. Bailey and M. Dolan (eds) *Adolescent Forensic Psychiatry.* London: Arnold, pp.27–39.

Tiffin, P. and Kaplan, C. (2004) 'Dangerous children: assessment and management of risk.' *Child and Adolescent Mental Health 9*, 56–64.

Webster, C.D., Eaves, D. Douglas, K.S. and Wintrup, A. (1995) *The HCR-20 Scheme: The Assessment of Dangerousness and Risk.* Vancouver: Mental Health Law and Policy Institute.

Worling, J.R. and Curwen, T. (2004) 'The Estimate of Risk of Adolescent Sexual Offense Recidivism (ERASOR): Preliminary psychometric data.' *Sexual Abuse: A Journal of Research and Treatment 16*, 3, 235–254.

Diagnostic issues in seriously disturbed adolescents

A psychiatric perspective

Robert Vermeiren

Case study

Peter is a 16-year-old adolescent who has been referred to a forensic psychiatric outpatient department because of repetitive rape of adult women. Because of the nature of the crimes, the juvenile judge has asked to write an expert report on the youth, in order to make the most appropriate decision with regard to further intervention. At the time of the referral, Peter was staying in a community institution (*Gemeenschapsinstelling*), which may be considered the Belgian version of a 'detention centre'. Reasons of referral were three consecutive rapes, committed over a period of some months, on three adult women, of whom the oldest was over 80 years old. The offences were physical assault, tearing of clothes and touching intimate places. There was no intention of robbery. Peter's history was one of severe family problems: e.g. his early divorced mother died in a car accident while a sibling was driving when drunk, with Peter being on the back seat. Because of family problems, Peter had been admitted to numerous institutions throughout his life. In most cases, he had stayed there for short periods, always less then one year. Also, a large number of mental health professionals had been consulted before, resulting in long lists of diagnoses, e.g. early attachment disorder of childhood, attention deficit hyperactivity disorder, oppositional defiant disorder, conduct disorder, post-traumatic stress disorder. Because the successive admissions to residential facilities occurred in many different places around the country, treatments were always of relatively short duration.

Many such stories can be written down, probably in every country in the world. One aspect that needs to be considered in these youths is the complexity of the diagnostic process: that is, the process of identifying the nature and cause of the problem through a thorough evaluation of the young person and their history. Throughout their multiple contacts with healthcare institutions, such youths face many different professionals, and adequate communication with regard to previous diagnostic decisions is often lacking. Because many countries lack adequate services for them, these individuals undergo a variety of consecutive interventions and placements, leaving family members and clinicians with substantial frustration. In Belgium, such youths are called 'hot potatoes', since the institutions are very reluctant to admit them, and once entered, the main purpose is often to find a 'more adequate' place. Although most professionals invest considerable effort and experience in these cases, diagnostic inconsistency is too often the confusing result. Because of the shortcomings of current classification systems, and the complexity of problems in such youths, most of them will end up with a heterogeneity of diagnoses. In this appendix, diagnostic issues will be discussed, and it will be explained that current classification systems lack the ability to describe these minors.

Classification of disorders

Psychiatric classification systems are used worldwide, most often for clinical purposes but also for administrative reasons. The best known systems are the *Diagnostic and Statistical Manual of Mental Diseases* (DSM, American Psychiatric Association 1994) and the *International Classification of Diseases* (ICD, World Health Organisation 1992). Both systems have developed descriptions of a number of specific disorders of childhood and adolescence, of which some are diagnosed with growing frequency in adults. The construction of specific diagnoses, and of the criteria a person should meet in order to receive a diagnosis, is done by experts during consensus meetings. Although this process is guided by scientific evidence, much depends on the opinion of the experts. For this reason, diagnoses have been redefined regularly throughout the different version of the classification systems, a process that is often accompanied by renaming of the diagnoses. For example, the current DSM diagnosis of attention deficit hyperactivity disorder (ADHD) was previously called minimal brain damage (MBD) or attention deficit disorder-hyperactivity (ADD-H), and has been called hyperkinetic disorder in ICD.

Clinicians often feel that the existing diagnoses do not fit some severely disordered individuals. This has to do with the shortcomings of diagnostic instruments, but also with specific aspects of these classification systems. In complex cases, it is a challenge to assess whether a specific symptom is present, but also to determine when a specific symptom has developed. Some diagnoses require criteria (e.g. for ADHD, autism and conduct disorder – early onset subtype) to be present before a specific age. When a particular youth has several disorders at the same time, it often proves impossible to disentangle the developmental antecedents. Furthermore, since parents are often unavailable or unreliable informants of symptoms, it may not be possible to determine the age of onset. Therefore, early onset may be very difficult to assess in adolescents with conduct disorder (Sanford *et al.* 1999; Vermeiren *et al.* 2002).

Problems of comorbidity

Another complication may be the limitations of classification systems when diagnosing some specific disorders occurring together in the same young person, called 'comorbidity'. A frequent disorder combination is ADHD and autism. According to the DSM, however, ADHD may not be diagnosed when autism is present. Whether there are sufficient arguments for this stance is still in debate, and the next version of DSM will show whether the consensus group has changed its opinion on this. Clinical practice does not profit from this situation because the presence of ADHD makes a considerable therapeutical difference. An autistic individual with ADHD poses many more problems behaviourally, and an appropriately structured educational and environmental milieu is required.

Evidence has proven that comorbidity is a frequent phenomenon in child psychiatry, and that many disorders co-occur more frequently than may be expected by chance alone (Angold *et al.* 1999). With regard to the topic of this book, seriously disordered youth, the comorbidity of internalising (e.g. depression, anxiety disorders) and externalising disorders (e.g. conduct disorder, ADHD) may be of particular importance. Since such youths bear a diversity of psychiatric problems, diagnostic and therapeutic interventions may prove difficult, with a high likelihood of failure.

Currently, there is discussion whether comorbidity should be addressed by giving an individual several independent disorders or by constructing specific disorder categories that combine diagnoses. An example of specific disorder category is the ICD-10 diagnosis of 'mixed disorder of conduct and emotions'. Studies of this mixed diagnosis have shown quite large prevalences, more than may be expected on the prevalence of each disorder alone (Graham and Rutter 1973). Clinically, however, there are debates over whether it should be preferable to assign one combined diagnosis or give different independent diagnoses. Both present problems; it may be expected that, when different specific categories are preferred, clinicians will tend to give fewer diagnoses. On the other hand, when mixed categories become more popular, they may be overused when criteria for the other diagnoses are less obvious. Also, it should be investigated what system should be preferred for therapeutical reasons.

Prevalence of seriously disordered young people

A substantial number of children and adolescents can be diagnosed at some point in their childhood or adolescence with a psychiatric disorder, but only a small group may bear a combination of several disorders (Angold *et al.* 1999). Although this last group has vast clinical needs, its prevalence remains unknown, as well as the nature of the diagnoses these youths bear.

There are several reasons why severely disordered minors are not considered in epidemiological studies. First, the prevalence of the phenomenon is (although unknown) probably quite low. Even in large population-based studies, these youths may not show up. Second, because of their problems, these youths tend to be present in residential facilities. For this reason, these youths may not appear in many population-based studies, and even in outpatient samples they may have a very low prevalence. Third, when specific disorders are investigated, focus is often on clear diagnostic cases. For reasons that are understandable from a scientific point of view, exclusion criteria often define that children with a number of other disorders cannot take part. Fourth, in most epidemiological studies, only a limited number of diagnoses are assessed, mainly because easy-to-administer instruments are lacking for many categories. Although a substantial number of severely disordered youth may carry a developmental disorder or an attachment disorder of early childhood, feasible instruments useful in large-scale epidemiological studies are not available for these disorders.

While general population studies may be unable to investigate this severely disordered population, studies in specific samples may give an idea of the extent of the problem. Incarcerated youths may be particularly interesting for this purpose, because many of them became incarcerated after many years of contact with healthcare services. Since adequate services for severely disordered youths are lacking in many countries, this group has an increased likelihood of becoming delinquent, resulting in contact with juvenile court and eventual detention.

Several studies have shown that a vast majority of youths in incarceration may be diagnosed with a psychiatric disorder, and that comorbidity occurs very frequently in this group (Ruchkin et al. 2002; Teplin et al. 2002; Vermeiren 2003). Some recent studies have demonstrated that apart from internalising (i.e. depression and anxiety) and externalising disorders (i.e. conduct disorder, oppositional defiant disorder), psychosis-related symptoms and substance abuse and dependence occur frequently (Teplin et al. 2002; Vreugdenhil et al. 2004). While most studies of adolescents in detention have focused on boys, some studies of girls in detention are available (Teplin et al. 2002; Vermeiren 2003). Although antisocial behaviour may be much less frequent in girls than boys, psychiatric pathology may occur much more often in detained girls, in particular depression and post-traumatic stress disorder. Furthermore, externalising disorders and substance abuse and dependence may reach similar high rates in detained boys and girls. For this reason, early diagnostic assessment of severely disordered youths should be given greater attention, since this must enable timely recognition of cases, resulting in targeted intervention.

Population based follow-up studies have shown that problematic youth can be identified at an early age. With regard to antisocial behaviour, the dual taxonomic model of Moffitt (1993) can be helpful. Apart from an adolescent onset delinquent group that tends to desist from crime later on (Adolescent Limited, AL), an early onset group with highly increased risk of persistency was distinguished (Life-Course Persistent, LCP). This LCP group is a very disordered one, characterised by a combination of intrinsic problems (e.g. attention problems, impulsivity, verbal intelligence deficits) and family problems (Moffitt 1993). Furthermore, although this group comprises only five per cent of the (male) population, they commit half of all offences by adolescents. Clinically, this model demonstrates the developmental specificity of diagnostic work. At specific ages, different combinations of disorders may be prognostically important.

Conclusion

This appendix has demonstrated that the case study of Peter, a seriously disordered delinquent boy who has received multiple diagnoses over time but little adequate help, may not be extraordinary. Although diagnostic classification systems are helpful for describing problems, a main problem is related to the lack of diagnostic categories that reflect the complexity of problems in these multiply disordered patients. No one diagnosis fits all symptoms, while a combination of several diagnoses may be considered overdiagnostic. Furthermore, substantial (developmental) information is often lacking for assigning a diagnosis, while diagnostic instruments are lacking for others. Since therapeutic interventions should rely on adequate diagnostic work and definition of problems, future research should target on the group of severely disordered youth in particular.

References

American Psychiatric Association (1994) *Diagnostic and Statistical Manual of Mental Disorders – Fourth Edition (DSM-IV)*. Washington, DC: APA.

Angold, A., Costello, E.J. and Erkanli, A. (1999) 'Comorbidity.' *Journal of Child Psychology and Psychiatry and Allied Disciplines 40*, 57–87.

Graham, P. and Rutter, M. (1973) 'Psychiatric disorder in the young adolescent: A follow-up study.' *Proceedings of the Royal Society of Medicine 66*, 1226–1229.

Moffitt, T.E. (1993) 'Adolescence-limited and life course persistent antisocial behaviour: A developmental taxonomy.' *Psychological Review 100*, 674–701.

Ruchkin, V.V., Schwab-Stone, M., Koposov, R., Vermeiren, R. and Steiner, H. (2002) 'Violence exposure, posttraumatic stress and personality in juvenile delinquents.' *Journal of the Academy of Child and Adolescent Psychiatry 41*, 3, 322–329.

Sanford, M., Boyle, M.H., Szatmari, P., Offord, D.R., Jamieson, E. and Spinner, M. (1999) 'Age-of-onset classification of conduct disorder: Reliability and validity in a prospective cohort study.' *Journal of the American Academy of Child and Adolescent Psychiatry 38*, 992–999.

Teplin, L.A., Abram, K.M., McClelland, G.M., Dulcan, M.K. and Mericle, A.A. (2002) 'Psychiatric disorders in youth in juvenile detention.' *Archives of General Psychiatry 59*, 1133–1143.

Vermeiren, R. (2003) 'Psychopathology and delinquency in adolescents: A descriptive and developmental perspective.' *Clinical Psychology Review 23*, 277–318.

Vermeiren, R., Schwab-Stone, M., Ruchkin, V., De Clippele, A. and Deboutte, D. (2002) 'Predicting recidivism in delinquent adolescents from psychological and psychiatric assessment.' *Comprehensive Psychiatry 43*, 142–149.

Vreugdenhil, C., Doreleijers, T.A. and Vermeiren, R. (2004) 'Psychiatric disorders in a representative sample of incarcerated boys in the Netherlands.' *Journal of the American Academy of Child and Adolescent Psychiatry 43*, 1, 97–104.

World Health Organisation (1992) *International Classification of Mental and Behavioural Disorders*. Geneva: WHO.

Disorganised attachments and psychological trauma in the lives of hard to place children

Jean Harris-Hendriks

Introduction

There is a great deal of interest in attachment disorders among the types of children who are violent, difficult to place with other children, or who sexually offend. This brief commentary sets out the proper diagnostic classifications and identifies some shortcomings in the existing systems, and identifies the need for continuing debate in this area.

Attachment disorders

Attachment disorders refer to a persistent disturbance in a child's ability to interact and relate to others across social situations. Such disorders usually begin before the age of five, and have roots in the child's earliest relationships with caregivers. They are distinguished from autism and pervasive developmental disorders because they are held to have largely social origins. Attachment disorders are associated with very poor early childcare, unresolved loss or trauma. It is worth noting that attachment theory is only just beginning to be applied to adolescence, and the existing classification systems do not properly take note of the different presentations of adolescent children compared with younger children. A certain amount of misunderstanding about the application of attachment theory ideas to the needs of difficult children exists among clinical, social and legal services (Byrne *et al.* 2005).

For an overview of the recent debates on attachment, Soloman and George (1999) provide a useful resource. The role of abuse and neglect in affecting brain development is discussed in Glaser (2000).

The *International Classification of Mental and Behavioural Disorders* (ICD-10, World Health Organization 1992) is one of the most widely used ways of thinking about and classifying problems of attachment. It distinguishes between reactive attachment disorder and disinhibited attachment disorder. The former would normally have arisen as a direct result of severe parental abuse or serious mishandling. It remits to a major degree if the child is placed in a normal rearing environment, which provides continuity in responsive caregiving. Disinhibited attachment disorder is thought to be due in part to a persistent failure of opportunity to develop selective attachments as a consequence of extremely frequent changes in caregivers. Box A3.1 identifies the main characteristics of these two types of attachment disorder within ICD-10.

Box A3.1 ICD-10 definitions of attachment disorder*

Reactive attachment disorder

- Occurs in infants and young children
- Persistent abnormalities in pattern of social relationships associated with emotional disturbance and reactive to changes in environmental circumstances
- Characterised by fearfulness and hypervigilance ('frozen watchfulness')
- Poor social interaction with peers
- Frequent aggression to self and others
- Evidence of misery, lack of emotional responsiveness, withdrawal
- Infants show contradictory or ambivalent social responses, gaze aversion, respond to care-givers with a mixture of approach, avoidance and resistance to comforting
- Growth failure may occur.

Disinhibited attachment disorder

- Arises in first five years of life
- Persistent despite changes in environment
- At 2 years, clinging and diffuse, non-selectively focused attachment behaviour
- At 4 years, clinging replace by attention-seeking and indiscriminately friendly behaviour
- In middle and later childhood, selective attachments may have developed but attention-seeking behavior often persists; poorly modulated peer interactions are usual, there may be associated emotional or behavioural disturbance.

* Text in Box A3.1 reproduced from American Psychiatric Association 1994, by permission of the World Health Organization.

The American Psychiatric Association provides a parallel diagnostic system called the *Diagnostic and Statistical Manual* (DSM-IV, APA 1994). In this there are similarly two subheadings under attachment disorder, entitled Inhibited Type and Disinhibited Type. DSM-IV criteria are displayed in more detail in Box A3.2.

Box A3.2 DSM-IV definitions of attachment disorder*

Reactive attachment disorder of infancy or early childhood

A. Markedly disturbed and developmentally inappropriate

- Persistent failure to initiate or respond in a developmentally appropriate way to most social interactions, as shown by excessively inhibited, hypervigilant or highly ambivalent and contradictory responses (e.g., the child may respond to caregivers with a mixture of approach, avoidance and resistance to comforting, or may exhibit frozen watchfulness).

- Diffuse attachments as manifest by indiscriminate sociability with marked inability to exhibit appropriate selective attachments (e.g. excessive familiarity with relative strangers or lack of selectivity in choice of attachment figure.

B. The disturbance in Criterion A is not accounted for solely by developmental delay (as in Mental Retardation) and does not meet the criteria for a Pervasive Developmental Delay

C. Pathogenic care as evidence by at least one of the following:

- Persistent disregard of the child's basic emotional needs for comfort, stimulation and affection

- Persistent disregard of the child's basic physical needs

- Repeated changes of primary caregiver that prevent formation of stable attachments
  (e.g. frequent changes in foster care).

D. There is a presumption that the care in Criterion C is responsible for the disturbed behaviour in Criterion A (e.g. the disturbances in Criterion A began following the pathogenic care in Criterion C).

Reactions to psychological trauma

Both ICD-10 and DSM-IV also include descriptions of reactions to psychological trauma. The ICD-10 (1992) classification is headed 'Reaction to Severe Stress and Adjustment Disorders' (section F43). The DSM-IV (1994) classification is Post-Traumatic Stress Disorder (section 309.81) and 'Acute Stress Disorder' (section 308.3). Yule (2002) provides an overview of current thinking on postraumatic stress disorder as this affects adolescents and children. Also useful are articles by Bolton *et al.* (2004), and Fergusson, Swain-Campbell and Horwood (2004).

It might be useful just to look at the DSM-IV classification of post-traumatic stress disorder, which is often reported as a symptom of very difficult and disturbed children (Box A3.3).

Box A3.3 DSM-IV definitions of post-traumatic stress disorder*

A. The person has been exposed to a traumatic event in which both of the following were present:

- The person experienced, witnessed or was confronted with an event or events that involved actual or threatened death or serious injury, or a threat to the physical integrity of self or others.
- The person's response involved intense fear, helplessness or horror (in children this may be expressed instead by disorganised or agitated behaviour).

B. The traumatic event is persistently re-experienced in at least one of the following ways:

- Recurrent and intrusive distressing recollections of the event
- Recurrent distressing dreams
- Acting or feeling as if the traumatic event were recurring
- Intense psychological distress and exposure to cues that symbolise or resemble an aspect of the event
- Physiological reactivity on exposure to cues that symbolise or resemble an aspect of the event.

C. Persistent avoidance of stimuli associated with the trauma and numbing by at least three of the following:

- Efforts to avoid thoughts, feelings or conversations associated with the trauma
- Efforts to avoid activities, places or people that arouse recollections of the trauma
- Inability to recall an important aspect of the trauma
- Markedly diminished interest or participation in significant activities
- Feeling of detachment or estrangement from others

- Restricted range of affect
- Sense of foreshortened future.

D. Persistent symptoms of arousal (not present before the trauma) as indicated by at least two of the following: difficulty in falling or staying asleep; irritability or outbursts of anger; difficulty concentrating; hypervigilance; exaggerated startle response.

E. Duration of the disturbance is more than one month.

F. The disturbance causes clinically significant distress or impairment in social, occupational or other important areas of functioning.

*Text in Boxes A3.2 and A3.3 reprinted with permission from the Diagnostic and Statistical Manual of Mental Disorders, Fourth Edition, Text Revision, copyright © American Psychiatric Association 2000.

Where from here?

While these classification systems are useful, they were not designed specifically with these difficult children in mind. What is needed is the development and refinement of a debate about the effects, both neurological and psychological, upon developing children who experience both disorganised attachments and psychological trauma. This might have come, for example, in the shape of abuse, neglect and inter-parental violence. It may have arisen from the effects of civil and international strife. Very few of the children who are the topic of this volume will have escaped without some kind of trauma in their lives. Many of these children and young people, as they progress into adolescence, have disorders that are then classifiable in their own right under the systems described. The categories may vary, but there are ways of describing their symptoms in these systems. Then, many of these young people, as they pass into late adolescence and early adulthood, turn out to meet the criteria for disorders of personality. The boundaries between attachment disorders and personality disorders require some further exploration for these types of children.

As they stand the classifications are useful, but do not do justice to the stories. What we need is a framework for considering children and young people that allows us to track their history, to mesh together images of deprivation, discontinuity and dislocation with evidence of psychological trauma so that classification becomes more subtle and, while retaining its place within a wider framework, provides meaning and clarification to our perception of each individual child. This will then help us to tailor the most appropriate interventions and treatments. We have a long way to go.

References

American Psychiatric Association (1994) *Diagnostic and Statistical Manual of Mental Disorders – Fourth Edition (DSM-IV)*. Washington, DC: APA.

Bolton, D., Hill, J., O'Ryan, D., Udwin, O., Boyle, S. and Yule, W. (2004) 'Long-term effects of psychological trauma on psychosocial functioning.' *Journal of Child Psychology and Psychiatry 45*, 1007–1014.

Byrne, J.G., O'Connor, T.G., Marvin, R.S. and Whelan, W.F. (2005) 'Practitioner review: The contribution of attachment theory to child custody assessments.' *Journal of Child Psychology and Psychiatry 46*, 2, 115–127.

Fergusson, D., Swain-Campbell, N. and Horwood, J. (2004) 'How does childhood economic disadvantage lead to crime?' *Journal of Child Psychology and Psychiatry 45*, 956–966.

Glaser, D. (2000) 'Child abuse and neglect on the brain: A review.' *Journal of Child Psychology and Psychiatry 41*, 97–116.

Soloman, H. and George, C. (1999) *Attachment Disorganisation*. New York: Guilford Press.

World Health Organization (1992) *International Classification of Mental and Behavioural Disorders*. Geneva: WHO.

Yule, W. (2002) 'Post-traumatic stress disorder.' In M. Rutter and E. Taylor (eds) *Child and Adolescent Psychiatry*, 4th edn. Oxford: Blackwell, pp.520–528.

Management of serious interpersonal violence in individuals with autistic spectrum disorders

Paul Devonshire

Clinical categories, particularly those relating to mental health and personality, are ever in a state of flux as new knowledge becomes available and/or dissatisfaction with existing categories grows amongst professionals using them. At present one such is the autistic spectrum disorders (ASD). According to the *Diagnostic Statistical Manual-IV* of the American Psychiatric Association (DSM-IV, APA 1994), this category includes at present the diagnostic labels of autistic disorder and Asperger's Syndrome, as well as Rett's Disorder and Childhood Disintegrative Disorder. As the title ASD implies, there is an assumption that the disorders are on some kind of continuum, with increasing severity in terms of either the presenting symptoms or the complexity of the underlying pathology, or indeed of a combination of the two. In addition, there is wide variation between individuals with the same diagnosis. The autistic spectrum disorders sit within the broader category of pervasive developmental disorders, highlighting that there is alteration in the normal development which persists throughout the lifespan, the 'disorder' lying in the areas of communication and social interaction, leading to difficulties in personal and social adjustment.

A 'qualitative impairment in social interaction' is an important diagnostic criteria for both autistic disorder and Asperger's Syndrome, with the impairment operating in both the understanding and expression of thoughts and feelings, both with spoken and non-verbal language. A major concept within ASD is *Theory of Mind*, which refers to the ability to understand that (a) the individual has a mind; (b) other people have minds; and (c) the individual and other people may not be thinking or feeling the same thing at the same time. Other cognitive difficulties can arise from a failure to operate with symbolic or representational concepts that make normal play behaviour difficult. Facial expressions, body language and even the tone of voice can also deviate from the cultural norm, leading to a presentation of oddness. One individual has been able to articulate her experiences writing: 'I do realise that I do not see the world as others do... The fact that (people) can see, hear, smell, touch, and relate to others is "normal". For me, these things are often pain-fully overwhelming, non-existent or just confusing' (Lawson 2005). This description marks a level of insight and articulation that might not be attained by many individuals with ASD but examples like this and Mark Haddon's *The Curious Incident of the Dog in the Night-time,* although a work of fiction, serve to illustrate the difficulties faced by those within the autistic spectrum.

Although the primary features relate to communication difficulties, other mental health issues, such as anxiety and depression, may accompany ASD as a consequence, though such subjective distress is not part of the diagnostic criteria. This can result in such subjective states being overlooked, professional concentration being on the primary symptoms. In higher functioning individuals it can present the problem of which service, Mental Health or People with Learning Difficulties, will address them.

Such impairments in function can obviously lead to difficulties within the mainstream school environment, both with regard to formal academic progress in the classroom and social assimilation within both the immediate peer group and the wider community. However, special abilities might also mark them out as different and make for difficulties in the conformist world of childhood. A proportion of those with ASD will be victims of bullying and exploitation. They can also sometimes be perpetrators. Thus the National Autistic Society in 2000 quotes figures that 21 per cent of children with ASD have been excluded from school on at least one occasion (Barnard, Prior and Potter 2000). The difficulty of social functioning can then persist into the adult world with difficulties in finding employment and other aspects of adult social life.

There has been an increase in the reported incidence of ASD within the school age population (Scott *et al.* 2002). Figures suggest an incidence of at least 1 in 110 for ASD as a whole and 1 in 300 for Asperger's Syndrome. Statistics of the general population with ASD have also included the variable of IQ, with figures quoted for those above and below IQ 70: thus for the former 417,000 and for the latter 117,600.

There is some debate about these figures since it might represent a greater preparedness to use the diagnosis rather than there being an actual increase in prevalence. Wing (1993), for example, found in a cross-cultural study marked variation in diagnosis between 3.3. to 16.00 per 10,000. However, the increase in figures has been acknowledged in the recent Learning Disability White Paper and therefore it can be assumed that this will have an impact upon social policy. One problem with ASD (viz. Asperger's Syndrome) is that the intellectual level can be outside the range for learning disability services and the presenting features might not accord with inclusion criteria for other mental health services (such as anxiety, depression, psychotic phenomena).

At present there are no statistics available detailing the incidence of criminal acts committed by individuals with ASD, though the proportion of those with ASD who do commit serious offences is low. Indeed it could be argued that certain features of ASD protect the individual from criminal activity, such as 'the particular affection for rules'. Strengths themselves, however, can become weaknesses. Thus a tendency towards an obsessive interest can be advantageous, but some objects of obsessions (viz. sex or weapons) can have dangers. However, from what are recognised as risk factors amongst violent offenders – poor peer relationships, poor problem-solving skills, early attachment difficulties, behavioural disturbances – it can be extrapolated that those with ASD, by the nature of the diagnostic criteria, will constitute a vulnerable population.

It will be important to identify the various routes by which an individual can arrive at criminal activity in order to avoid a one-stop mentality in the provision of treatment or management. As Jordan and Jones (1996) have observed: 'It is not possible to say that one form of provision is best for all pupils...child and school characteristics as well as parental wishes will help determine the best setting for each individual Service's need to recognise the range of factors involved and take each into account in individualising interventions.' The routes can be divided into three broad categories:

1. *Reactive.* One explanation of violent behaviour is the 'frustration hypothesis', whereby the individual reacts to present frustrations by an angry outburst. It can be expected that the various limitations in an ASD individual's coping skills will lead to frustration that will elicit a violent reaction, either directed at another person or objects. Such offending can be conceptualised as impulsive and unplanned, reflecting poor behavioural controls of emotion and poor understanding.

2. *Active.* Through the lack of empathy or perspective taking, ASD individuals will be predisposed to engage in antisocial acts that they might otherwise be inhibited from committing by some kind of moral awareness, a regard for other people, or simple fear of punishment.

3. *Instrumental.* There may be occasion when the individual with ASD learns through normal reinforcement principles to achieve certain personal goals through acting out behaviour of one kind or another.

There is a convention in the psychological understanding of behaviour that each act fulfils some meaningful purpose or function for the individual, and therefore there is in all behaviour, including offending behaviour, a metacommunication that deserves understanding. Although there is some validity in this approach, there are dangers that, in solely applying this approach, other important factors that determine behaviour are not taken into account. The clinical presentation of ASD exposes the challenge of determining how much the behaviour is purposeful and motivated as opposed to deficiencies in functional capacity. Thus is the social ineptness of the ASD individual some sign of disapproval of the human race or a symptom of some underlying defect or impairment in social behaviour?

A major challenge is to understand the nature of the communication difficulties, both in terms of any receptive (viz. comprehension) and expressive difficulties, and then devising ways in which these can be improved or, if this is not possible or limited, accommodated. The former implies changes in the individual to accommodate to society, whilst the latter requires changes in those in the immediate environment to accommodate the individual. In the home this would include parents and relatives; in the school, both teachers and fellow students; in the workplace, employers and colleagues; if in the criminal justice system, legal personnel, police and court officials. To achieve this requires specialist knowledge about the nature of the communication difficulties, ignorance of which can lead to unwarranted parental guilt at their perceived failure and indeed amongst professionals working with individuals with ASD to their frustration at the lack of adequate or expected progress. Quick and easy therapeutic progress is not something that can be guaranteed in every instance, and whilst achievements are to be celebrated, managing the disappointments is also important.

Communication can be something that is taken for granted, and therefore when it goes wrong, people can lack a proper understanding of the 'how' of communication. It is important, therefore, to be able to deconstruct what has contributed to an individual's miscommunication. However, it might not always be possible for the individual with ASD to achieve a sufficient level of insight with which the ability to operate autonomously in a different way can develop. This can be a challenge to the professional since it might encourage a more paternalistic approach which would run counter to present ideologies rooted in empowerment and inclusiveness. The concept of treatment in the sense of achieving a predetermined change in behaviour will not be so appropriate, but rather the individual's behaviour will be 'managed' by the quality of the environment in which the individual operates, in what can be called a 'prophylactic milieu'. A corollary of this is that those in the individual's environment need some kind of counselling/training/education to help them understand the underlying impairments and thereby modify their own understanding and reactions. Such an approach can address the stigma that might attach to the individual who may be seen as just stupid or malicious, through others adopting attributions that do not take account of the underlying impairments.

In October 2005, the National Autistic Society launched a Criminal Justice System information campaign in order to increase the understanding of autism and Asperger's Syndrome among professionals. Such initiatives are important in enabling a better service for those who may become caught up in the system.

References

American Psychiatric Association (1994) *Diagnostic and Statistical Manual – IV*. Washington, DC: APA.

Barnard, J., Prior, A. and Potter, D. (2000) *Inclusion and Autism: Is It Working?* London: National Autistic Society.

Haddon, M. (2003) *The Curious Incident of the Dog in the Night-time*. London: Jonathan Cape.

Jordan, R. and Jones, G. (1996) 'Educational provision for children with autism in Scotland: Final report.' Birmingham: University of Birmingham.

Lawson, W. (2005) *Sex, Sexuality and the Autism Spectrum*. London: Jessica Kingsley Publishers.

Scott, F., Baron-Cohen, S., Bolton, P. and Brayne, C. (2002) 'Prevalence of autism spectrum conditions in children aged 5–11 years in Cambridgeshire, UK.' *Autism* 6, 3, 231–237.

Wing, L. (1993) 'The definition of prevalence of autism: A review.' *European Child and Adolescent Psychiatry* 2, 61–74.

Meeting the needs of young people who are dangerous within the English/Welsh context

A social care management perspective

David Derbyshire

This short appendix sets out a series of issues about the social care of young people who are judged by professionals to be dangerous to others, from the experience of a former social services manager in London local authorities. It seeks to set out some helpful ways forward but does so from a basis of standing back from daily realities for managers in local authority children's services and seeks to ask questions of how services are currently configured and whether better outcomes could be achieved by doing things differently.

What are the issues?

As the chapters in this volume have shown, the size of the problem around such young people is small, but the amount of planning time at front line and senior levels that each case consumes is vast in relation. This reflects that not only are there no easy answers to the provision of effective care or education for these young people, but also that each young person in this group is a risk to the reputation of the council with whose children's services she or he is in contact.

Such young people are likely in the main to be those considered to be at risk of sexually abusing younger children as a result of a previous child protection investigation, or an allegation or concern. Relatively few such young people are convicted of an offence because of the difficult nature of the task for the Crown Prosecution Service in judging matters of consent, dealing with notions of 'sexual experimentation' between young people and because a trial might frequently be more of an ordeal than a relief for the victim. This means that it is difficult to know where and how to have the discussions about managing the risk they pose. In England and Wales, the Criminal Justice and Courts Services Act 2000 required police and probation services to establish arrangements for assessing and managing the risks posed by sexual and violent offenders. However, few such young people fall within the legal definition of category one or two considerations for the resulting Multi-Agency Public Protection Panel (MAPPP) meetings. Category three considerations do permit MAPPP discussion of people without convictions, but only in exceptional circumstances, and the practice around this category varies considerably from authority to authority. Some local Area Child Protection Committees (ACPCs) have got around this to some extent by creating a local version of meetings for those falling outside the remit of MAPPP meetings, but these will generally lack the same levels of access to measures such as intensive supervision or commitment of resources for the police as the major crime prevention lead agency.

In addition, a small number of young people present issues around service provision because of general propensity to violent crime, rather than sexual offending. Most of these are concerns to schools, which find themselves frequently trying to avoid exclusion and expulsion from school because of local and national policy around social inclusion, but struggling also to safeguard the well-being and educational progress of other children in the school. These children can also be a serious problem within residential care settings.

If the children have come to the attention of the youth justice system, then those with serious convictions or charges against them are likely to be found in secure accommodation centres and secure training centres until conviction and sentencing. They are at this point likely to be the main responsibility of Youth Offending Teams (YOTs), which will be responsible for pre-sentencing reports and supervision in the community, although not responsible generally for welfare issues such as determining placement needs for looked after children. More of these young people are boys than girls. For all these young people, the questions around planning services are these:

- How can a series of agencies best come together to provide services to assess and meet the needs of a young person who does not wish to have her/his needs met by these agencies and who offers no verbal insight into the danger that they might pose?
- How can harm to the reputation of the organisation be avoided by preventing a young person from offending in a way which is likely to result in adverse media exposure?
- How can other children in the organisation's care be properly protected?

What happens now?

Agencies concerned with child welfare and safeguarding are currently striving to meet the needs of this group throughout England and Wales. Below are some of the standard practices of local authorities to plan social care for these young people, although this appendix is too brief to detail standard practices around use of temporary exclusions, and other rewards and sanctions around behaviour in schools.

Referral to mental health services

This frequently fails as local mental health services and many other less local services require a greater degree of cooperation and insight and stability around placement than can be offered by many of these young people. Where such insight exists even in partial form, there is some reason to hope that risky behaviours might be curtailed through exposure to intensive psychological, psychiatric and social care interventions, most commonly obtained in specialist residential placements for dealing with young abusers. However, there is a shortage of placements available for such young people, and there is likely to be pressure on managers and practitioners to limit any open-ended 'therapeutic' interventions in such placements because of a need to provide more objective evidence-based indicators of likely placement success. In addition, each placement of this kind is likely to cost in excess of £3000 per week for each child and children's placements budgets are traditionally the greatest pressure on service budgets.

Multi-agency Public Protection Panels (MAPPP)

Issues pertaining to the local MAPPP were mentioned above. Where a persistent young offender or an unconvicted potential offender presents a concern, further complexities arise in considering a likelihood of offending when the civil liberties of the young person concerned come into play, i.e. authorities are asked whether it is reasonable to plan an intervention about reducing likelihood of offending for a young person under 18 who has not yet been convicted or cautioned. Local MAPPP meetings held under the auspices of ACPC procedures have had some success in alerting different agencies to likely risks and in ensuring, for instance, that schools are better placed to deal with specific issues of 'stranger danger'. However, the requirement for a conviction before the formal MAPPP meeting around category one and two offenders is problematic in some instances. A review of the effectiveness of formulaic assessment tools used in the probation and youth offending services might assist in generating confidence that such models can accurately predict risk of future serious offending. However, as such models are heavily weighted to an analysis of previous convictions, they are unlikely to have much benefit for the management of unconvicted potentially dangerous offenders. Dealing with young people who pose a serious risk, but who have not yet hurt anyone, thus poses a real problem within current arrangements.

Social work intervention

Some social care services run by local authorities will have access to specialist resources although these tend to be concentrated in teams of practitioners whose aim is broadly to limit the admission of teenagers to the care and accommodation system. Field social work intervention with individual children is often limited in terms of frequency and, given the high turnover rates for staff in London, this can easily translate into a young person receiving around 12 to 15 such contacts per year from a variety of different social workers and their assistants. Most training has also tended to concentrate on an in-house basis on safeguarding younger children or assisting young people who are at risk of exploitation such as through prostitution. Social services managers might also find themselves facing a shortage of social work staff with particular skills in communicating with teenagers. It is worth noting that the Crime and Disorder Act 1998 led to the setting up of YOTs in England and Wales to work with those who have been convicted of offences, although there are moves in places to enable them to work with young people simply at risk of offending as well.

Use of care and accommodation

Social work intervention may lead to admission to local authority care or accommodation. Specialist placements in residential care have been developed on a small-scale basis to deal with young sex abusers. The notion of treatment foster care, where a family is supported by intensive supports from mental health, education and social care professionals, is now gathering apace, although its benefits for those who are considered dangerous are not yet fully evaluated. Local authorities may seek to avoid or limit the use of care both for reasons of expense as indicated above, but also because young people in this category are not likely to generate positive educational or other outcomes on which local authority performance is measured at a critical level within the performance management framework set by government.

Secure accommodation

Relatively few young people are looked after in secure accommodation on welfare grounds as the criteria require a sound assessment of likely harm to self or others, a history of absconding and a care plan which supports a view that a young person's welfare will be better assisted in secure accommodation on a reasonably time-limited basis than not. Few young people who are a risk to others necessarily meet all such criteria and there is often a shortage of appropriate beds in secure units that would be able to provide sustainable assistance for these young people. This is not a criticism but more a reflection of the fact that social care and other agencies have little understanding of how best to assist such young people. A number of young people will be placed in care or accommodation in highly staffed units where staff to resident ratio is normally 2:1 and where there are likely to be only one or two other young people who fit a similar profile. These placements are mainly provided by private or voluntary care organisations. They pose questions around the human rights of young people who are effectively detained long distances from home without recourse to an order and where there is often little attention to their educational needs.

Ways forward?

There are no easy solutions to this issue and the mere integration of children's services pursuant to the Children Act 2004 and associated guidance will not alone assist. Key issues to consider to assist local authority planning and to assist outcomes for such young people would be as follows:

1. To extend use of formal MAPPP processes to those who are not convicted but who have a behavioural history and professional analysis that suggests a high risk of significant harm being caused in future and to ensure that this approach is adopted across the country. Specific MAPPPs for young people would be able to consider planning and specialist assessment for young people based on full inter-agency consideration of needs. Such meetings could be constructed under the auspices of present MAPPPs or the new and emerging Safeguarding Children Boards in order to ensure that a focus on promoting the welfare of the child is maintained. Such meetings would also have access to supervision and early identification techniques used by the police service and partners in attempting to prevent crime as required by the Crime and Disorder Act 1998. Overall, such meetings would ensure that young people thought to be posing a risk to others would receive levels of support, assessment and supervision in the community similar to those with similar risk assessments in the adult convict population. It will be important for such meetings to be able to base their assessments on holistic perspectives and not only on the tools provided in the ASSET formula used currently by YOTs.

2. To develop the role of the YOTs and others involved in antisocial behaviour units in local authorities to take on responsibility for this wider group of young people. This would ensure that those dealing with young people were those most skilled and interested in working with this group. Essentially, this would not seek to place more children into the court arena but would broaden the role of the YOT so that its focus is not only on offending but also the welfare issues behind offending. This suggestion would also have the potential for local authorities of easing resource difficulties where two social workers from the YOT and social services are required to work with the same child with two different attendant management and administration systems and costs.

3. Workforce development strategies both locally and nationally should pay particular attention to the question of developing a workforce which is best able to deal with teenagers in general, and those posing a risk to others in particular. This may need to call more heavily upon those with a background in the likes of youth work or work for Connexions or other such organisations, where direct contact with teenagers has been a requirement of the job. For local authorities, it is important that guidance allows sufficient flexibility so as to enable authorities to employ the best staff for the job rather than merely relying on a particular group of staff to undertake certain case-holding functions.

4. Continued emphasis should be placed through training and other quality assurance and management activities to ensure that actions taken in planning for the welfare of young children are taken with a view to the

rest of childhood in mind. This will not remove the problem of young people who act dangerously entirely, but it would close some of the gaps in cases where the young person's level of dangerousness is related to a personal history of abuse or neglect which might have been detected by more analytical intervention earlier than later.

5. Development of local mental health services for young people where the mental health practitioner does not require willingness to work or insight as a prerequisite would assist multi-agency working enormously. It is to be hoped but yet to be seen whether the National Service Framework modules around safeguarding and Child and Adolescent Mental Health Services will deliver this mode of intervention into reality.

6. Greater emphasis in individual service planning for young people on their educational needs being met in order to avoid further drift away from mainstream societal norms for young people with highly deviant likely criminal behaviours.

7. Development likewise of placement resources for young people who pose a risk to others where insight is not a prerequisite. This would present a problem in that the service would need to work hard to do more than contain young people with this style of presentation and to meet needs and promote welfare. Nevertheless, care would be provided in properly staffed and equipped units with high staffing ratios. In view of the small number of highly dangerous young people in any local authority area, this development will require regional commissioning by local authorities and a willingness to open such a unit by either one of those local authorities or one of the major national voluntary or private care providers.

8. Multi-agency planning through the likes of panel reviews of involvement with young people who pose a risk would help to ensure earlier identification of a problem across agencies and provision of services. This should be more easily achieved through the integration of education and social services departments now taking place across authorities as a result of the Children Act 2004.

Overall, the number of possible helpful new initiatives in England and Wales does hold out hope that things can get better in this difficult area of service provision. However, the key message has to be one around ensuring that local authorities and partners do not practise on a basis of service being made available only to those who are likely to perform well in life and who are therefore more easily found placement and other support services. The challenge is a commissioning challenge and one where new children's trusts in England and Wales will have an opportunity to reshape services for a highly vulnerable and dangerous collection of young people. In short, the challenge is to renew services and not to give up on them or on the young people whose needs services must meet.

Service provision in Bulgaria for children who commit extreme acts of interpersonal violence

Daniela Kolarova

The context for services for children in need in Bulgaria

The context for Bulgaria's approach to children who commit extreme acts of interpersonal violence is a picture of a country in some flux with regard to provision for children in need. Bulgaria's European Union accession date is set for January 2007. One of the prerequisites for European accession is decreasing the number of children in institutions. According to figures from the National Statistics Institute and a State Agency for Child Protection estimate Bulgaria has the highest number of infants in state institutions in Europe or the former Soviet Union. Recent statistics show that Bulgaria has almost 22,000 children in institutional care.

Despite this country's adoption of the Child Protection Act in 2000, which stipulates that children should be placed in institutions if no family-based solution can be found, the number of children in care has not decreased significantly. Many of these children have disabilities, come from socially disadvantaged families or have been abandoned, but very few of them are orphans. (Children's institutions are commonly referred to as 'orphanages', even though a majority have living relatives, and a number of NGOs are concerned that inadequate steps are being taken to return or reintegrate children back into the family sphere.) This is the biggest problem facing Bulgaria as it slowly reforms its child welfare system. Out of the total number of children in institutions about 3000 are infants, representing a staggering segment of a population of only 7,450,000, of which around 1 million (14%) are children between the ages of 0–14 years. Some 65 per cent of these infants are Roma, far disproportionate to the Bulgarian Roma population. Despite the high numbers in institutional care, the population of children in Bulgaria is decreasing. Recent demographic data from the National Statistics Institute show that the number of children is currently 150,000 fewer than in the year 2000.

A number of political, economical and demographic changes are thus happening which impact on the experiences of children in Bulgaria. The process of transition is very difficult especially for children at risk. At present some 3000 to 5000 are estimated to be living or working on the street. A further 45,000 children are dropping out of school each year and the approximate number of children at risk of severe social and family marginalisation is twice as high.

Against this context, the year 2004 may well be seen as a turning point for Bulgarian society with regard to fuller acknowledgement of the phenomenon of extreme acts of violence committed by children. Three separate cases drew huge media attention and provoked widespread public concern. One of the cases involved two 14-year-old girls who, it was reported, 'coldbloodedly' killed their best friend for a mobile phone. They apparently 'showed no remorse'. Soon after another two cases were reported. One involved the murder and dismemberment of a 14-year-old boy committed by his friend, and the other concerned a young teenage boy who killed his mother and brother. In all of the cases the children were assessed as 'sane' and therefore responsible for the crimes they committed.

But behind the language of sensationalism of the media and the apparent oversimple representation of such extreme acts of violence as 'sane' or 'insane', there is another story of a developing recognition of complexity and subtlety. Underpinning this is the emergence of a new and more child-centred perspective that is beginning to permeate society at every level. The policy of inclusion at the level of central government is being adopted within every aspect of the social care and education system. The challenge for the country is to articulate this policy at the local practice level and, more specifically, to the most complex circumstances and children in need. Not least in this respect is the way services are delivered for children who pose a serious risk of harm to others.

The Bulgarian State Agency for Child Protection (SACP)

The key development within the range of institutional responses to child protection and also to violence committed by children is the creation of the Bulgarian State Agency for Child Protection (SACP). Originally set up in 2001 to complement existing services concerned with child welfare, the SACP focuses on the broad aim of prevention of abuse against children. One feature of this concerns developing a strategy for combating violence and other forms of abuse in specialised institutions for children, including those that provide for young offenders.

The SACP analysis concerning conditions in existing institutions providing for children and young offenders draws attention to a worrying range of deficiencies including lack of staff training and the impact of institutional living conditions such as depersonalisation, anonymity of care and separation of/lack of contact with family and community. They note the close association between these factors in relation to the risk of abuse including sexual and violent abuse carried out by children against children.

However, there is little or no available data concerning prevalence of abuse committed by children against children, and there are also indications that sexualised forms of abuse in particular may be inadequately recognised and reported.

The SACP is an important instrument for the promotion of better and more child-centred approaches to the treatment and support of all children in need. But the extent to which this agency can impact policy and, in particular, care and treatment practices towards children who may commit extreme acts of interpersonal violence is unclear. This is partly a problem of separation of function of this agency from the youth justice system and from those childcare institutions providing for children who may have committed such offences. Furthermore, this is not helped by the relatively complex administrative arrangements and institutional roles and responsibilities concerning child and young offenders.

Broadly there are various levels of intervention in Bulgaria relating to the seriousness or degree of risk posed or represented by the case. A case manager or 'examiner' has the special role of carrying out an assessment of the various contributory factors linked to the offending behaviour. The information collected is used to determine course of treatment and nature of intervention. Decision making concerning this, as well as the initial assessment of seriousness or degree of risk, is the responsibility of the Local Commission for Combating Antisocial Acts of Minors and Adolescents. This commission is made up of psychologists, social services representatives, jurors, the police, the district prosecutor's office, education specialists, and may also include medical doctors and local public figures. They operate closely with the court. Less serious offences and those that involve low risk place greater emphasis on interventions within the child's family home and the normal range of community settings including the child's school.

Issues in service provision for children who are seriously violent

The route followed by a child who has committed a serious act of interpersonal violence is invariably towards placement in a 'correctional boarding school'. This type of school is essentially a form of detention in which the child is required to engage in a programme aimed at eventual social reintegration. The programme is formulated by a multiprofessional group.

With regard to the capacity of these institutions to provide appropriate and safe conditions for all children placed within them, and the efficacy and precise nature of interventions, there is little available data. The apparent lack of transparency concerning methodology and outcomes is a cause for concern. There is also an absence of other details relating to how the institutions manage and support children who all may have complex needs and behaviours, some of which may pose risk of harm to others. Continuing concern can be expressed over the generally low level of resources available to properly maintain quality of life and to safeguard the interests of all children in residential care and correctional boarding schools. The issue of low levels of staff training alongside an apparent absence of standards formalised in policy and practice guidelines also point the way to necessary and important action.

In conclusion it is clear that significant steps have been taken at all levels to improve the childcare system and to embrace a child-centred approach to care and support. The transference of policy at governmental level to practices that ensure safety for all children, including children who may commit extreme acts of interpersonal violence, is gradually filtering through a complex system despite it being greatly disadvantaged by inadequate funding and resources. There remains much to do to improve service quality for some of the country's most needy children.

The Our Family care model in Russia as an effective prevention scheme for children in care who commit extreme acts of interpersonal violence

Maria Ternovskaya, Maria Kapilina and Tatiana Gubina

Russian context

The increasing growth of poverty and family crisis levels (6 million children are living below the poverty line) in Russia in recent years has caused the considerable increase in numbers of street and runaway children and children in care of the state. Levels of crime among these children including interpersonal violence acts have been cause for concern. Figure A7.1 demonstrates the increase in numbers of children in care in Russia from 1993 to 2004, which doubled over this period.

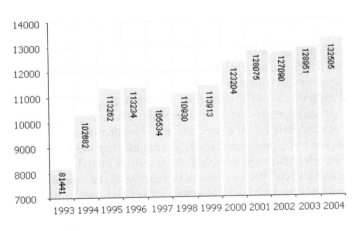

Figure A7.1 Numbers of children in care in Russia from 1993 to 2004

The traditional Russian care system for children without parental care does not prevent criminal acts among the children and one might argue it even stimulates them. In Moscow about 100 children in state orphanages commit acts of serious interpersonal violence every year. In 2004, six children murdered other children, and 72 were recorded as having run away from orphanages and committed crime acts in the streets. Some of these children were missing for more than three years. Correctional institutions for young offenders do not actually provide behaviour 'correction', and young people released from such institutions in 98 per cent of cases commit criminal acts again.

The Our Family model

In 1992, The Our Family project was started in Moscow, partly state funded, and since then has been duplicated by 29 more Russian regions as a new care model that aims to meet the needs of each child and to provide family care (fostering and adoption) for them. Unlike traditional provision, this model is child centred and rehabilitative for the child, his or her environment and family network. We believe that it does provide a significant preventive tool with regards to minimising any child's criminal activity, including elimination of interpersonal violence acts.

The Our Family model believes that every child should be brought up in a natural family environment. Every effort should be made in order to help a child to live with his or her own birth parents or, if this is no longer possible, with foster or adoptive parents. The Our Family project, through consultation, training and research, supports childcare reform in the Russian Federation, which we hope will eventually allow every child to live with and be brought up in a family.

The Our Family project believes that children in need are best served when professionals from all child-related disciplines work in very close cooperation. Therefore at Our Family a multidisciplinary team of childcare professionals works together under one roof and contributes to childcare planning and direct service provision.

Before being placed with foster families, most children spend some time living at one of three Our Family's residential rehabilitation units, which are family-style homes for up to ten children. Here they receive any medical, psychological and educational support they may need from the multidisciplinary team, as well as loving family care, to prepare them for foster family placements or to return to their own birth families. Based on the same site as the residential units, the foster-care team assesses and trains prospective foster parents and then together with the reha- bilitation team selects the most suitable foster family for each child. Both foster and adoptive parents and children continue to be supervised and supported by the Our Family multidisciplinary team after placement. The Our Family project services for children are as follows:

1. First-stop (medical and psychological diagnostics) unit for street children (for ten children).

2. Rehabilitation unit for children from other cities and for those whose legal situation is not yet clarified (for 10 to 16 children). A 'social mother' is leader of the unit.

3. The 'social family' unit for preparation of very disturbed children for family placements (for 8 to 14 children). Social parents are leaders of the unit.

4. The rehabilitation team (a multidisciplinary team with a paediatrician, child psychologists, psychiatrist, special needs specialist, speech therapist, social workers).

5. The child protection and monitoring team (social workers visit foster homes and provide legal protection of children's rights).

6. The fostering team.

7. The family support (family preservation) team.

How does the Our Family model help to prevent crime and violence among the children?

International research has shown that the following factors may determine an ability of a child to commit interpersonal crime: social, personality and biological factors. It is usually hard to define the main reason for a particular child behaving in a certain way as these factors act on different levels and in complicated interactions. The main reasons for development of crime and violence have of course been extensively researched (see Lösel and Bender, Chapter 3 of this volume) and can include the following:

*   neglect
*   child abuse that causes aggressive behaviour and gives an example to follow
*   broken attachments (secure attachment can potentially act as a deterrent factor as a child is afraid to lose love of a parent and a good attitude)
*   borderline disorders that provoke interpersonal violence under certain circumstances
*   self-control problems that can cause aggression and impulsive acts
*   psychiatric and mental health problems
*   learning disabilities (the child does not understand what he or she does).

Since its inception Our Family has cared for about 300 children and 100 per cent have been diagnosed with having at least one of these problems at the time of admission. For 45 per cent the risk of interpersonal violence was very high as a number of factors occurred at once. Some examples below demonstrate these results.

Alex

Alex, age 11, had severe mental disability, was physically very fit, trustful in person-ality, followed others, was sensitive and touchy, and had suffered from physical and sexual abuse in early childhood as well as severe neglect. At admission Alex was aggressive and had a high risk for interpersonal violence as used by criminals in his social circle and guided by them, and because of lack of understanding of the implications of his acts. At Our Family he was placed with a professional foster carer who knew how to work with mentally disabled kids and how to manage aggression. Since coming to the project, he feels more secure in the family and has developed attachment. As a result his behaviour and emotional condition were sta-bilised.

Our experience shows that the main difficulty is to control children who have attachment disorders (disorganised attachment disorder). Such children can be controlled by setting boundaries. They try to show their ability to get what they want, which is self-destructive and dangerous for other children. The ways to control and influence the child are limited as it is not possible to change biological background, but in our experience on the project it is possible to influence the social context and the personal behaviour and life choices of these children.

Social context and attachment relationships aspects

The younger the child the more important are social context and attachment rela-tionships. Here are two examples where two children demonstrate the importance of the creation of the proper social context. Both were placed with the project at the age of five and went on to achieve normal intellectual development.

Andrew

Andrew is 15 now. He was destructive, showed no empathy for other people, liked risks and breaking rules, did not seem to gain any satisfaction from any intellectual activities and education and did not develop any attachments, although he was raised by loving foster parents. He liked freedom, financial success (despite having no motivation for work), understood power and risks and looked for relationships with criminals. A special foster family was found for this boy where the father of the family had a strong character. He developed a strong relationship with Andrew and has involved him in sports, work activities and helps him to balance independ-ence and control.

Alexander

A gypsy child who suffered from physical and emotional abuse, Alexander had problems with his central nervous system, aggressive and chaotic behaviour. He was placed with loving adoptive parents where he received extensive psychother-apy. He attends a school for gifted children, which has helped him to develop good education motivation and a strong attachment to his new parents. He also has positive memories of all those who cared for him well and keeps up a relationship with them. Three years since his adoption, he now has few emotional outbreaks or shows of aggression.

In order to prevent acts of violence it is very important to create the proper social context for each child according to his or her needs and personal character.

The influence of social context at the time of critical developmental points

For each of the children there are critical points when their system of values is revised. These are at the age of puberty and at the time they leave foster care. Extensive therapy and supervision are important at these times. For example, Rustam was eight years old when placed with Our Family. He had bipolar disorder (aggression frequently interchanged with depression). He was closed up, did not communicate, aggressively reacted to any interaction, and hit or bit anybody who touched him. He was placed with the Our Family rehabilitation family group where he achieved stable relationships, warm attitudes, safe life conditions and a stable acceptance reaction in the face of his aggressive acts. He also received continuous psychotherapy. In time his intellectual development improved and after five years he was ready to develop an attachment relationship with new parents and was adopted through the Our Family scheme at the time of entering puberty.

About 20 young people who have left the care of Our Family since its opening ten years ago were able to go through the leaving care crisis period with the support of both foster parents and Our Family services. This was crucial and allowed normal socialisation and the development of new relationships with former foster parents.

Life or social support systems developed by Our Family, which work to reduce the implication of biological risk factors and to create safe attachment relationships and a system of supportive and social relationships for children and young people, also allow the minimisation of significant risks for interpersonal criminal and violence acts.

Outcomes for children from Our Family project

According to official statistics in Russia, only 10 per cent of young people leaving the care of the state have normal life chances: 40 per cent become criminals, 10 per cent commit suicide, 40 per cent start drinking and leave their own children in orphanages.

Our records at the Our Family project suggest much better results. Child development seems to be normalised by being part of the project, and only one young person out of the 300 cared for over ten years has a significant risk of interpersonal acts of violence in the future.

The Contributors

Dr Helen Agathonos DSW, BSc, MA, PhD, Psychologist, Consultant on Child Protection. Head, Department of Family Relations, Institute of Child Health (1979–2003). Dr Agathonos has over 30 years of professional experience in research and in clinical work on child maltreatment of all types, institutional care for children, social exclusion, child and family policy. Her work has been published at national and at international levels. At EU level, she has wide experience in lobbying for children's position and in collaborative research on children's issues.

Professor Susan Bailey OBE, FRCPsych, Professor of Child and Adolescent Forensic Mental Health, University of Central Lancashire, and Registrar, Royal College of Psychiatrists. Professor Bailey's research and clinical interests centre on needs led risk managed multi-agency service delivery for young people at high risk to others wherever these children are in systems.

Dr Doris Bender is senior lecturer in psychology at the Institute of Psychology at the University of Erlangen-Nuremberg, Germany. She teaches in the fields of clinical psychology, assessment and evaluation, developmental psychopathology, health psychology and psychology and law. Her main research interests address the origins and development of aggression and delinquency from childhood to young adulthood, resilience and protective factors, marital quality and stability. She has published numerous articles on these issues and is co-editor of three books.

Professor Gwyneth Boswell is Professor in the School of Allied Health Professions at the University of East Anglia. For the last 12 years, Gwyneth has researched and published widely on the subject of violent young offenders, both in the UK and South Africa. She is also co-author, with Davies and Wright, of *Contemporary Probation Practice* (Avebury 1993), author of *Young and Dangerous* (Avebury 1996), editor of *Violent Children and Adolescents: Asking the Question Why* (Whurr 2000) and co-author, with Wedge, of *Imprisoned Fathers and their Children* (Jessica Kingsley Publishers 2002).

David Derbyshire, MSc, CQSW, PGCE, is currently Service Development Director at NCH – The Bridge Child Care Development Service and provides strategic advice around a range of childcare planning and safeguarding issues to a diverse range of clients in the public and voluntary and community sectors. David has a strong history in managing child protection services in local authorities and has worked as Head of Service in a children's social services where he managed an improvement programme to improve outcomes for vulnerable children and raise the performance rating of the authority concerned.

Paul Devonshire is a Chartered Member and Associate Fellow of the British Psychological Society in the Clinical/Neuropsychology and Forensic Psychology Divisions. Paul has 30 years' experience in the NHS in various clinical settings, including high and medium security working with mentally abnormal offenders. He is a part-time tutor in the Psychology Department, University of Surrey and honorary lecturer at St George's Hospital Medical School. He is currently engaged in private practice with medico-legal work and teaching.

Dr Kevin J. Epps has spent most of his career working in mental health, prison and secure and open childcare settings with children and adolescents presenting with serious forms of antisocial behaviour. As well as 11 years working at the Department of Health's Glenthorne Youth Treatment Centre, Kevin has also been Lead Psychologist with the Birmingham and Solihull Mental Health Trust Forensic Child and Adolescent Mental Health Service, and has worked in independent practice.

Tatiana Gubina is a psychologist working with the Our Family Centre in Moscow. Her work includes training foster carers and social workers and consulting to carers in relation to difficult behaviour in children.

Dr Ann Hagell is currently Research Development Adviser at The Nuffield Foundation, one of the UK's best known charitable trusts. Previously she was Co-director and Co-founder of the Policy Research Bureau in London. She is a chartered psychologist specialising in social policy research on high-risk young people, and has undertaken research in both the UK and USA. She edits the multidisciplinary *Journal of Adolescence* and is author/co-author of a range of articles, reports and contributions to books on at-risk young people, and is a former Fulbright scholar. She is also a Trustee of the Prison Reform Trust.

Dr Jean Harris-Hendriks, MB, ChB, DPM, FRC Psych, has been a Consultant in Child and Adolescent Psychiatry for 32 years and is currently Honorary Consultant to the Traumatic Stress Clinic, Camden and Islington Mental Health NHS Trust, London and Honorary Senior Lecturer to the Royal Free Hospital and University College Hospital Medical Schools, London. She has a special interest in child and adolescent forensic psychiatry and in particular concerning the effects upon children of psychological trauma, and is widely published in this area.

Emily Hill was working as a Research Fellow at the Policy Research Bureau, an independent, social policy research centre based in London specialising on research on the family and young people, at the time of contributing to this volume. She has since moved on to work as a practitioner in South London with young people at risk of developing offending behaviour.

Renuka Jeyarajah-Dent is Executive Director of NCH – The Bridge Child Care Development Service which provides consultancy, training and forensic services to those agencies concerned with the protection of children from abuse and neglect. Renuka is an Educational Psychologist and an Associate Fellow and Chartered Psychologist of The British Psychological Society. She is a Trustee of Shaftesbury and Arethusa (a provider of residential care for children and young people in the care of the state), and has a series of publications in the field of violence, danger and risk.

Maria Kapilina is a child psychologist working with the Our Family project in the Russian Federation.

Dr Daniela Kolarova is the Director of Partners Bulgaria Foundation. The mission of the organisation is to facilitate the ongoing process of democratic transition in Bulgaria by supporting various civil initiatives, including many connected to improving life for children at risk. Daniela is a social psychologist and since 1990 has been a lecturer at Sofia University 'St Kl. Ohridski'. Daniela has an established reputation for leading projects that have been of benefit to vulnerable children and marginalised people.

Professor Friedrich Lösel is Director of the Institute of Criminology at Cambridge University, UK, and Professor of Psychology at the University of Erlangen-Nuremberg, Germany. Previously, he has worked at the Universities of Erlangen, Bamberg and Bielefeld and in Advanced Research Centres funded by the German Research Council. Much of his research addresses the origins, development, prevention and treatment of delinquency and violence. He has published 16 books and approximately 250 articles and has received the Lifetime Award of the European Association of Psychology and Law and the Sellin-Glueck Award of the American Society of Criminology.

Patricia Moran works as an independent chartered research psychologist. Patricia has a long-standing collaboration with the Psychology Department at Royal Holloway, University of London, where she has worked in the Lifespan Research Group. She also has extensive experience of social policy research with other organisations including the Policy Research Bureau, National Society for the Prevention of Cruelty to Children, and NCH. Patricia also works as a counsellor and psychological coach in private practice.

Paul Nieuwbeerta is Senior Research Fellow at the Netherlands Institute for the Study of Crime and Law Enforcement.

Graeme Richardson manages a psychology team within a Forensic Mental Health Service for young people, working with mentally disordered young offenders. He has published in the areas of adolescent sexual offending, interrogative suggestibility and risk assessment.

Angeliki Skoubourdi, DSW, Social Worker, Department of Family Relations, Institute of Child Health. Areas of professional interest and experience include research and clinical work in child maltreatment and institutional care for children.

Dr Maria Ternovskaya, a physicist by training, is now the Director of the Our Family project in the Russian Federation. This multiprofessional project both demonstrates and disseminates good practice in relation to substitute family replacement, family support and child protection.

Dr Paul A. Tiffin, MBBS, BMedSci (Hons), MRCPsych, trained and works as a psychiatrist in North East England. He currently holds a joint clinical and academic post as Consultant in the Psychiatry of Adolescence. Clinical and research interests include psychosis, violence risk assessment and psychiatric epidemiology.

Vivi Tsibouka, DSW, MA, is a Social Worker and Social Anthropologist, Department of Family Relations, Institute of Child Health. Areas of professional interest and experience include research and clinical work in child maltreatment, institutional care for children, social exclusion and community intervention.

Professor Peter van der Laan is Senior Research Fellow at the Netherlands Institute for the Study of Crime and Law Enforcement in Leiden, and Professor of Social and Educational Care at the University of Amsterdam.

Professor Robert Vermeiren, child and adolescent psychiatrist, is Professor of Forensic Psychiatry and works in the Netherlands at the VU University Medical Center, Amsterdam and the University of Leiden, Faculty of Law. In addition, Robert Vermeiren has an appointment at the Yale Child Study Center in the USA.

Dr Eileen Vizard, FRCPsych, is a child psychiatrist and psychoanalyst who has worked with abused children and their families for 25 years. Dr Vizard is Clinical Director of the NSPCC Young Abusers Project, a specialist assessment and treatment service for children with sexually harmful behaviour, based in North London, and Honorary Senior Lecturer at University College London. Dr Vizard has published, researched and taught widely within the field of childcare and child abuse. Dr Vizard's current research interest is the early origins of juvenile sexual offending and emerging severe personality disorder traits in childhood.

Subject Index

Page numbers in *italics* refer to figures, tables and boxes

Author Index